FROM
MEDICINE MEN
TO MUHAMMAD

FROM MEDICINE MEN TO MUHAMMAD

A Thematic Source Book of the
History of Religions

Part 4 of *FROM PRIMITIVES TO ZEN*

MIRCEA ELIADE

1817

HARPER & ROW, PUBLISHERS

NEW YORK, EVANSTON, SAN FRANCISCO, LONDON

ISBN: 0-06-062138-9

LIBRARY OF CONGRESS CATALOG CARD NUMBER: 73-20204

First Harper & Row paperback published 1974.
This book contains chapters V and VI of FROM PRIMITIVES TO ZEN.

Preface to the Paperback Edition

The instigation for this anthology of religious texts and its three companion volumes came during my first years of teaching History of Religions at the University of Chicago. In discussing a specific problem, I expected my students to read at least some of the basic original sources; but I soon discovered that I was unable to recommend to them any single work where one might find a number of essential texts regarding, for example, high gods, cosmogonic myths, conceptions of death and the afterlife, etc. Although we have many source books, some of them excellent, for the most important religions, there were then no comprehensive anthologies in English presenting religious documents according to themes and topics. It seems to me that only by reading a certain number of religious texts related to the same subject (cosmogony, initiation, myths on the origin of death, etc.) is a student able to grasp their structural similarities and their differences.

Any thematic classification of religious documents implies a certain amount of arbitrariness. Some of the texts located under one classification could just as well have been integrated into another classification. But this source book is designed to be *read* first, from beginning to end, and only afterward to be *consulted*. A cross-reference index will help the reader, if he so wishes, to examine consecutively all the documents related to a specific religion or a particular cultural-geographic area such as Mesopotamia, Ancient Greece, India (or again just one segment of Indian religion: Vedism, Brahmanism, Buddhism, etc.), or the 'primitives' (but also just Australia, Oceania, Africa, Asia, North or South America).

A disturbing problem was raised by the respective proportions to be allotted to the documents representing the different religions and cultural-geographic areas. I was understandably eager to include the most representative religious texts; on the other hand, the thematic classification compelled me to illustrate all the important religious beliefs, conceptions, rituals, and institutions. Thus, for example, because I selected copiously from the *Tao Tê Ching,* the Vedic hymns, and the *Upanishads,* I was compelled to be sparing with Chinese and Indian rituals.

For obvious reasons, only a limited number of documents could be reprinted *in toto.* Omissions in the body of the text are indicated by ellipsis points. In the case of long documents, portions omitted are summarized. In rare cases, when the text was unusually long, I gave a résumé with long quotations. Explanatory notes are restricted to bare essentials; in many instances, I made use of or adapted the translator's notes. When it seemed necessary, I introduced a document or a group of documents with a brief comment. My own comments are printed in italics. Commentaries by others are printed in the same type as the documents they accompany; credit is given in the source line for the document. The use of parentheses and brackets within the documents reprinted follows the style of the book from which the particular selection was taken.

I have tried to avoid using materials from books and periodicals that are rare or hard to get. Thus the reader interested in a specific topic can find additional documents in rather easily accessible publications. The selective bibliography at the end of the volume was prepared with the same end in view: only the most useful and important books are listed. Whenever I could cite a monograph on a specific subject containing a rich and well-organized bibliography, I thought it unnecessary to quote other works.

I have made use only of existing English translations of sacred texts. In the case of Ancient Near Eastern, Indian, Greek, Chinese, and Japanese texts, I chose from all the competent translations available, in order to convey to the reader the various possibilities for rendering such abstruse and nonfamiliar texts. In selecting documents related to the 'primitive,' pre-literate societies, I followed the same principle: I limited my choice to works written in, or translated into, English. I hasten to add that although the term 'primitive' is misleading, and should be replaced by 'pre-literate' or 'archaic,' I have kept it, with the majority of authors, for reasons of convenience.

I have tried to include documents from almost all the important religious traditions, from primitive religion to the Ancient Near East to Islam, late Buddhism, and Zen. I have not included Hittite and Ugaritic texts, however, because their fragmentary condition would have demanded too extensive a commentary; furthermore, there are many readily available and competent translations of such texts. A more serious omission is that of Judaism and Christianity. But one cannot present these religions without quoting extensively from the Old and New Testaments, and it seemed unwise to increase the bulk and price of this source book considerably by reproducing such well-known texts. However, companion volumes presenting the Judaic and Christian documents on a somewhat similar thematic basis would be timely. For the moment, the omission of Judaism and Christianity may give the reader a rather inexact idea of the novelty and uniqueness of Muhammad's prophetic experience and of Islamic mystical and theological speculations on the One God. But of course I am assuming that the majority of readers will know something of the other two older monotheistic traditions.

No author of such anthology can hope to satisfy all of his colleagues or, even less so, all of his readers. No matter how 'objective' an author may be in collecting, classifying, and presenting religious documents, his choice is ultimately a personal one. But I should like to point out that this book must be judged as a whole, and not from the particular viewpoint of the anthropologist, or the classical scholar, or the orientalist. As I have already said, the book was conceived as one to be read from beginning to end, and not merely consulted. For the same reason I have tried to limit the scientific apparatus to a minimum. I have not intended to bring out another scholarly work for the exclusive use of the scholar, but a simple and readable book accessible to any *honnête homme* curious about the religious beliefs of his fellow men.

I have to thank my friend and colleague Professor Joseph Kitagawa for helping me in the selection of Japanese materials, Mrs. Rehova Arthur for carefully typing a great portion of the manuscript, Mr. Alan Miller for reading a number of Islamic texts, and Mr. David Knipe for editing and providing notes (not otherwise credited) to the Indian and Scandinavian materials. I am grateful to Miss Nancy Auer for typing and editing most of the Mesopotamian documents, for helping me at various stages of the work, and also for reading and correcting the proofs. Finally, I am thankful to my wife not only for typing a certain number of texts, but especially for encouraging me to continue and complete this work, which kept me inter- mittently busy for five years. Of course, had I known that so much work would be involved, I would not have dared to embark on such a project. My one consolation for the time and energy consumed is that this source book and its three companion volumes will help the student and the inter- ested reader to confront and understand the religious life of ancient and non-Western man.

MIRCEA ELIADE

University of Chicago

Publisher's Note to the Paperback Edition

The selections in *From Primitives to Zen* are numbered consecutively from no. 1 to no. 306. The consecutive numbering is retained in this paperback edition to facilitate the use of the cross-reference system. Nos. 1-74 are contained in *Gods, Goddesses, and Myths of Creation;* nos. 75-157 in *Man and the Sacred;* nos. 158-197 in *Death, Afterlife, and Eschatology;* nos. 198-306 in *From Medicine Men to Muhammad.*

Contents

Contents

Contents

Contents

CHAPTER II

SPECULATIONS ON MAN AND GOD

Contents

Contents

Contents

CHAPTER I

Specialists of the Sacred:
From Medicine Men to Mystics
and Founders of Religions

A. SHAMANS AND MEDICINE MEN

Shamanism is a religious phenomenon characteristic of Siberian and Ural-Altaic peoples. The word 'shaman' is of Tungus origin (saman) and it has passed, by way of Russian, into European scientific terminology. But shamanism, although its most complete expression is found in the Arctic and central Asian regions, must not be considered as limited to those countries. It is encountered, for example, in southeast Asia, Oceania, and among many North American aboriginal tribes. A distinction is to be made, however, between the religions dominated by a shamanistic ideology and by shamanistic techniques (as is the case with Siberian and Indonesian religions) and those in which shamanism constitutes rather a secondary phenomenon.

The shaman is medicine man, priest, and psychopompos; that is to say, he cures sickness, he directs the communal sacrifices, and he escorts the souls of the dead to the other world. He is able to do all this by virtue of his techniques of ecstasy, i.e., by his power to leave his body at will. In Siberia and in northeast Asia a person becomes a shaman by hereditary transmission of the shamanistic profession or by spontaneous vocation or 'election.' More rarely a person can become a shaman by his own decision or upon request of the clan, but the self-made shamans are regarded as weaker than those who inherit the profession or who are 'elected' by the supernatural beings. In North America, on the other hand, the voluntary 'quest' for the powers constitutes the principal method. No matter how the selection takes place, a shaman is recognized as such only following a series of initiatory trials after receiving instruction from qualified masters.

In North and Central Asia as a rule the trials take place during an indefinite period of time during which the future shaman is sick and stays in his tent or wanders in the wilderness, behaving in such an eccentric way that it could be mistaken for madness. Several authors went so far as to explain Arctic and Siberian shamanism as the ritualized expression of a psychomental disease, especially of Arctic hysteria. But the 'chosen' one becomes a shaman only if he can interpret his pathological crisis as a religious experience and succeeds in curing

3

himself. The serious crises that sometimes accompany the 'election' of the future shaman are to be regarded as initiatory trials. Every initiation involves the symbolic death and resurrection of the neophyte. In the dreams and hallucinations of the future shaman may be found the classical pattern of the initiation: he is tortured by demons, his body is cut in pieces, he descends to the nether world or ascends to heaven and is finally resuscitated. That is to say, he acquires a new mode of being, which allows him to have relations with the supernatural worlds. The shaman is now enabled to 'see' the spirits, and he himself behaves like a spirit; he is able to leave his body and to travel in ecstasy in all cosmic regions. However, the ecstatic experience alone is not sufficient to make a shaman. The neophyte must be instructed by masters in the religious traditions of the tribe, and he is taught to recognize the various diseases and to cure them.

Among certain Siberian peoples the consecration of the shaman is a public event. Among the Buriats, for example, the neophyte climbs a birch, a symbol of the world tree, and in doing this he is thought to ascend to heaven. The ascension to heaven is one of the specific characteristics of Siberian and central Asian shamanism. At the occasion of the horse sacrifice, the Altaic shaman ascends to heaven in ecstasy in order to offer to the celestial god the soul of the sacrificed horse. He realizes this ascension by climbing the birch trunk, which has nine notches, each symbolizing a specific heaven.

The most important function of the shaman is healing. Since sickness is thought of as a loss of the soul, the shaman has to find out first whether the soul of the sick man has strayed far from the village or has been stolen by demons and is imprisoned in the other world. In the former case the healing is not too difficult: the shaman captures the soul and reintegrates it in the body of the sick person. In the latter case he has to descend to the nether world, and this is a complicated and dangerous enterprise. Equally stirring is the voyage of the shaman to the other world to escort the soul of the deceased to its new abode; the shaman narrates to those present all the vicissitudes of the voyage as it takes place.

198. THE MAKING OF A MEDICINE MAN: WIRADJURI TRIBE (SOUTHEAST AUSTRALIA)

My father is Yibai-dthulin. When I was a small boy he took me into the bush to train me to be a Wulla-mullung. He placed two large quartz crystals against my breast, and they vanished into me. I do not know how they went, but I felt them going through me like warmth. This was to make me clever and able to bring things up. He also gave me some things like quartz crystals in water. They looked like ice and the water tasted sweet. After that I used to see things that my mother could not see. When out with her I would say, 'What is out there like men walking?' She used to say, 'Child, there is nothing.' These were the *jir* (ghosts) which I began to see.

When I was about ten years old, I was taken to the Burbung[1] and saw what the old men could bring out of themselves; and when my tooth was out the old men chased me with the *wallungs*[2] in their mouths, shouting, 'Ngai, Ngai,' and moving their hands towards me. I went into the bush for a time, and while there my old father came out to me. He said, 'Come here to me'; and he then showed me a piece of quartz crystal in his hand, and when I looked at it he went down into the ground and I saw him come up all covered with red dust. It made me very frightened. He then said, 'Come to me,' and I went to him, and he said, 'Try and bring up a Wallung.' I did try, and brought one up. He then said, 'Come with me to this place.' I saw him standing by a hole in the ground, leading to a grave. I went inside and saw a dead man, who rubbed me all over to make me clever, and who gave me some Wallung. When we came out, my father pointed to a Gunr (tiger-snake) saying 'That is your *budjan*;[3] it is mine also.' There was a string tied to the tail of the snake, and extending to us. It was one of those strings which the doctors bring up out of themselves, rolled up together.

He took hold of it, saying, 'Let us follow him.' The tiger-snake went through several tree trunks, and let us through. Then we came to a great Currajong tree, and went through it, and after that to a tree with a great swelling round its roots. It is in such places that Daramulun lives. Here the Gunr went down into the ground, and we followed him, and came up inside the tree, which was hollow. There I saw a lot of little Daramuluns, the sons of Baiame. After we came out again the snake took us into a great hole in the ground in which were a number of snakes, which rubbed themselves against me, but did not hurt me, being my *Budjan*. They did this to make me a clever man, and to make me a *Wulla-mullung*. My father then said to me, 'We will go up to Baiame's camp.' He got astride of a *Mauir* (thread) and put me on another, and we held by each other's arms. At the end of the thread was Wombu, the bird of Baiame. We went through the clouds, and on the other side was the sky. We went through the place where the Doctors go through, and it kept opening and shutting very quickly. My father said that, if it touched a Doctor when he was going through, it would hurt his spirit, and when he returned home he would sicken and die. On the other side we saw Baiame sitting in his camp. He was a very great old man with a long beard. He sat with his legs under him and from his shoulders extended two great quartz crystals to the sky above him. There were also numbers of the boys of Baiame and of his people, who are birds and beasts.

Notes

1 The initiation ceremonies.
2 Quartz crystals.
3 *Budjan* is a secret personal totem.

A. W. Howitt, *The Native Tribes of South-East Australia* (London, 1904), pp. 406-8

199. A MEDICINE MAN'S INITIATION: KURNAI TRIBE (SOUTHEAST AUSTRALIA)

The Medicine Man speaks:

'When I was a big boy about getting whiskers I was at Alberton camped with my people. Bunjil-gworan was there and other old men. I had some dreams about my father, and I dreamed three times about the same thing. The first and the second time, he came with his brother and a lot of other old men, and dressed me up with lyre-bird's feathers round my head. The second time they were all rubbed over with Naial (red ochre), and had Bridda-briddas on. The third time they tied a cord made of whale's sinews round my neck and waist, and swung me by it and carried me through the air over the sea at Corner Inlet, and set me down at Yiruk [Wilson's Promontory]. It was at the front of a big rock like the front of a house. I noticed that there was something like an opening to the rock. My father tied something over my eyes and led me inside. I knew this because I heard the rocks make a sound as of knocking behind me. Then he uncovered my eyes, and I found that I was in a place as bright as day, and all the old men were

6

round about. My father showed me a lot of shining bright things, like glass, on the walls, and told me to take some. I took one and held it tight in my hand. When we went out again my father taught me how to make these things go into my legs, and how I could pull them out again. He also taught me how to throw them at people. After that, he and the other old men carried me back to the camp and put me on the top of a big tree. He said, "Shout out loud and tell them that you are come back." I did this, and I heard the people in the camp waking up, and the women beginning to beat their rugs for me to come down, because now I was a Mulla-mullung. Then I woke up and found that I was lying along the limb of a tree. The old men came out with firesticks, and when they reached the tree, I was down, and standing by it with the thing my father had given me in my hand. It was like glass, and we call it Kiin. I told the old men all about it, and they said that I was a doctor. From that time I could pull things out of people, and I could throw the Kiin like light in the evening at people, saying to it Blappan (go!). I have caught several in that way. After some years I took to drinking, and then I lost my Kiin and all my power, and have never been able to do anything since. I used to keep it in a bag made of the skin of a ring-tail opossum, in a hole of a tree. One night I dreamed that I was sleeping in the camp, and my wife threw some kruk [menstrual blood] at me, and after that my Kiin went out of my bag. I do not know where. I have slept under the tree where I left it, thinking that my power might come back, but I have never found the Kiin, and I never dream any more about it.'

A. W. Howitt, The Native Tribes of South-East Australia (London, 1904), pp. 408-10

200. THE INITIATION OF A BINBINGA MEDICINE MAN (CENTRAL AUSTRALIA)

The Binbinga hold that medicine men are consecrated by the spirits Mundadji and Munkaningi (father and son). The magician Kurkutji told how, entering a cave one day, he came upon the old Mundadji, who caught him by the neck and killed him.

Mundadji cut him [Kurkutji] open, right down the middle line, took out all of his insides and exchanged them for those of himself, which he placed in the body of Kurkutji. At the same time he put a number

7

of sacred stones in his body. After it was all over the younger spirit, Munkaninji, came up and restored him to life, told him that he was now a medicine man, and showed him how to extract bones and other forms of evil magic out of men. Then he took him away up into the sky and brought him down to earth close to his own camp, where he heard the natives mourning for him, thinking that he was dead. For a long time he remained in a more or less dazed condition, but gradually he recovered and the natives knew that he had been made into a medicine man. When he operates the spirit Munkaninji is supposed to be near at hand watching him, unseen of course by ordinary people. When taking a bone out, an operation usually conducted under the cover of darkness, Kurkutji first of all sucks very hard at the stomach of the patient and removes a certain amount of blood. Then he makes passes over the body, punches, pounds and sucks, until at last the bone comes out and is then immediately, before it can be seen by the onlookers, thrown in the direction of the spot at which Munkaninji is sitting down quietly watching. Kurkutji then tells the natives that he must go and ask Munkaninji if he will be so kind as to allow him, Kurkutji, to show the bone to them, and permission having been granted, he goes to the spot at which he has, presumably, previously deposited one, and returns with it.

B. Spencer and F. J. Gillen, *The Northern Tribes of Central Australia* (London, 1904), pp. 487-8

201. THE INITIATION OF AN AUSTRALIAN MEDICINE MAN: UNMATJERA TRIBE (CENTRAL AUSTRALIA)

Just as in the case of northern Asiatic or American shamanism, in Australia too one becomes a shaman in three ways: by inheriting the profession, by call or election, or by personal quest. But whatever way he has taken, a candidate is not recognized as a medicine man until he has been accepted by a certain number of medicine men or been taught by some of them, and, above all, after a more or less laborious initiation. In the majority of instances, the initiation consists in an ecstatic experience, during which the candidate undergoes certain operations performed by mythical Beings, and undertakes ascents to Heaven or descents to the subterranean World. (Cf. M. Eliade, Shamanism: Archaic Techniques of Ecstasy [New York: Bollingen Series LXXVI, 1964], pp. 45 ff.)

8

Shamans and Medicine Men

Following are the words of Ilpailurkna, a famous magician of the Unmatjera tribe, as reported by Spencer and Gillen.

When he was made into a medicine man, a very old doctor came one day and threw some of his *atnongara* stones[1] at him with a spear-thrower. Some hit him on the chest, others went right through his head, from ear to ear, killing him. The old man then cut out all his insides, intestines, liver, heart, lungs—everything in fact, and left him lying all night long on the ground. In the morning the old man came and looked at him and placed some atnongara stones inside his body and in his arms and legs, and covered his face with leaves. Then he sang over him until his body was all swollen up. When this was so he provided him with a complete set of new inside parts, placed a lot more *atnongara* stones in him, and patted him on the head, which caused him to jump up alive. The old medicine man then made him drink water and eat meat containing *atnongara* stones. When he awoke he had no idea as to where he was, and said, 'Tju, tju, tju'—'I think I am lost.' But when he looked round he saw the old medicine man standing beside him, and the old man said, 'No, you are not lost; I killed you a long time ago.' Ipailurkna had completely forgotten who he was and all about his past life. After a time the old man led him back to his camp and showed it to him, and told him that the woman there was his lubra, for he had forgotten all about her. His coming back this way and his strange behaviour at once showed the other natives that he had been made into a medicine man.

Note

1 These *atnongara* stones are small crystalline structures which every medicine man is supposed to be able to produce at will from his body, through which it is believed that they are distributed. In fact it is the possession of these stones which gives his virtue to the medicine man.

B. Spencer and J. Gillen, *The Northern Tribes of Central Australia* (London, 1904), pp. 480-1

202. HOW LEBID BECAME A SHAMAN (KWAKIUTL INDIAN)

'Lebid had been sick for a long time,' said the one who told the tale. 'For three winters he had been sick abed and he was just bones. It was real mid-winter and it was very cold. . . .

[*After Lebid had died, his body was wrapped in blankets and laid at the far end of the village site. It was too cold to bury him.*]

Night came. When all the Gwasila lay down, a wolf began to howl behind Gwekelis. It was not long that one wolf was howling, when many wolves began to howl. They gathered at the place where Lebid was wrapped up on the rock. Then the Gwasila guessed that the wolves were going to eat him. Probably the wolves were sitting around the dead one, for they were all howling together. The Gwasila did not sleep for they were afraid. When it was near daylight the wolves were still howling, many. Then all the Gwasila heard Lebid singing his sacred song among the howling wolves and they knew that Lebid had now become a shaman. When day came in the morning the many howling wolves went back into the woods, and Lebid went also into the woods, singing his sacred song. He kept together with the wolves. Now the sisters of Lebid and his late wife, Maxmaklodalaogwa were running about in vain, looking at the place where he had been wrapped up on the rocks. They saw the tracks of Lebid who had been walking among the wolves. Now the Gwasila were asked by the shamans of the Nakwaxdax that they should all go and wash, with the women and children in the morning and in the evening, so that they should all purify themselves. Then they did so. Now he had been away for two days, then he was heard singing his sacred song inland from the village of Gwekelis. . . . When day came in the morning the Gwasila went to get fire wood. Lebid's wife and daughters and sisters cleared Lebid's house so as to make it clean. . . . All the Gwasila were purified. When it got dark in the evening he came singing his sacred song. They could hardly hear him in the woods. Now at once the Gwasila started a fire in the middle of the house. All the men and the women who were not menstruating and the children went in. Now the shaman of Nakwaxdax told all those who went into the house to carry batons. When they were all holding the batons the shaman of the Nakwaxdax, whose name was Making-alive (Qwequlagila) told the Gwasila to beat fast time together. They all beat time together. For a long time they were beating time. Then they stopped beating time and the sound of Lebid came nearer as he was singing his sacred song behind the village. Three times the Gwasila beat fast time. Then the sound of the sacred song came to the front of the house. Again they beat fast time; the fourth time Lebid came into the door, really naked, only hemlock was wound around his head and hemlock was wound around his neck. He was really lean. The Gwasila beat fast time. He went around the fire in the middle of the house still singing his sacred song. These are the words of his sacred song:

1. *I was taken away far inland to the edge of the world by the magical power of heaven, the treasure, ha, wo, ho.*
2. *Only then was I cured by it, when it was really thrown into me, the past life bringer of Naualakume, the treasure, ha, wo, ho.*
3. *I come to cure with this means of healing of Naualakume, the treasure. Therefore I shall be a life bringer, ha, wo, ho.*
4. *I come with the water of life given into my hand by Naualakume, the means of bringing to life, the treasures, ha, wo, ho.*

Then Lebid sang his other sacred song:

1. *He turns to the right side, poor one, this supernatural one, so as to obtain the supernatural one, ha, wo, ho.*
2. *Let the supernatural one be the life bringer, the supernatural one, ha, wo, ho.*
3. *That the poor one may come to life with the lifebringer of Naualakume, ha, wo, ho.*
4. *The poor one comes, this supernatural one, to give protection with the means of giving protection of Naualakume, ha, wo, ho.*

After he had danced, all those went out of the house who were not shamans. Then the real shamans of the Gwasila sat down in the house. Lebid sat down on a new mat in the rear of the house. All had their faces blackened, the old shamans, and all had on their heads the shamans' head rings of red cedar bark. All had around their necks shamans' neck rings of red cedar bark. Then they all lay on their backs and there was no talking. Only Lebid, the new shaman who had come back to life was sitting on his new mat. . . . They were waiting for all the men and women who were not shamans to go to sleep. When they thought they were all asleep they sent four real shamans to go and look into the doors of all the houses of the Gwasila to see whether they were not barred. Then they found that all the doors of the houses were barred. They came into the meeting house of the shamans and they barred the door of the house. Then they sat down. They were sitting quite a while in silence, then arose one of the shamans, whose name was Bringing-Life-out-of-the-Woods (Qulamol-telsila). He spoke and said, 'Indeed, friends, indeed, this is the way it is done, for we came here to this house, that Lebid, who is newly added to us, our friend, may tell us how it was brought right down to this shaman. Now he will tell us why he came to life again. He will keep nothing hidden from his friends.' Thus he said and sat down.

Then Lebid spoke and said, 'Indeed, friends, you fellow-shamans, thus you must do to a new shaman. Now I will tell you, friends. I was very sick, and a man came into the place where I was lying in another house and invited me to follow him. Immediately I arose and followed him. Then I saw that my body was still lying here groaning. We had not gone far into the woods before we arrived at a house and we entered the house. I was asked by the other man to go and sit down in the rear of the house. When I had seated myself, then spoke the man who was sitting on the right hand side of the doorway of the house. He said, "Go on, speak, Naualakume, he who is the great shaman, of what we shall do to him who has come and is sitting among us," said he. Then a man came who had tied around his head a thick ring of red cedar bark and a thin neck ring of cedar bark. He spoke and said, "Our friend will not stay away, for I wish him to go back to his tribe so that he may become a great shaman and that he may cure the sick in his tribe. And he shall have my name for his name. Now he shall have the name Naualakume. And I shall take out the breath from his body so that I may keep it," said he as he went out of the door of the house. It was not long before he came back. He spoke and said, "Now his body is dead on the ground, for I am holding his breath, which is the owner of the soul of our friend. Now I shall give him my shamanistic power," said he and he vomited a quartz crystal. Then all the men beat fast time on the boards. He sang his sacred song as he threw the quartz crystal into the lower part of my sternum, and now I had become a shaman after this as it was getting daylight. Then Naualakume said, "Again we shall beat time for our friend tonight," said he. Then all the wolves who were now men, went to sleep. In the evening they all went into the house, for Lebid was still sitting there. And when the men were all in, Naualakume came singing his sacred song outside the house. Then he came in. There was a wolf carved out of yew wood on the back of his rattle. He went around the fire in the middle of the house. After he had gone around four times he sat down near me and pressed (on top) with his right hand on the top of my head, and he put down his rattle and pressed with his left hand the top of my head; then he sang his sacred song. Then he pressed down with both his hands on both sides of my head, down to the lower end of my trunk.' And so he brought his hands together, put his hands flat together, and raised his hands throwing up the sickness of Lebid. After he had done this four times he finished. . . . Then all the men put on their wolf masks and when they were

all dressed, they all went out of the door of the house, and also Lebid.
As soon as all had come out, all the wolves howled. Lebid walked
among them, and also Naualakume kept the breath of the body of
Lebid, for only his soul had been taken by the wolves. Now they went
to where the body of Lepid was wrapped on the rocks. As soon as
they had arrived there, Naualakume asked the other wolves to take
off the mat that had been spread over the body and the wrapping of
two pairs of blankets. As soon as all had been taken off, Naualakume
went there. He called Lebid to sit by his side. He took his breath and
drew it into his mouth. Then he blew it into the mouth of Lebid's
body. He asked the many wolves that they all should lick the body
of the dead one. 'Now my soul was sitting on the ground and was just
watching the wolves as they were licking the body. They had not
been licking it long when it began to breathe. Then Naualakume
pressed both his hands on the head of the soul of Lebid and he pressed
down with both his hands on his head. Then the soul began to get
small and it was of the size of a large fly. He took it and put it on
top of the head of Lebid and blew it in. Immediately Lebid arose and
sang his sacred song. Now he was singing among the wolves who
were howling and they went back into the woods and went home to
their house. Lebid also followed them. Again the wolves beat time at
night. And now they really taught Lebid who had now the name
Naualakume how to treat the sick. He said that he could not throw
(sickness); and other Gwasila say that he could throw (sickness), he
who had now the name Naualakume. Then said the great shaman of
the wolves [i.e. Lebid] that he would always make him dream "about
what I should do when curing really sick ones, as he was giving instructions to me." Now I came into this house where we are sitting now.'

Franz Boas, *The Religion of the Kwakiutl Indians*, vol.
II (New York: Columbia University Press, 1930), pp.
46-50

203. THE 'ENLIGHTENMENT' OF THE ESKIMO SHAMANS (IGLULIK)

*During the shaman's initiation, the master helps the disciple to obtain
'lighting' or 'enlightenment,' angákok, also called quamanek.*

The *angákoq* consists 'of a mysterious light which the shaman suddenly feels in his body, inside his head, within the brain, an inexplicable searchlight, a luminous fire, which enables him to see in the dark, both literally and metaphorically speaking, for he can now, even with closed eyes, see through darkness and perceive things and coming events which are hidden from others: thus they look into the future and into the secrets of others.'

The candidate obtains this mystical light after long hours of waiting, sitting on a bench in his hut and invoking the spirits. When he experiences it for the first time 'it is as if the house in which he is suddenly rises; he sees far ahead of him, through mountains, exactly as if the earth were one great plain, and his eyes could reach to the end of the earth. Nothing is hidden from him any longer; not only can he see things far, far away, but he can also discover souls, stolen souls, which are either kept concealed in far, strange lands or have been taken up or down to the Land of the Dead.'

M. Eliade, *Shamanism: Archaic Techniques of Ecstasy* (New York: Bollingen Series LXXVI, 1964), pp. 60-1, based on and quoted from Knud Rasmussen, *Intellectual Culture of the Iglulik Eskimos* (Copenhagen, 1930), pp. 112-13

204. AN INITIATORY DREAM OF A SAMOYED SHAMAN

A. A. Popov gives the following account concerning a shaman of the Avam Samoyed. Sick with smallpox, the future shaman remained unconscious for three days and so nearly dead that on the third day he was almost buried. His initiation took place during the time. He remembered having been carried into the middle of a sea. There he heard his Sickness (that is, smallpox) speak, saying to him: 'From the Lords of the Water you will receive the gift of shamanizing. Your name as a shaman will be *Huottarie* (Diver).' Then the Sickness troubled the water of the sea. The candidate came out and climbed a mountain. There he met a naked woman and began to suckle at her breast. The woman, who was probably the Lady of the Water, said to him: 'You are my child; that is why I let you suckle at my breast. You will meet many hardships and be greatly wearied.' The husband of the Lady of the Water, the Lord of the Underworld, then gave him two guides, an ermine and a mouse, to lead him to the underworld. When they came to a high place, the guides showed him seven tents with torn roofs. He entered the first and there found the inhabitants of the underworld and the men of the Great Sickness (syphilis). These men tore out his heart and threw it into a pot. In other tents he met the Lord of Madness and the Lords of all the nervous disorders, as well as the evil shamans. Thus he learned the various diseases that torment mankind.

Still preceded by his guides, the candidate then came to the Land of the Shamanesses, who strengthened his throat and his voice. He was then carried to the shores of the Nine Seas. In the middle of one of them was an island, and in the middle of the island a young birch tree rose to the sky. It was the Tree of the Lord of the Earth. Beside it grew nine herbs, the ancestors of all the plants on earth. The tree was surrounded by seas, and in each of these swam a species of bird with its young. There were several kinds of ducks, a swan, and a sparrow-hawk. The candidate visited all these seas; some of them were salt, others so hot he could not go near the shore. After visiting the seas, the candidate raised his head and, in the top of the tree, saw men of various nations: Tavgi Samoyed, Russians, Dolgan, Yakut, and Tungus. He heard voices: 'It has been decided that you shall have a drum (that is, the body of a drum) from the branches of this tree.' He began to fly with the birds of the seas. As he left the shore, the Lord of the Tree called to him: 'My branch has just fallen; take it and make a drum of it that will serve you all your life.' The branch had three forks, and the Lord of the Tree bade him make three drums from it, to be kept by three women, each drum being for a special ceremony—the first for shamanizing women in childbirth, the second for curing the sick, the third for finding men lost in the snow.

The Lord of the Tree also gave branches to all the men who were in the top of the tree. But, appearing from the tree up to the chest in human form, he added: 'One branch only I give not to the Shamans, for I keep it for the rest of mankind. They can make dwellings from it and so use it for their needs. I am the Tree that gives life to all men.' Clasping the branch, the candidate was ready to resume his flight when again he heard a human voice; this time revealing to him the medicinal virtues of the seven plants and giving him certain instructions concerning the art of shamanizing. But, the voice added, he must marry three women (which, in fact, he later did by marrying three orphan girls whom he had cured of smallpox).

And after that he came to an endless sea and there he found trees and seven stones. The stones spoke to him one after the other. The first had teeth like bears' teeth and a basket-shaped cavity, and it revealed to him that it was the earth's holding stone; it pressed on the fields with its weight, so that they should not be carried away by the wind. The second served to melt iron. He remained with these stones for seven days and so learned how they could be of use to men.

Then his two guides, the ermine and the mouse, led him to a high, rounded mountain. He saw an opening before him and entered a bright cave, covered with mirrors, in the middle of which there was something like a fire. He saw two women, naked but covered with hair, like reindeer. Then he saw that there was no fire burning but that the light came from above, through an opening. One of the women told him that she was pregnant and would give birth to two reindeer; one would be the sacrificial animal of the Dolgan and Evenki, the other that of the Tavgi. She also gave him a hair, which was to be useful to him when he shamanized for reindeer. The other woman also gave birth to two reindeer, symbols of the animals that would aid man in all his works and also supply his food. The cave had two openings, toward the north and toward the south; through each of them the young women sent a reindeer to serve the forest people (Dolgan and Evenki). The second woman, too, gave him a hair. When he shamanizes, he mentally turns toward the cave.

Then the candidate came to a desert and saw a distant mountain. After three days' travel he reached it, entered an opening, and came upon a naked man working a bellows. On the fire was a cauldron 'as big as half the earth.' The naked man saw him and caught him with a huge pair of tongs. The novice had time to think, 'I am dead!' The man cut off his head, chopped his body into bits, and put everything in the cauldron. There he boiled his body for three years. There were also three anvils, and the naked man forged the candidate's head on the third, which was the one on which the best shamans were forged. Then he threw the head into one of three pots that stood there, the one in which the water was the coldest. He now revealed to the candidate that, when he was called to cure someone, if the water in the ritual pot was very hot, it would be useless to shamanize, for the man was already lost; if the water was warm, he was sick but would recover; cold water denoted a healthy man.

The blacksmith then fished the candidate's bones out of a river, in which they were floating, put them together, and covered them with flesh again. He counted them and told him that he had three too many; he was therefore to procure three shaman's costumes. He forged his head and taught him how to read the letters that are inside it. He changed his eyes; and that is why, when he shamanizes, he does not

16

see with his bodily eyes but with these mystical eyes. He pierced his ears, making him able to understand the language of plants. Then the candidate found himself on the summit of a mountain, and finally he woke in the yurt, among the family. Now he can sing and shamanize indefinitely, without ever growing tired.

M. Eliade, *Shamanism: Archaic Techniques of Ecstasy* (New York: Bollingen Series, LXXVI, 1964), pp. 38-42; translating and summarizing A. A. Popov, Tavgytsy. *Materialy po etnografii avamskikh i vedeyevskikh tavgytsev* (Moscow and Leningrad, 1936, pp. 84 ff.

205. MYSTICAL MARRIAGE OF A SIBERIAN (GOLDI) SHAMAN

The Goldi clearly distinguish between the tutelary spirit (ayami), which chooses the shaman, and the helping spirits (syvén), which are subordinate to it and are granted to the shaman by the ayami itself. According to Sternberg the Goldi explain the relations between the shaman and his ayami by a complex sexual emotion. Here is the report of a Goldi shaman.

Once I was asleep on my sick-bed, when a spirit approached me. It was a very beautiful woman. Her figure was very slight, she was no more than half an arshin (71 cm.) tall. Her face and attire were quite as those of one of our Gold women. Her hair fell down to her shoulders in short black tresses. Other shamans say they have had the vision of a woman with one half of her face black, and the other half red. She said: 'I am the "ayami" of your ancestors, the Shamans. I taught them shamaning. Now I am going to teach you. The old shamans have died off, and there is no one to heal people. You are to become a shaman.'

Next she said: 'I love you, I have no husband now, you will be my husband and I shall be a wife unto you. I shall give you assistant spirits. You are to heal with their aid, and I shall teach and help you myself. Food will come to us from the people.'

I felt dismayed and tried to resist. Then she said, 'If you will not obey me, so much the worse for you. I shall kill you.'

She has been coming to me ever since, and I sleep with her as with my own wife, but we have no children. She lives quite by herself without any relatives in a hut, on a mountain, but she often changes her abode. . . . Sometimes she comes under the aspect of an old woman, and sometimes under that of a wolf, so she is terrible to look at. Sometimes she comes as a winged tiger. I mount it and she takes me to show me different countries. I have seen mountains, where only old men and women live, and villages, where you see nothing but young people, men and women : they look like Golds and speak Goldish, sometimes those people are turned into tigers.

Now my ayami does not come to me as frequently as before. Formerly, when teaching me, she used to come every night. She has given me three assistants—the 'jarga' (the panther), the 'doonto' (the bear) and the 'amba' (the tiger). They come to me in my dreams, and appear whenever I summon them while shamaning. If one of them refuses to come, the 'ayami' makes them obey, but, they say, there are some who do not obey even the 'ayami.' When I am shamaning, the 'ayami' and the assistant spirits are possessing me; whether big or small, they penetrate me, as smoke or vapour would. When the 'ayami' is within me, it is she who speaks through my mouth, and she does everything herself. When I am eating the 'sukdu' (the offerings) and drinking pig's blood (the blood of pigs is drunk by shamans alone, lay people are forbidden to touch it), it is not I who eat and drink, it is my 'ayami' alone.

M. Eliade, *Shamanism, op. cit.*, pp. 72-3, quoting Leo Sternberg, 'Divine Election in Primitive Religion' (1924), pp. 476 *ff.* Cf. *Shamanism*, pp. 421 *ff.*, for autobiographies of South-Indian Savara shamans and shamanesses, whose marriages to spirits are in striking parallel to the documents collected by Sternberg

206. A POWERFUL SHAMAN (APACHE)

'My white brother,' an Apache shaman told Reagan, 'you probably will not believe it, but I am all powerful. I will never die. If you shoot me, the bullet will not enter my flesh, or if it enters it will not hurt me. . . . If you stick a knife in my throat, thrusting it upwards, it will come out through my skull at the top of my head. . . . I am all powerful. If I wish to kill any one, all I need to do is to thrust out my hand and touch him and he dies. My power is like that of a god.'

Albert B. Reagan, *Notes on the Indians of the Fort Apache Region*, American Museum of Natural History, Anthropological Papers, XXXV, part V (1930), p. 391

207. SOUL-LOSS AND MAGICAL CURE (APINAYÉ OF EASTERN BRAZIL)

When Meōka's little daughter had the dysentery at the age of six months, Ka'ta'm (according to the story he told me [Nimiendaju]) effected the cure as follows:

'I was walking toward the brook with Iré [Ka'ta'm's wife] to bathe. Passing the plantation, I heard a little child crying. "Do you hear something?" I asked Iré. "No," she said, "I do not hear anything." But I myself heard it distinctly and thought, "Who could this be?" Letting my wife wait, I walked toward the sound. There I saw the shadow of Meōka's daughter sitting in the plantation, right in the middle of the shadows of the white watermelons, which had already been harvested and eaten, and of which only the stalks remained. For that is the very time when the shadows of all cultivated fruits dance in the plantation. They had taken the little one to the farm and allowed her to taste of the watermelon, and the shadows of the fruits had retained the child's.

'I went to her mother and told her not to cry, for her little child would recover. I advised her to wait for several days, then the shadow would spontaneously return. The grandmother thought the girl's body was already too feeble and would not be able to hold out. Then I went thither and fetched back the shadow.'

I [Nimiendaju] witnessed this last-mentioned procedure. Ka'ta'm had himself painted in the afternoon and went down to the plantation by himself. The mother sat down in front of the door, with her sick child on her lap, surrounded by a number of women. After a while Ka'ta'm slowly returned from the farm. He was carrying the child's invisible shadow-soul precisely as though its body were in his arms. When the women caught sight of him, they burst out crying aloud, imagining how the little patient's shadow had spent days all alone, surrounded only by the shadows of the fruits, without fire and shelter. Ka'ta'm put the shadow on the child's head and stroked it down her body.

Some time before this accident Ka'ta'm had similarly cured his own child, whose shadow had been captured by the fruits' shadows; and several days later he discovered the shadow of another sick child at the bathing-hole in the creek and brought it back. Its mother had taken the child along to bathe, and while so engaged it had lost its shadow in the water. Ka'ta'm heard and learned the pitiful song of the lost soul, and sang it in the evening for the women, who at first wept, then took up the tune.

Curt Nimuendaju, *The Apinayé* (Washington, D.C., 1937), pp. 144-5

208. A YUKAGIR SHAMANISTIC SÉANCE (NORTHEASTERN SIBERIA)

The shaman sits down on the ground and, after drumming for a long time, invokes his tutelary spirits, imitating the voices of animals. 'My fore-father, my ancestors, stand near by me. In order to help me, stand near me, my girl spirits. . . .' He begins drumming again and, rising with the help of his assistant, goes to the door and breathes deeply, in order to swallow the souls of his ancestors and other spirits that he has summoned. 'The soul of the patient, it seems, has travelled along the road to the Kingdom of Shadows,' the spirits of the ancestors announce through the shaman's voice. The patient's relatives encourage him: 'Be strong, strength do not spare!' The shaman drops his drum and lies face down on the reindeer skin; he remains motionless, the sign that he has left his body and is journeying in the beyond. He has descended into the Kingdom of Shadows 'through the drum as through a lake.' For a long time he does not stir and all those present patiently wait for him to wake. His return is indicated by a few motions. Two girls massage his legs, and, now completely restored to himself, he replaces the soul in the patient's body. He then goes to the door and dismisses his helping spirits.

At the end of such a séance the shaman gave Jochelson the particulars of his ecstatic journey. Accompanied by his helping spirits, he had followed the road that leads to the Kingdom of Shadows. He came to a little house and found a dog that began to bark. An old woman, who guarded the road, came out of the house and asked him if he had come for ever or for a short time. The shaman did not answer her; instead, he addressed his spirits: 'Do not listen to the old woman's words, walk on without stopping.' Soon they came to a stream. There was a boat, and on the other bank the shaman saw tents and men. Still accompanied by his spirits, he entered the boat and crossed the stream. He met the souls of the patient's dead relatives, and entering their tent, found the patient's soul there too. As the relatives refused to give it to him, he had to take it by force. To carry it safely back to the earth, he inhaled the patient's soul and stuffed his ears to prevent it from escaping.

M. Eliade, *Shamanism, op. cit.*, pp. 247-8; summarizing Waldemar Jochelson, *The Yukaghir and the Yukaghirize Tungus* (Leiden and New York, 1924-6) pp. 196-9

209. AN ESKIMO SHAMAN DESCENDS TO THE BOTTOM OF THE OCEAN

Descent to the abode of Takánakapsâluk, the Mother of the Sea Beasts, is undertaken at an individual's request, sometimes because of illness, sometimes because of bad luck in hunting; only in the latter case is the shaman paid. But it sometimes happens that no game at all is to be found and the village is threatened with famine; then all the villagers gather in the house where the seance is held, and the shaman's ecstatic journey is made in the name of the whole community. Those present must unfasten their belts and laces, and remain silent, their eyes closed. For a time the shaman breathes deeply, in silence, before summoning his helping spirits. When they come the shaman begins to murmur, 'The way is made ready for me; the way opens before me!' and the audience answer in chorus: 'Let it be so.' And now the earth opens, and the shaman struggles for a long time with unknown forces before he finally cries: 'Now the way is open.' And the audience exclaim in chorus: 'Let the way be open before him; let there be way for him.' Now, first under the bed, then farther away, under the passage, is heard the cry, 'Halala-he-he-he, Halala-he-he-he'; this is the sign that the shaman has set off. The cry grows more and more distant until it is no longer heard.

During this time the audience sing in chorus, their eyes closed, and sometimes the shaman's clothes—which he had taken off before the séance—come to life and start flying about the house, over the heads of the audience. The signs and deep breathing of people long dead are also heard; they are dead shamans come to help their colleague on his dangerous journey. And their signs and their breathing seem to come from very far under water, as if they were sea beasts.

Reaching the bottom of the ocean, the shaman finds himself facing three great stones in constant motion barring his road; he must pass between them at the risk of being crushed. (This is another image

21

of the 'strait gate' that forbids access to the plane of higher being to anyone but an 'initiate,' that is, one who can act like a 'spirit.') Successfully passing this obstacle, the shaman follows a path and comes to a sort of bay; on a hill stands Takánakapsâluk's house, made of stone and with a narrow entrance. The shaman hears sea beasts blowing and panting, but does not see them. A dog with bared teeth defends the entrance; the dog is dangerous to anyone who is afraid of it, but the shaman passes over it, and it understands that he is a very powerful magician. (All these obstacles oppose the ordinary shaman, but the really powerful shamans reach the bottom of the sea and the presence of Takánakapsâluk directly, by diving beneath their tent or snow hut, as if slipping through a tube.)

If the goddess is angry with men, a great wall rises before her house. And the shaman has to knock it down with his shoulder. Others say that Takánakapsâluk's house has no roof, so that the goddess can better see men's acts from her place by the fire. All kinds of marine animals are gathered in a pool to the right of the fire, and their cries and breathings are heard. The goddess's hair hangs down over her face and she is dirty and slovenly; this is the effect of men's sins, which have almost made her ill. The shaman must approach her, take her by the shoulder, and comb her hair (for the goddess has no fingers with which to comb herself). Before he can do this, there is another obstacle to be overcome; Takánakapsâluk's father, taking him for a dead man on the way to the land of shades, tries to seize him, but the shaman cries, 'I am flesh and blood!' and succeeds in passing.

As he combs Takánakapsâluk's hair, the shaman tells her that men have no more seal. And the goddess answers in the spirit language: 'The secret miscarriages of the women and breaches of taboo in eating boiled meat bar the way for the animals.' The shaman now has to summon all his powers to appease her anger; finally she opens the pool and sets the animals free. The audience hears their movements at the bottom of the sea, and soon afterward the shaman's gasping breathing, as if he were emerging from the surface of the water. A long silence follows. Finally the shaman speaks: 'I have something to say.' All answer. 'Let us hear, let us hear.' And the shaman, in the spirit language, demands the confession of sins. One after another, all confess their miscarriages or their breaches of taboos and repent.

M. Eliade, *Shamanism, op. cit.,* pp. 294-6; summarizing Knud Rasmussen, *Intellectual Culture of the Iglulik Eskimos* (Copenhagen, 1930), pp. 124 *ff.*

210. BLACK MAGIC: AN AUSTRALIAN SORCERER (ARNHEM LAND)

One of the most noted killers in the southeastern Murngin country was Laindjura, who had destroyed many victims by black magic. As an individual he was not very different from the ordinary man in the tribe, although possibly a bit more alert. He was a good hunter as well as an excellent wood carver, and had several wives and a number of children. There was nothing sinister, peculiar, or psychopathic about him; he was perfectly normal in all of his behaviour. Among his own people the attitudes were no different toward him than toward any other man in the clan. It was extremely difficult, however, to obtain Laindjura's confidence to the point where he would talk about his activities as a sorcerer. Although he and I were on very friendly terms, it was not until my second field trip into the area that he gave me long accounts of his various killings.

It is impossible definitely to evaluate how far Laindjura and other killers believed the case histories which they gave me. There was no doubt in my own thinking that Laindjura believed a great part of them. Since he was constantly credited and blamed by friends and enemies for certain deaths, he may at first have taken an attitude 'as if' he had done these things and ultimately have come to believe that he had actually performed the operations he claimed he had. A black sorcerer who is credited with many killings has a rather difficult time among the people surrounding his own group, and under most circumstances it is more difficult and unpleasant to be so classed than as an ordinary man; hence a man would not practise such complete duplicity as these stories might indicate unless the setting were extraordinary from our point of view.

The Killing of Bom-li-tjir-i-li's wife—'All of us were camping at Marunga Island. We were looking for oysters. This woman I was about to kill was hunting for lilies that day, for the other women had gone another way to search for oysters. I carried a hatchet with me and watched her. The woman gathered her lily bulbs, then left the swamp, went back on to the sandy land and lay down in the shade. She covered herself with paper bark to keep warm because she had been in the lily pond and felt cold. Only her head came out from the bark. She could not see.

'I sneaked up and hit her between the eyes with the head of a tomahawk. She kicked and tried to raise up but she couldn't. Her eyes turned up like she was dead. I picked her up under the arms and dragged her to a mangrove jungle and laid her down. She was a young girl.

'I split a mangrove stick from off a tree and sharpened it. I took some djel-kurk (orchid bulb) first and got it ready. I did not have my spear-thrower with me, so I took the handle off my tomahawk and jabbed about the skin on her Mount of Venus which was attached to her vagina and pushed it back. I pushed the skin up to her navel.

'Her large intestine protruded as though it were red calico. I covered my arm with orchid juice. I covered the killing stick with it too. I put the stick in the palm of my hand so that I could push the point upward with my thumb. When she inhaled, I pushed my arm in a little. When she exhaled I stopped. Little by little I got my hand inside her. Finally I touched her heart. I pushed the killing stick with my thumb up over the palm, which pressed the stick against my fingers, into her heart. She had a very large heart and I had to push harder than usual.

'I pulled the stick out. I stood back of her and held her up with her breasts in my hands. She was in a squatting position.

'Her heart's blood ran out into the paper-bark basket I had left to catch it in. It ran slower and slower and then stopped. I laid her down and took the blood away. I hid it. I came back and broke a nest of green ants off a tree. I laid it near her. I put the live ants on her skin. I did not squeeze them, for I was in a hurry because I was afraid her relatives would come looking for her. The skin, when bitten by the ants, moved by itself downward from her navel and covered her bones over her Mount of Venus.

'I then took some dry mud from an old lily pond. I put my sweat on the mud and warmed it over the fire. I put it against her to heal the wound so that no trace would be left of what I had done. I was careful none of her pubic hair would be left inside her vagina so that it would be felt by her husband or seen by the women. I kept up the mud applications until the vagina looked as it did before. I put blood and sweat in the mud and warmed it and put it inside the uterus. I did this again, using the mud, sweat, and blood. I did this six or eight times. The inside now was like it was before.

'I turned her over. Her large intestine stuck out several feet. I shook some green ants on it. It went in some little way. I shook some more on, and a little receded. I shook some more, and all of it went in. Everything was all right now. There was no trace of the wound.

'I took the tomahawk handle which had her heart's blood on it

I whirled it around her head. Her head moved slowly. I whirled it again. She moved some more. The spirit that belonged to that dead woman went into my heart then. I felt it go in. I whirled the stick again and she gasped for breath. I jumped over her and straightened her toes and fingers. She blew some breath out of her mouth, and was all right.

'It was noontime. I said to her, "You go eat some lilies." The woman got up and walked away. She went round another way. I said to that woman "You will live two days. One day you will be happy, the next day you will be sick." The woman went to the place where I had found her. She went to sleep. I took her blood and went away. The other women came from where they had been gathering oysters. They were laughing and talking. They awakened the girl. She picked up her lily bulbs and went to the camp with the women.

'The next day she walked around and played, laughed, talked and made fun and gathered a lot of oysters and lilies. She came back to camp that night. She brought the things she had gathered into camp. She laid down and died that night.'

W. Lloyd Warner, A Black Civilization (New York, 1958), pp. 188-90

B. HOLY PERSONAGES

211. AN AFRICAN DIVINE KING (NYASALAND)

Mbande is a hill on the plain of north Nyasaland with a commanding view of the surrounding country and well suited to defence. The west side is precipitous and below the scarp edge there used to be a marsh; to the north the hill is protected by a wide reach of the Lukulu river. It is a sacred place and for many generations was the home of the 'divine king,' the Kyungu. Like the Lwembe he was the living representative of a hero, and was selected by a group of hereditary nobles from one of two related lineages, the office alternating (if suitable candidates were available) between the two. They sought a big man, one who had begotten children and whose sons were already married, not a young man for, the nobles said, 'young men always want war, and destroy the country.' He must be a man of wisdom (*gwa mahala*) and generous in feeding his people.

The Kyungu's life was governed by taboos even more rigorous than those surrounding the Lwembe. He must not fall ill, or suffer a wound, or even scratch himself and bleed a little, for his ill health, or his blood falling on the earth would bring sickness to the whole country. 'Men feared when Kyungu's blood fell on the ground, they said, "It is his life."' 'If he had a headache his wives (if they loved him) told him not to mention it, they hid his illness; but if the nobles entered and found him ill they dug the grave and put him in it, saying, "He is the ruler (*ntemi*), it's taboo for him to be ill." Then he thought: "Perhaps it is so" (with a gesture of resignation).'

Great precautions were taken to preserve his health. He lived in a separate house with his powerful medicines. His food was prepared by boys below the age of puberty lest a menstruating woman, or a youth who had laid with a woman, should touch it and so bring sickness upon him; and his numerous wives were immured in the royal enclosure—a great stockade—and jealously guarded, for any infidelity on their part was thought to make their husband ill, and with him the whole country.

When the Kyungu did fall ill he was smothered by the nobles who lived around him at Mbande, and buried in great secrecy, with a score or more of living persons—slaves—in the grave beneath him, and one or two wives and the sons of commoners above. And in the midst of all this slaughter the nobles brought a sheep to look into the grave that the dead Kyungu might be gentle (*mololo*) like the sheep!

The living Kyungu was thought to create food and rain, and his breath and the growing parts of his body—his hair and nails and the constantly replaced mucus of his nose—were believed to be magically connected with the fertility of the Ngonde plain. When he was killed his nostrils were stopped so that he was buried 'with the breath in his body'; while portions of his hair and nails and of his nasal mucus were taken from him beforehand and buried by the nobles of Ngonde in the black mud near the river. This was 'to defend the country against hunger,' to close up the land, to keep it rich and heavy and fertile as it was when he himself lived in it.'

His death was kept secret—a relatively easy matter since he lived in seclusion—and one of the nobles (Ngosi) impersonated him wearing his clothes. After a month or two when the nobles had decided whom to choose as the new Kyungu, the luckless man was summoned to Mbande: 'Your father calls you.' Then he came with his companions and entered the house to make obeisance; they seized him and put the sacred cloth on him and set him on the stool 'Kisumbi,' saying, 'Thou Kyungu, thou art he,' and he became the Kyungu. Then they struck the drum, Mwenekelwa, and everyone knew that the Kyungu had died and another had been installed. Men feared greatly to be seized as the Kyungu, just as they feared to be seized as the Lwembe, because the life of a divine king was short. Ngonde historians quote a number of cases of sons of the Kyungu who fled to escape being set on the stool; once they had sat on it they dared not flee lest they die. . . .

In time of drought the nobles of Ngonde would go to a diviner to inquire who it was who was angry; they would mention all the names of the sacred groves of the Kyungus in turn and he would tell them that it was so and so. They would inform the living Kyungu and he would give them a bull or a sheep, together with some beer—they would take one of the pots of beer from his own house, brought by his people as tribute. And he would give them some flour and cloths also. Then they would go with them into the grove and build a miniature hut. Next they would kill the beast and hang some of the meat up on a tree—the rest they would eat later outside the grove. Then they would tear up the cloths and fasten some of the pieces on to the hut in the grove—an action they would explain as 'giving him cloths.' And finally, they would pour out some of the beer and the flour. Nearly always, in time of drought, they would thus build a hut and make an offering in the grove of the Kyungu whom the diviner had mentioned.

But occasionally, if one of the chiefs had recently insulted the Kyungu, they concluded that it was the living Kyungu himself who was angry. They would go to a diviner and mention all the names of the dead Kyungus, but he would refuse to accept any of them: 'No . . . no.' And at length he would tell them that it was the living Kyungu who was angry because so-and-so had insulted him. Then there would be no sacrifice at the grove at all, but the nobles of Ngonde would go to the one who had insulted the Kyungu and charge him with it, asking him what he meant by thus killing them all, would not the whole land starve? And so the wrongdoer would take a cow to the Kyungu who, thereupon, would address the nobles of Ngonde, saying: 'If it was my anger which brought the drought then it will rain (for I am no longer angry). But if the rain does not come then it cannot have been my anger, it must have been someone [of the dead Kyungus] whom you forgot to ask about it.' 'And if, after that, the rain came soon, then it was not likely that anyone would insult the Kyungu again.'. . .

Thus to insult Kyungu was not only treasonable, it was blasphemous, and the whole plain was believed to be cursed with drought or disease in reply. An 'insult' might mean any neglect of the obligations of the chiefs and nobles and commoners of the plain to their lord. . . .

The majesty (*ubusisya*) of the Kyungu was cultivated in a variety of ways. He smeared himself with ointment made from lion fat, and his bed was built up with elephant tusks and lion pelts. He was enthroned on the sacred iron stool called Kisumbi, he had a spear, Kamisa, and Mulima, a porous piece of iron 'like a mouth organ' used to make rain, all handed down from the first Kyungu. His zebra tails, set with medicines in horn handles, were waved in war and during prayer to the shades, and he also had the famous drum on which the blood of a child was poured.

But the majority of their subjects only worshipped from afar in fear and trembling. At Mbande no ordinary commoner was ever conducted into the sacred enclosure, but only the territorial nobles and the elder chiefs, and they only occasionally; while when the Kyungu travelled through his country all men save the very oldest fled from his approach. Even in speech fearful circumlocutions were used to refer to his journeying—'The country is on the move'—'the great hill is moving'—'the mystery is coming.' It was taboo both for the old men who stayed to see him, and for those who entered the sacred enclosure, ever to greet him in the usual way. Falling down and clapping the hands was the only greeting for the Kyungu.

From the wives of the Kyungu also men fled in terror, fearing lest they be compromised and thrown over the cliff of Mbande, and this both added to the atmosphere of terror which surrounded him and was an expression of it.

Monica Wilson, *Communal Rituals of the Nyakyusa*
(London: Oxford University Press, 1959), pp. 40-6

212. THE DEATH OF ORPHEUS

Orpheus, the son of Oiagros, and of Kalliope, one of the Muses, was king of the Macedonians and of the country of the Odrysai. He was skilled in music and particularly in the lyre; and, since the Thracians and Macedonians are a music-loving race, he won great favour with the people thereby. The manner of his death was this: he was torn in pieces by the women of Thrace and Macedonia because he would not allow them to take part in his religious rites, or it may be on other pretexts too; for they do say that after the misfortune that he had with his own wife he became the foe of the whole sex. Now on appointed days a throng of armed Thracians and Macedonians used to gather at Leibethra, and come together in a certain building which was large and well adapted for the performance of initiatory rites; and when they entered to take part in the rites, they laid down their arms before the door. The women watched for this, and, filled with anger at the slight put upon them, seized the arms, slew those who attempted to overpower them, and rending Orpheus' limb from limb, cast the scattered remains into the sea. No requital was exacted from the women, and a plague afflicted the land. Seeking relief from their troubles, the inhabitants received an oracle, saying that if they should find the head of Orpheus and bury it, then they should have rest. After much difficulty they found it through a fisherman at the mouth of the river Meles. It was still singing, and in no way harmed by the sea, nor had it suffered any of the other dreadful changes which the fates of man bring upon dead bodies. Even after so long time it was fresh, and blooming with the blood of life. So they took it and buried it under a great mound, and fenced off a precinct around it, which at first was a hero-shrine but later grew to be a temple. That is, it is honoured with sacrifices and all the other tributes which are paid to gods. No woman may ever set foot within it.

Konon, *Fab.* 45, printed in Kern, *Testt.* 39 and 115. Translated by W. K. C. Guthrie, in Guthrie, *Orpheus and the Greek Religion* (London: Methuen, 1935), pp. 61-2

See also nos. 147, 148-54

213. EMPEDOCLES GOES AMONG MEN AS AN IMMORTAL

Friends who dwell throughout the great town of golden Acragas, up by the citadel, men mindful of good deeds, unversed in wickedness, havens of respect for strangers, all hail. I go about among you all an immortal god, mortal no more, honoured as is my due and crowned with garlands and verdant wreaths. Whenever I enter the prosperous townships with these my followers, men and women both, I am revered; they follow me in countless numbers, asking where lies the path to gain, some seeking prophecies, while others, for many a day stabbed by grievous pains, beg to hear the word that heals all manner of illness. (*Frag.* 112.)

But at the end they come among men on earth as prophets, bards, doctors and princes; and thence they arise as gods mighty in honour, sharing with the other immortals their hearth and their table, without part in human sorrows or weariness. (*Frags.* 146, 147.)

Translation by G. S. Kirk and J. E. Raven, *The Presocratic Philosophers* (Cambridge, Eng.: Cambridge University Press, 1957), p. 354

214. THE FLAMEN DIALIS AND HIS WIFE

(Aulus Gellius, 'Attic Nights,' x, 15)

A great many ceremonies are imposed upon the Flamen Dialis [the priest of Jupiter], and also many restraints [*castus multiplices*, taboos], about which we read in the books *On The Public Priesthoods* and also in Book I of Fabius Pictor's work. Among them I recall the following: it is forbidden [*religio est*] the Flamen Dialis to ride a horse; it is likewise forbidden him to view the 'classes arrayed' outside the pomerium [the sacred boundary of Rome], i.e., armed and in battle order; hence only rarely is the Flamen Dialis made a consul, since [the conduct of] wars is entrusted to the consuls; it is likewise unlawful [*fas numquam est*] for him ever to take an oath by Jupiter [*jurare dialem*]; it is likewise unlawful for him to wear a ring, unless it is cut through and empty [i.e., without a jewel?]. It is also unlawful to carry out fire from the *flaminia*, i.e., the Flamen Dialis' dwelling, except for a sacral purpose; if a prisoner in chains enters the house he must be released and the chains must be carried up through the *impluvium* [the opening in the roof above the *atrium* or living room] onto the roof tiles and dropped down from there into the street. He must have no knot in his head gear or in his girdle or in any other part of his attire. If anyone is being led away to be flogged and falls at his feet as a suppliant, it is unlawful [*piaculum est*] to flog him that day. The hair of the [Flamen] Dialis is not to be cut, except by a free man. It is customary [*mos est*] for the Flamen neither to touch nor even to name a female goat, or raw (?) meat, ivy, or beans.

He must not walk under a trellis for vines. The feet of the bed on which he lies must have a thin coating of clay, and he must not be away from this bed for three successive nights, nor is it lawful for anyone else to sleep in this bed. At the foot of his bed there must be a box containing a little pile of sacrificial cakes. The nail trimmings and hair of the Dialis must be buried in the ground beneath a healthy tree. Every day is a holy day [*feriatus est*] for the Dialis. He must not go outdoors [*sub divo*] without a head-covering—this is now allowed indoors, but only recently by decree of the pontiffs, as Masurius Sabinus has stated; it is also said that some of the other ceremonies have been remitted and cancelled.

It is not lawful for him to touch bread made of fermented meal [i.e., with yeast]. His underwear ['inner tunic'] he does not take off except in covered places, lest he appear nude under the open sky, which is the same as under the eye of Jove. No one else outranks him in the seating at a banquet except the *Rex sacrificulus*. If he loses his his wife, he must resign his office. His marriage cannot be dissolved [*dirimi ius non est*] except by death. He never enters a burying ground, he never touches a corpse. He is, however, permitted [*non est religio*] to attend a funeral.

Almost the same ceremonial rules belong to the Flaminica Dialis [i.e., his wife]. They say that she observes certain other and different ones, for example, that she wears a dyed gown, and that she has a twig from a fruitful tree tucked in her veil [which was worn over her head at a sacrifice], and that it is forbidden [*religiosum est*] for her to ascend more than three rungs of a ladder (except what the Greeks call 'ladders' [steps?]) and even that when she goes to the Argei [when twenty-four puppets were thrown into the Tiber] she must neither comb her head nor arrange her hair.

Translation by Frederick G. Grant, in his *Ancient Roman Religion*, Library of Religion paperbook series (New York, 1957), pp. 30-2

215. AUGUSTUS—'FATHER OF HIS OWN FATHERLAND' (HALICARNASSUS)

Following is an inscription found at Halicarnassus, dating from some time after 2 B.C.

Since the eternal and deathless nature of the universe has perfected its immense benefits to mankind in granting us as a supreme benefit, for our happiness and welfare, Caesar Augustus, Father of his own Fatherland, divine Rome, Zeus Paternal, and Saviour of the whole human race, in whom Providence has not only fulfilled but even surpassed the prayers of all men : land and sea are at peace, cities flourish under the reign of law, in mutual harmony and prosperity; each is at the very acme of fortune and abounding in wealth; all mankind is filled with glad hopes for the future, and with contentment over the present; [it is fitting to honour the god] with public games and with statues, with sacrifices and with hymns.

Translation by Frederick C. Grant, *Ancient Roman Religion, op. cit.,* pp. 174-5

216. NICHIREN PROCLAIMS HIMSELF THE 'BODHISATTVA OF SUPERB ACTION

Nichiren (1222-82) was a Japanese religious teacher.

I, Nichiren, a man born in the ages of the Latter Law, have nearly achieved the task of pioneership in propagating the Perfect Truth, the task assigned to the Bodhisattva of Superb Action (Vishishtachāritra). The eternal Buddhahood of Shākyamuni, as he revealed himself in the chapter on Life-duration, in accordance with his primeval entity; the Buddha Prabhūtaratna, who appeared in the Heavenly Shrine, in the chapter on its appearance, and who represents Buddhahood in the manifestation of its efficacy; the Saints [bodhisattvas] who sprang out of the earth, as made known in the chapter on the Issuing out of Earth —in revealing all these three, I have done the work of the pioneer [among those who perpetuate the Truth]; too high an honour, indeed, for me, a common mortal! . . .

I, Nichiren, am the one who takes the lead of the Saints-out-of-Earth. Then may I not be one of them? If I, Nichiren, am one of them, why may not all my disciples and followers be their kinsmen? The Scripture says 'If one preaches to anybody the Lotus of Truth, even just one clause of it, he is, know ye, the messenger of the Tathāgata, the one commissioned by the Tathāgata, and the one who does the work of the Tathāgata.' How, then, can I be anybody else than this one? . . .

By all means, awaken faith by seizing this opportunity! Live your life through as the one who embodies the Truth, and go on without hesitation as a kinsman of Nichiren! If you are one in faith with Nichiren, you are one of the Saints-out-of-Earth; if you are destined to be such, how can you doubt that you are the disciple of the Lord Shākyamuni from all eternity? There is assurance of this in a word of Buddha, which says: 'I have always, from eternity, been instructing and quickening all these beings.' No attention should be paid to the difference between men and women among those who would propagate the Lotus of the Perfect Truth in the days of the Latter Law. To utter the Sacred Title is, indeed, the privilege of the Saints-out-of-Earth. . . .

When the Buddha Prabhūtaratna sat in the Heavenly Shrine side by side with the Tathāgata Shākyamuni, the two Buddhas lifted up the banner of the Lotus of the Perfect Truth, and declared themselves to be the Commanders [in the coming fight against vice and illusion]. How can this be a deception? Indeed, they have thereby agreed to raise us mortal beings to the rank of Buddha. I, Nichiren, was not present there in the congregation, and yet there is no reason to doubt the statements of the Scripture. Or, is it possible that I was there? Common mortal that I am, I am not well aware of the past, yet in the present I am unmistakably the one who is realizing the Lotus of Truth. Then in the future I am surely destined to participate in the communion of the Holy Place. Inferring the past from the present and the future, I should

33

think that I must have been present at the Communion in the Sky. [The present assures the future destiny, and the future destiny is inconceivable without its cause in the past.] The present, future, and past cannot be isolated from one another. . . .

In this document, the truths most precious to me are written down. Read, and read again; read into the letters and fix them into your mind! Thus put faith in the Supreme Being, represented in a way unique in the whole world! Ever more strongly I advise you to be firm in faith, and to be under the protection of the threefold Buddhahood. March strenuously on in the ways of practice and learning! Without practice and learning the Buddhist religion is nullified. Train yourself, and also instruct others! Be convinced that practice and learning are fruits of faith! So long as, and so far as, there is power in you, preach, if it be only a phrase or a word [of the Scripture]! *Namu Myōhō-renge-kyō! Namu Myōhō-renge-kyō!* [Adoration to the Lotus of Perfect Truth.]

Masaharu Anesaki, *Nichiren, the Buddhist Prophet* (Cambridge, Mass., 1916), pp. 83-5; as quoted in Wm. Theodore de Bary (ed.), *Sources of Japanese Tradition* (New York: Columbia University Press, 1958), pp. 228-9

217. NICHIREN'S TRANSFIGURATION WHILE LIVING IN RETIREMENT

This spot among the mountains is secluded from the worldly life, and there is no human habitation in the neighbourhood—east, west, north, or south. I am now living in such a lonely hermitage; but in my bosom, in Nichiren's fleshly body, is secretly deposited the great mystery which the Lord Shākyamuni revealed on Vulture Peak, and has entrusted to me. Therefore I know that my breast is the place where all Buddhas are immersed in contemplation; that they turn the Wheel of Truth upon my tongue; that my throat is giving birth to them; and that they are attaining the Supreme Enlightenment in my mouth. This place is the abode of such a man, who is mysteriously realizing the Lotus of Truth in his life; surely such a place is no less dignified than the Paradise of Vulture Peak. As the Truth is noble, so is the man who embodies it; as the man is noble, so is the place where he resides. We read in the chapter on the 'Mysterious Power of the Tathāgata' as follows:

Holy Personages

'Be it a forest, or at the foot of a tree, or in a monastery . . . on that spot erect a stūpa dedicated to the Tathāgata. For such a spot is to be regarded as the place where all Tathāgatas have arrived at the Supreme Perfect Enlightenment; on that spot all Tathāgatas have turned the Wheel of Truth, on that spot all Tathāgatas have entered the Great Decease.' Lo, whoever comes to this place will be purged of all sins and depravities which he has accumulated from eternity, and all his evil deeds will at once be transformed into merits and virtues.

Masaharu Anesaki, *Nichiren, the Buddhist Prophet* (Cambridge, Mass., 1916), p. 129, as quoted in Wm. Theodore de Bary (ed.), *Sources of Japanese Tradition* (New York: Columbia University Press, 1958), p. 231

See also nos. 157, 193, 246

C. FORMS OF ASCETICISM

218. THE INDIAN ASCETIC

('The Laws of Manu,' VI, 33-65)

33. But having thus passed the third part of (a man's natural term of) life in the forest, he may live as an ascetic during the fourth part of his existence, after abandoning all attachments to worldly objects.[1]

34. He who after passing from order to order, after offering sacrifices and subduing his senses, becomes, tired with (giving) alms and offerings of food, an ascetic, gains bliss after death.

35. When he has paid the three debts, let him apply his mind to (the attainment of) final liberation; he who seeks it without having paid (his debts) sinks downwards.

36. Having studied the Vedas in accordance with the rule, having begat sons according to the sacred law, and having offered sacrifices according to his ability, he may direct his mind to (the attainment of) final liberation. . . .

41. Departing from his house fully provided with the means of purification (Pavitra),[2] let him wander about absolutely silent, and caring nothing for enjoyments that may be offered (to him).

42. Let him always wander alone, without any companion, in order to attain (final liberation), fully understanding that the solitary (man, who) neither forsakes nor is forsaken, gains his end.

43. He shall neither possess a fire, nor a dwelling, he may go to a village for his food, (he shall be) indifferent to everything, firm of purpose, mediating (and) concentrating his mind on Brahman. . . .

45. Let him not desire to die, let him not desire to live; let him wait for (his appointed) time, as a servant (waits) for the payment of his wages.

46. Let him put down his foot purified by his sight,[3] let him drink water purified by (straining with) a cloth, let him utter speech purified by truth, let him keep his heart pure.

47. Let him patiently bear hard words, let him not insult anybody, and let him not become anybody's enemy for the sake of this (perishable) body.

48. Against an angry man let him not in return show anger, let him bless when he is cursed, and let him not utter speech, devoid of truth, scattered at the seven gates.[4]

49. Delighting in what refers to the Soul,[5] sitting (in the postures prescribed by the Yoga), independent (of external help), entirely abstaining from sensual enjoyments, with himself for his only companion, he shall live in this world, desiring the bliss (of final liberation). . . .

60. By the restraint of his senses, by the destruction of love[6] and hatred, and by the abstention from injuring the creatures,[7] he becomes fit for immortality.

61. Let him reflect on the transmigrations of men, caused by their sinful deeds, on their falling into hell, and on the torments in the world of Yama,

62. On the separation from their dear ones, on their union with hated men, on their being overpowered by age and being tormented with diseases,

63. On the departure of the individual soul from this body and its new birth in (another) womb, and on its wanderings through ten thousand millions of existences,

64. On the infliction of pain on embodied (spirits), which is caused by demerit, and the gain of eternal bliss, which is caused by the attainment of their highest aim, (gained through) spiritual merit.

65. By deep meditations, let him recognize the subtle nature of the supreme Soul,[8] and its presence in all organisms, both the highest and the lowest.

Notes

1 Reference here is to the ideal four stages (*āshramas*) of the Brahman's life: student (*brahmacārin*), householder (*grihastha*), hermit or forest-dweller (*vānaprastha*), and finally, ascetic or mendicant (*yati, bhikshu, parivrājaka, samnyāsin*).

2 Construed as either his capacities after having completed three states of life, or his 'equipment' such as staff and water-pot.

3 Lest he injure any small animal, or step on something impure.

4 The seven bodily orifices?

5 *Ātman.*

6 Or, affection, passion (*rāga*).

7 *Ahimsā,* non-injury.

8 Brahman.

Translation by G. Bühler in *Sacred Books of the East,* XXV (Oxford, 1886), pp. 204-10

219. GOTAMA BUDDHA TALKS OF HIS ASCETIC PRACTICES

('Majjhima-nikāya,' XII *['Māha-sīhanāda-sutta'])*

Gotama Buddha is speaking to Sāriputta, one of his favourite disciples.

Aye, Sāriputta, I have lived the fourfold higher life;—I have been an ascetic of ascetics; loathly have I been, foremost in loathliness, scrupulous have I been, foremost in scrupulosity; solitary have I been, foremost in solitude.

(i) To such a pitch of asceticism have I gone that naked was I, flouting life's decencies, licking my hands after meals, never heeding when folk called to me to come or to stop, never accepting food brought to me before my rounds or cooked expressly for me, never accepting an invitation, never receiving food direct from pot or pan or within the threshold or among the faggots or pestles, never from (one only of) two people messing together, never from a pregnant woman or a nursing mother or a woman *in coitu*, never from gleanings (in time of famine) nor from where a dog is ready at hand or where (hungry) flies congregate, never touching flesh or spirits or strong drink or brews of grain. I have visited only one house a day and there taken only one morsel; or I have visited but two or (up to not more than) seven houses a day and taken at each only two or (up to not more than) seven morsels; I have lived on a single saucer of food a day, or on two, or (up to) seven saucers; I have had but one meal a day, or one every two days, or (so on, up to) every seven days, or only once a fortnight, on a rigid scale of rationing. My sole diet has been herbs gathered green, or the grain of wild millets and paddy, or snippets of hide, or water-plants, or the red powder round rice-grains within the husk, or the discarded scum of rice on the boil, or the flour of oil-seeds, or grass, or cow-dung. I have lived on wild roots and fruit, or on windfalls only. My raiment has been of hemp or of hempen mixture, of cerements, of rags from the dust-heap, of bark, of the black antelope's pelt either whole or split down the middle, of grass, of strips of bark or wood, of hair of men or animals woven into a blanket or of owl's wings. In fulfilment of my vows, I have plucked out the hair of my head and the hair of my beard, have never quitted the upright for the sitting posture, have squatted and never risen up, moving only a-squat, have couched on thorns, have gone down to the water punctually thrice before nightfall to wash (away the evil within). After this wise, in divers fashions, have I lived to torment and to torture my body—to such a length in asceticism have I gone.

(ii) To such a length have I gone in loathliness that on my body I have accumulated the dirt and filth of years till it dropped off of itself—even as the rank growths of years fall away from the stump of a tinduka-tree. But never once came the thought to me to clean it off with my own hands or to get others to clean it off for me;—to such a length in loathliness have I gone.

(iii) To such a length in scrupulosity have I gone that my footsteps out and in were always attended by a mindfulness so vigilant as to awake compassion within me over even a drop of water lest I might harm tiny creatures in crevices;—to such a length have I gone in scrupulosity.

(iv) To such a length have I gone as a solitary that when my abode was in the depths of the forest, the mere glimpse of a cowherd or neatherd or grasscutter, or of a man gathering firewood or edible roots in the forest, was enough to make me dart from wood to wood, from thicket to thicket, from dale to dale, and from hill to hill,—in order that they might not see me or I them. As a deer at the sight of man darts away over hill and dale, even so did I dart away at the mere glimpse of cowherd, neatherd, or what not, in order that they might not see me or I them;—to such a length have I gone as a solitary.

When the cowherds had driven their herds forth from the byres, up I came on all fours to find a subsistence on the droppings of the young milch-cows. So long as my own dung and urine held out, on that I have subsisted. So foul a filth-eater was I.

I took up my abode in the awesome depths of the forest, depths so awesome that it was reputed that none but the passion-less could venture in without his hair standing on end. When the cold season brought chill wintry nights, then it was that, in the dark half of the months when snow was falling, I dwelt by night in the open air and in the dank thicket by day. But when there came the last broiling month of summer before the rains, I made my dwelling under the baking sun by day and in the stifling thicket by night. Then there flashed on me these verses, never till then uttered by any:

> Now scorched, now froze, in forest dread, alone,
> naked and fireless, set upon his quest,
> the hermit battles purity to win.

In a charnel ground I lay me down with charred bones for pillow.

When the cowherds' boys came along, they spat and staled upon me, pelted me with dirt and stuck bits of wood into my ears. Yet I declare that never did I let an evil mood against them arise within me.—So poised in equanimity was I.

[80] Some recluses and brahmins there are who say and hold that purity cometh by way of food, and accordingly proclaim that they live exclusively on jujube-fruits, which, in one form or other, constitute their sole meat and drink. Now I can claim to have lived on a single jujube-fruit a day. If this leads you to think that this fruit was larger in those days, you would err; for, it was precisely the same size then that it is today. When I was living on a single fruit a day, my body grew emaciated in the extreme; because I ate so little, my members, great and small, grew like the knotted joints of withered creepers; like a buffalo's hoof were my shrunken buttocks; like the twists in a rope were my spinal vertebrae; like the crazy rafters of a tumble-down roof, that start askew and aslant, were my gaunt ribs; like the starry gleams on water deep down and afar in the depths of a well, shone my gleaming eyes deep down and afar in the depths of their sockets; and as the rind of a cut gourd shrinks and shrivels in the heat, so shrank and shrivelled the scalp of my head,—and all because I ate so little. If I sought to feel my belly, it was my backbone which I found in my grasp; if I sought to feel my backbone, I found myself grasping my belly, so closely did my belly cleave to my backbone;—and all because I ate so little. If for ease of body I chafed my limbs, the hairs of my body fell away under my hand, rotted at their roots;—and all because I ate so little.

Other recluses and brahmins there are who, saying and holding that purity cometh by way of food, proclaim that they live exclusively on beans—or sesamum—or rice—as their sole meat and drink.

[81] Now I can claim to have lived on a single bean a day—on a single sesamum seed a day—or a single grain of rice a day; and [the result was still the same]. Never did this practice or these courses or these dire austerities bring me to the ennobling gifts of super-human knowledge and insight. And why?—Because none of them lead to that noble understanding which, when won, leads on to Deliverance and guides him who lives up to it onward to the utter extinction of all ill.

Translation by Lord Chalmers, *Further Dialogues of the Buddha,* I (London, 1926), pp. 53-7

220. GOTAMA BUDDHA PRACTISED THE MOST SEVERE ASCETICISM AND BECAME A MASTER IN YOGA

('Majjhima-nikāya,' XXXVI *['Mahā-saccaka-sutta'])*

Thought I then to myself:—Come, let me, with teeth clenched and with tongue pressed against my palate, by sheer force of mind restrain, coerce, and dominate my heart. And this I did, till the sweat streamed from my armpits. Just as a strong man, taking a weaker man by the head or shoulders, restrains and coerces and dominates him, even so did I, with teeth clenched and with tongue pressed against my palate, by sheer force of mind restrain, coerce, and dominate my heart, till the sweat streamed from my armpits. Resolute grew my perseverance which never quailed; there was established in me a mindfulness which knew no distraction,—though my body was sore distressed and afflicted, because I was harassed by these struggles as I painfully struggled on.— Yet even such unpleasant feelings as then arose did not take possession of my mind.

Thought I to myself:—Come, let me pursue the Ecstasy that comes from not breathing. So I stopped breathing, in or out, through mouth and nose; and then great was the noise of the air as it passed through my ear-holes, like the blast from a smith's bellows. Resolute grew my perseverance . . . did not take possession of my mind.

Thought I to myself:—Come, let me pursue further the Ecstasy that comes from not breathing. So I stopped breathing, in or out, through mouth and nose and ears; and then violent winds wracked my head, as though a strong man were boring into my skull with the point of a sword. Resolute grew my perseverance . . . did not take possession of my mind.

Thought I to myself:—Come, let me pursue still further the Ecstasy that comes from not breathing. So I kept on stopping all breathing, in or out, through mouth and nose and ears; and then violent pains attacked my head, as though a strong man had twisted a leather thong round my head. Resolute grew my perseverance . . . did not take possession of my mind.

Thought I to myself:—Come, let me go on pursuing the Ecstasy that comes from not breathing. So I kept on stopping breathing, in or out, through mouth and nose and ears; and then violent winds pierced my inwards through and through,—as though an expert butcher or his man were hacking my inwards with sharp cleavers. Resolute grew my perseverance . . . did not take possession of my mind.

Thought I to myself:—Come, let me still go on pursuing the Ecstasy that comes from not breathing. So I kept on stopping all breathing, in or out, through mouth and nose and ears; and then there was a violent burning within me,—as though two strong men, taking a weaker man by both arms, were to roast and burn him up in a fiery furnace. Resolute grew my perseverance . . . did not take possession of my mind.

At the sight of me, some gods said I was dead; others said I was not dead but dying; while others again said that I was an Arahat and that Arahats lived like that !

Thought I to myself:—Come, let me proceed to cut off food altogether. Hereupon, gods came to me begging me not so to do, or else they would feed me through the pores with heavenly essences which would keep me alive. If, thought I to myself, while I profess to be dispensing with all food whatsoever, these gods should feed me all the time through the pores with heavenly essences which keep me alive, that would be imposture on my part. So I rejected their offers, peremptorily.

Thought I to myself:—Come, let me restrict myself to little tiny morsels of food at a time, namely the liquor in which beans or vetches, peas or pulse, have been boiled. I rationed myself accordingly, and my body grew emaciated in the extreme. My members, great and small, grew like the knotted joints of withered creepers . . . (etc., as in Sutta XII) . . . rotted at their roots; and all because I ate so little.

Thought I to myself:—Of all the spasms of acute and severe pain that have been undergone through the ages past—or will be undergone through the ages to come—or are now being undergone—by recluses or brahmins, mine are pre-eminent; nor is there aught worse beyond. Yet, with all these severe austerities, I fail to transcend ordinary human limits and to rise to the heights of noblest understanding and vision. Could there be another path to Enlightenment?

A memory came to me of how once, seated in the cool shade of a rose-apple tree on the lands of my father the Shākyan, I, divested of pleasures of sense and of wrong states of mind, entered upon, and abode in, the First Ecstasy, with all its zest and satisfaction,—a state bred of inward aloofness but not divorced from observation and reflection. Could this be the path to Enlightenment? In prompt response to this memory, my consciousness told me that here lay the true path to Enlightenment.

Thought I to myself:—Am I afraid of a bliss which eschews pleasures of sense and wrong states of mind?—And my heart told me I was not afraid.

Thought I to myself:—It is no easy matter to attain that bliss with a body so emaciated. Come, let me take some solid food, rice and junket; and this I ate accordingly.

With me at the time there were the Five Almsmen, looking for me to announce to them what truth I attained; but when I took the rice and junket, they left me in disgust, saying that luxuriousness had claimed me and that, abandoning the struggle, I had reverted to luxuriousness.

Having thus eaten solid food and regained strength, I entered on, and abode in, the First Ecstasy.—Yet, such pleasant feelings as then arose in me did not take possession of my mind; nor did they as I successively entered on, and abode in, the Second, Third, and Fourth Ecstasies.

Translation by Lord Chalmers, Further Dialogues of the Buddha, I (London, 1926), pp. 174-7

See also nos. 225-30, 282-9

221. JAIN DOCTRINES AND PRACTICES OF NONVIOLENCE (AHIMSĀ): THE EXAMPLE OF MAHĀVĪRA

('Akārānga-sūtra, I, 8, i.3—iv.8)

Vardhamāna Mahāvīra ('The Great Hero') was a contemporary of the Buddha. He is said to have left his home at the age of thirty and wandered for twelve years in search of salvation. At the age of forty-two he obtained enlightenment and became a 'conqueror' (jina, term from which the Jain took their name). Mahāvīra founded an order of naked monks and taught his doctrine of salvation for some thirty years. He died in 468 B.C., at the age of seventy-two, in a village near Patna.

I. 3. For a year and a month he did not leave off his robe. Since that time the Venerable One, giving up his robe, was a naked, world-relinquishing, houseless (sage).

4. Then he meditated (walking) with his eye fixed on a square space before him of the length of a man. Many people assembled, shocked at the sight; they struck him and cried.

5. Knowing (and renouncing) the female sex in mixed gathering places, he meditated, finding his way himself: I do not lead a worldly life.

6. Giving up the company of all householders whomsoever, he meditated. Asked, he gave no answer; he went and did not transgress the right path.

7. For some it is not easy (to do what he did), not to answer those who salute; he was beaten with sticks, and struck by sinful people. . . .

10. For more than a couple of years he led a religious life without using cold water; he realized singleness, guarded his body, had got intuition, and was calm.

11. Thoroughly knowing the earth-bodies and water-bodies and fire-bodies and wind-bodies, the lichens, seeds, and sprouts,

12. He comprehended that they are, if narrowly inspected, imbued with life, and avoided to injure them; he, the Great Hero.

13. The immovable (beings) are changed to movable ones, and the movable beings to immovable ones; beings which are born in all states become individually sinners by their actions.

14. The Venerable One understands thus: he who is under the conditions (of existenece), that fool suffers pain. Thoroughly knowing (karman), the Venerable One avoids sin.

15. The sage, perceiving the double (karman), proclaims the incomparable activity, he, knowing one; knowing the current of worldliness, the current of sinfulness, and the impulse.

16. Practising the sinless abstinence from killing, he did no acts, neither himself nor with the assistance of others; he to whom women were known as the causes of all sinful acts, he saw (the true sate of the world). . . .

III. 7. Ceasing to use the stick (i.e. cruelty) against living beings, abandoning the care of the body, the houseless (Mahāvīra), the Venerable One, endures the thorns of the villages (i.e. the abusive language of the peasants), (being) perfectly enlightened.

8. As an elephant at the head of the battle, so was Mahāvīra there victorious. Sometimes he did not reach a village there in Ladha.

9. When he who is free from desires approached the village, the inhabitants met him on the outside, and attacked him, saying, 'Get away from here.'

10. He was struck with a stick, the fist, a lance, hit with a fruit, a clod, a potsherd. Beating him again and again, many cried.

11. When he once (sat) without moving his body, they cut his flesh, tore his hair under pains, or covered him with dust.

12. Throwing him up, they let him fall, or disturbed him in his religious postures; abandoning the care of his body, the Venerable One humbled himself and bore pain, free from desire.

13. As a hero at the head of the battle is surrounded on all sides, so was there Mahāvīra. Bearing all hardships, the Venerable One, undisturbed, proceeded (on the road to Nirvāna). . . .

IV. 1. The Venerable One was able to abstain from indulgence of the flesh, though never attacked by diseases. Whether wounded or not wounded, he desired not medical treatment.

2. Purgatives and emetics, anointing of the body and bathing, shampooing and cleaning of the teeth do not behove him, after he learned (that the body is something unclean).

3. Being averse from the impressions of the senses, the Brāhmana wandered about, speaking but little. Sometimes in the cold season the Venerable One was meditating in the shade.

4. In summer he exposes himself to the heat, he sits squatting in the sun; he lives on rough (food); rice, pounded jujube, and beans.

5. Using these three, the Venerable One sustained himself eight months. Sometimes the Venerable One did not drink for half a month or even for a month.

6. Or he did not drink for more than two months, or even six months, day and night, without desire (for drink). Sometimes he ate stale food.

7. Sometimes he ate only the sixth meal, or the eighth, the tenth, the twelfth; without desires, persevering in meditation.

8. Having wisdom, Mahāvīra committed no sin himself, nor did he induce other to do so, nor did he consent to the sins of others.

Translation from Prākrit by Herman Jacobi, *Jaina Sūtra*, part I, in *Sacred Books of the East*, (Oxford, 1884), pp. 85-7

222. MILAREPA EXTOLS HIS 'FIVE COMFORTS'

Milarepa (Mi-la-ras-pa, 1040-1123), magician, yogi and poet, disciple of Mar-pa of Lho-brag (1012-97), is perhaps the most famous figure in the religious history of Tibet. His complete poetical works, Mila Gnubum, 'The Hundred Thousand Songs of Milarepa,' have been recently translated into English by Garma C. C. Chang (New York: University Books, 1962). The following selection is from Mila Khabum, the 'Biography of Milarepa,' written by a mysterious yogi, 'The mad yogi from gTsan' in the latter part of the twelfth or in the beginning of the thirteenth century.

One night, a person, believing that I possessed some wealth, came and, groping about, stealthily pried into every corner of my cave. Upon my observing this, I laughed outright, and said, 'Try if thou canst find anything by night where I have failed by daylight.' The person himself could not help laughing, too; and then he went away.

About a year after that, some hunters of Tsa, having failed to secure any game, happened to come strolling by the cave. As I was sitting in Samādhi, wearing the above triple-knotted apology for clothing, they prodded me with the ends of their bows, being curious to know whether I was a man or a bhūta. Seeing the state of my body and clothes, they were more inclined to believe me a bhūta. While they were discussing this amongst themselves, I opened my mouth and spoke, saying, 'Ye may be quite sure that I am a man.' They recognized me from seeing my teeth, and asked me whether I was Thöpaga. On my answering in the affirmative, they asked me for a loan of some food, promising to repay it handsomely. They said, 'We heard that thou hadst come once to thy home many years ago. Hast thou been here all the while?' I replied, 'Yes; but I cannot offer you any food which ye would be able to eat.' They said that whatever did for me would do for them. Then I told them to make fire and boil nettles. They did so, but as they expected something to season the soup with, such as meat, bone, marrow, or fat, I said, 'If I had that, I should then have food with palatable qualities; but I have not had that for years. Apply the nettles in place of the seasoning.' Then they asked for flour or grain to thicken the soup with. I told them if I had that, I should then have food with sustaining properties; but that I had done without that for some years, and told them to apply nettle tips instead. At last they asked for some salt, to which I again said that salt would have imparted taste to my food; but I had done without that also for years, and recommended the addition of more nettle tips in place of salt. They said, 'Living upon such food, and wearing such garments as thou hast on now, it is no wonder that thy body hath been reduced to this miserable plight. Thine appearance becometh not a man. Why, even if thou should serve as a servant, thou wouldst have a bellyful of food and warm clothing. Thou art the most pitiable and miserable person in the whole world.' I said, 'O my friends, do not say that. I am one of the most fortunate and best amongst all who have obtained the human life. I have met with Marpa the Translator, of Lhobrak, and obtained from him the Truth which conferreth Buddhahood in one lifetime; and now, having entirely given up all worldly thoughts, I am passing my life in strict asceticism and devotion in these solitudes, far away from human habitations. I am obtaining that which will avail me in Eternity. By denying myself the trivial pleasures to be derived from food, clothing, and fame, I am subduing the Enemy [Ignorance] in this very lifetime. Amongst the World's entire human population I am one of the most courageous, with the highest aspirations. . . .

I then sang to them a song about my Five Comforts:
'Lord! Gracious Marpa! I bow down at Thy Feet!
Enable me to give up worldly aims.
'Here is the Dragkar-Taso's Middle Cave,
On this the topmost summit of the Middle Cave,
I, the Yogi Tibetan called Repa,
Relinquishing all thoughts of what to eat or wear, and this life's aims,
Have settled down to win the perfect Buddhahood.

'Comfortable is the hard mattress beneath me,
Comfortable is the Nepalese cotton-padded quilt above me,
Comfortable is the single meditation-band which holdeth up my knee,
Comfortable is the body, to a diet temperate inured,
Comfortable is the Lucid Mind which discerneth present clingings and
    the Final Goal;
Nought is there uncomfortable; everything is comfortable.

'If all of ye can do so, try to imitate me;
But if inspired ye be not with the aim of the ascetic life,
And to the error of the Ego Doctrine will hold fast,
I pray that ye spare me your misplaced pity;
For I a Yogi am, upon the Path of the Acquirement of Eternal Bliss.

'The Sun's last rays are passing o'er the mountain tops;
Return ye to your own abodes.
And as for me, who soon must die, uncertain of the hour of death,
With self-set task of winning perfect Buddhahood,
No time have I to waste on useless talk;
Therefore shall I into the State Quiescent of Samādhi enter now.'

Translation by W. Y. Evans-Wentz and Lama Kazi Dawa-Samdup, in Evans-Wentz, *Tibet's Great Yogi Milarepa* (Oxford, 1928), pp. 199-202

223. AL-HASAN EXTOLS ASCETICISM

Al-Hasan al-Basrī flourished in the eighth century A.D. *(died* A.D. *728=
110* A.H.*).*

Beware of this world *(dunyā)* with all wariness; for it is like to a snake,
smooth to the touch, but its venom is deadly. . . . The more it pleases
thee, the more thou be wary of it, for the man of this world, whenever
he feels secure in any pleasure thereof, the world drives him over
into some unpleasantness, and whenever he attains any part of it and
squats him down in it, the world turns him upside down. And again
beware of this world, for its hopes are lies, its expectations false; its
easefulness is all harshness, muddied its limpidity. . . . Even had the
Almighty not pronounced upon the world at all or coined for it any
similitude . . . yet would the world itself have awakened the slum-
berer and roused the heedless; how much more then, seeing that God
has Himself sent us a warning against it! . . . For this world has
neither worth nor weight with God, so slight it is. . . . It was offered
to our Prophet, with all its keys and treasures . . . but he refused
to accept it, and nothing prevented him from accepting it—for there
is naught that can lessen him in God's sight—but he disdained to
love what his creator hated, and to exalt what his Sovereign had
debased. As for Muhammad, he bound a stone upon his belly when he
was hungry; and as for Moses . . . it is said of him in the stories
that God revealed to him, 'Moses, when thou seest poverty approaching,
say, 'Welcome to the badge of the righteous!' And when thou seest
wealth approaching, say, 'Lo! a sin whose punishment has been put on
aforetime.' If thou shouldst wish, thou mightest name as a third the
Lord of the Spirit and the Word [Jesus], for in his affair there is a
marvel; he used to say, 'My daily bread is hunger, my badge is fear,
my raiment is wool, my mount is my foot, my lantern at night is
the moon, and my fire by day is the sun, and my fruit and fragrant
herbs are such things as the earth brings forth for the wild beasts and
the cattle. All the night I have nothing, yet there is none richer than I!'

Translation by A. J. Arberry, in his *Sufism* (London,
1950), pp. 33-5; as abridged by John Alden Williams,
Islam (New York, 1961), pp. 139-40

D. PROPHETS AND FOUNDERS OF RELIGIONS

224. ZARATHUSTRA IS BEING REPULSED BY EVERYBODY

('Yasna' 46)

At the beginning of the *Yasna* 46 Zarathustra is being repulsed by everybody. He knows the reason for his lack of success: his poverty 'in men and in cattle.' Therefore he turns to the wise Lord—Ahura Mazda—as a friend to a friend (stanza 2). In his prayers he calls for the reform of existence which is to be accomplished one day through the action of the saviour. He, Zarathustra, was chosen by the Lord to announce this good news (stanza 3). The following stanzas—4, and 7 to 11—depict the hosility which those who promote the Righteousness have to face from the wicked. In stanzas 12 to 17 the scene is changed; here Zarathustra enumerates his protectors. Whoever works at the renewal of the world on his, Zarathustra's, behalf, will obtain prosperity in the future life (stanzas 18-19).

1. *To what land shall I flee? Where bend my steps?*
   I am thrust out from family and tribe;
   I have no favour from the village to which I would belong,
   Nor from the wicked rulers of the country:
   How then, O Lord, shall I obtain thy favour?

2. *I know, O Wise One, why I am powerless:*
   My cattle are few, and I have few men.
   To thee I address my lament: attend unto it, O Lord,
   And grant me the support which friend would give to friend.
   As Righteousness teach the possession of the Good Mind.

3. *When, O Wise One, shall the wills of the future saviours come*
      forth,
   The dawns of the days when, through powerful judgment,
   The word shall uphold Righteousness?
   To whom will I help come through the Good Mind?
   To me, for I am chosen for the revelation by thee, O Lord.

49

4. The wicked one, ill-famed and of repellent deeds,
   Prevents the furtherers of Righteousness from fostering the cattle
   In the district and in the country.
   Whoever robs him of Dominion or of life, O Wise One,
   Shall walk foremost in the ways of the doctrine. . . .

7. Who, O Wise One, shall be sent as a protector to such as I am,
   If the evil one seeks to do me harm?
   Who but thy fire and thy mind, O Lord,
   Whose acts shall bring Righteousness to maturity?
   Do thou proclaim this mystery to my conscience!

8. Whoever seeks to injure my living possessions,
   May danger not come to me through his deeds!
   May all his actions turn against him with hostility, O Wise One,
   And take him from the good life, not the bad life!

   (A listener):

9. Who is he, the zealous man who first
   Taught me to honour thee as the most powerful,
   As the righteous Lord, holy in his action?
   (Zarathustra:)
   What he said to thee, to thee as Righteousness,
   What he said to Righteousness, the creator of the cattle,
   They ask it of me through thy Good Mind.

10. Whoever, man or woman, O wise Lord,
    Shall give me what thou knowest is the best of this existence,
    —To wit: reward for Righteousness and the Dominion (?) with
       (?) the Good Mind—
    And all those whom I shall induce to worship such as you,
    With all those will I cross the Bridge of the Separator!

11. The sacrificers and the sorcerer princes
    Have subdued mankind to the yoke of their Dominion,
    To destroy existence through evil deeds;
    They shall be tortured by their own soul and their own conscience,
    When they come to the Bridge of the Separator,
    For ever to be inmates of the house of Evil. . . .

13. Whoever among mortals pleases Spitama Zarathustra (? by his
       readiness?),
    He is worthy to be heard.
    To him shall the Wise One give existence,
    And as Good Mind he shall further his living possessions,

*(?) For his Righteousness (?) we shall consider him your faithful
    friend,
(To you and to Righteousness?). . . .*

18. Whoever is true to me, to him I promise, through the Good Mind,
     *That which I myself do most desire;
     But oppression to him who seeks to oppress us.
     O Wise One, I strive to satisfy your wish through Righteousness.
     Thus the decision of my will and of my mind.*

19. He who for me, who for Zarathustra,
     *According to Righteousness will bring to pass
     That which is most renewing by the will (of the Lord),
     To him as a reward, when he attains the future life,
     Shall come two pregnant cows with the ox and all that he desires
         through the Mind.
     This thou hast revealed to me, O Wise One, thou who knowest
         best!*

Translation and introductory commentary by Jacques
Duchesne-Guillemin, in his *The Hymns of Zarathustra*
(London, 1952), pp 75-83

225. PRINCE SIDDĀRTHA ENCOUNTERS OLD AGE,
SICKNESS AND DEATH

('Dīgha-nikāya,' XIV ['Mahāpadāna suttanta'])

Now the young lord Gotama, when many days had passed by, bade
his charioteer make ready the state carriages, saying: 'Get ready the
carriages, good charioteer, and let us go through the park to inspect
the pleasaunce.' 'Yes, my lord,' replied the charioteer, and harnessed
the state carriages and sent word to Gotama: 'The carriages are ready,
my lord; do now what you deem fit.' Then Gotama mounted a state
carriage and drove out in state into the park.

Now the young lord saw, as he was driving to the park, an aged
man as bent as a roof gable, decrepit, leaning on a staff, tottering as
he walked, afflicted and long past his prime. And seeing him Gotama
said: 'That man, good charioteer, what has he done, that his hair
is not like that of other men, nor his body?'

'He is what is called an aged man, my lord.'

'But why is he called aged?'

'He is called aged, my lord, because he has not much longer to live.'

'But then, good charioteer, am I too subject to old age, one who has not got past old age?'

'You, my lord, and we too, we all are of a kind to grow old; we have not got past old age.'

'Why then, good charioteer, enough of the park for today. Drive me back hence to my rooms.'

'Yea, my lord,' answered the charioteer, and drove him back. And he, going to his rooms, sat brooding sorrowful and depressed, thinking, 'Shame then verily be upon this thing called birth, since to one born old age shows itself like that!'

Thereupon the rāja sent for the charioteer and asked him: 'Well, good charioteer, did the boy take pleasure in the park? Was he pleased with it?'

'No, my lord, he was not.'

'What then did he see on his drive?'

(And the charioteer told the rāja all.)

Then the rāja thought thus: We must not have Gotama declining to rule. We must not have him going forth from the house into the homeless state. We must not let what the brāhman soothsayers spoke of come true.

So, that these things might not come to pass, he let the youth be still more surrounded by sensuous pleasures. And thus Gotama continued to live amidst the pleasures of sense.

Now after many days had passed by, the young lord again bade his charioteer make ready and drove forth as once before. . . .

And Gotama saw, as he was driving to the park, a sick man, suffering and very ill, fallen and weltering in his own water, by some being lifted up, by others being dressed. Seeing this, Gotama asked: 'That man, good charioteer, what has he done that his eyes are not like others' eyes, nor his voice like the voice of other men?'

'He is what is called ill, my lord.'

'But what is meant by ill?'

'It means, my lord, that he will hardly recover from his illness.'

'But I am too, then, good charioteer, subject to fall ill; have I not got out of reach of illness?'

'You, my lord, and we too, we are all subject to fall ill; we have not got beyond the reach of illness.'

'Why then, good charioteer, enough of the park for today. Drive me back hence to my rooms. 'Yea, my lord,' answered the charioteer, and drove him back. And he, going to his rooms, sat brooding sorrow-

ful and depressed, thinking: Shame then verily be upon this thing
called birth, since to one born decay shows itself like that, disease
shows itself like that.

Thereupon the rāja sent for the charioteer and asked him: 'Well,
good charioteer, did the young lord take pleasure in the park and was
he pleased with it?'

'No, my lord, he was not.'

'What did he see then on his drive?'

(And the charioteer told the rāja all.)

Then the rāja thought thus: We must not have Gotama declining
to rule; we must not have him going forth from the house to the
homeless state; we must not let what the brāhman soothsayers spoke
of come true.

So, that these things might not come to pass, he let the young man
be still more abundantly surrounded by sensuous pleasures. And thus
Gotama continued to live amidst the pleasures of sense.

Now once again, after many days . . . the young lord Gotama
. . . drove forth.

And he saw, as he was driving to the park, a great concourse of
people clad in garments of different colours constructing a funeral
pyre. And seeing this he asked his charioteer: 'Why now are all
those people come together in garments of different colours, and making
that pile?'

'It is because someone, my lord, has ended his days.'

'Then drive the carriage close to him who has ended his days.'

'Yea, my lord,' answered the charioteer, and did so. And Gotama saw
the corpse of him who had ended his days and asked: 'What, good
charioteer, is ending one's days?'

'It means, my lord, that neither mother, nor father, nor other kinsfolk
will now see him, nor will he see them.'

'But am I too then subject to death, have I not got beyond reach
of death? Will neither the rāja, nor the ranee, nor any other of my
kin see me more, or shall I again see them?'

'You, my lord, and we too, we are all subject to death; we have not
passed beyond the reach of death. Neither the rāja, nor the ranee,
nor any other of your kin will see you any more, nor will you see
them.'

'Why then, good charioteer, enough of the park for today. Drive
me back hence to my rooms.'

'Yea, my lord,' replied the charioteer, and drove him back.

And he, going to his rooms, sat brooding sorrowful and depressed, thinking: Shame verily be upon this thing called birth, since to one born the decay of life, since disease, since death shows itself like that!

Thereupon the rāja questioned the charioteer as before and as before let Gotama be still more surrounded by sensuous enjoyment. And thus he continued to live amidst the pleasures of sense.

Now once again, after many days . . . the lord Gotama . . . drove forth.

And he saw, as he was driving to the park, a shaven-headed man, a recluse, wearing the yellow robe. And seeing him he asked the charioteer, 'That man, good charioteer, what has he done that his head is unlike other men's heads and his clothes too are unlike those of others?'

'That is what they call a recluse, because, my lord, he is one who has gone forth.'

'What is that, "to have gone forth"?'

'To have gone forth, my lord, means being thorough in the religious life, thorough in the peaceful life, thorough in good action, thorough in meritorious conduct, thorough in harmlessness, thorough in kindness to all creatures.'

'Excellent indeed, friend charioteer, is what they call a recluse, since so thorough in his conduct in all those respects, wherefore drive me up to that forthgone man.'

'Yea, my lord,' replied the charioteer and drove up to the recluse. Then Gotama addressed him, saying, 'You master, what have you done that your head is not as other men's heads, nor your clothes as those of other men?'

'I, my lord, am one whose has gone forth.'

'What, master, does that mean?'

'It means, my lord, being thorough in the religious life, thorough in the peaceful life, thorough in good actions, thorough in meritorious conduct, thorough in harmlessness, thorough in kindness to all creatures.'

'Excellently indeed, master, are you said to have gone forth since so thorough is your conduct in all those respects.' Then the lord Gotama bade his charioteer, saying: 'Come then, good charioteer, do you take the carriage and drive it back hence to my rooms. But I will even here cut off my hair, and don the yellow robe, and go forth from the house into the homeless state.'

'Yea, my lord,' replied the charioteer, and drove back. But the prince Gotama, there and then cutting off his hair and donning the yellow robe, went forth from the house into the homeless state.

Now at Kapilavatthu, the rāja's seat, a great number of persons, some eighty-four thousand souls, heard of what prince Gotama had done and thought: Surely this is no ordinary religious rule, this is no common going forth, in that prince Gotama himself has had his head shaved and has donned the yellow robe and has gone forth from the house into the homeless state. If prince Gotama has done this, why then should not we also? And they all had their heads shaved and donned the yellow robes, and in imitation of the Bodhisat they went forth from the house into the homeless state. So the Bodhisat went up on his rounds through the villages, towns and cities accompanied by that multitude.

Now there arose in the mind of Gotama the Bodhisat, when he was meditating in seclusion, this thought: That indeed is not suitable for me that I should live beset. 'Twere better were I to dwell alone, far from the crowd.

So after a time he dwelt alone, away from the crowd. Those eighty-four thousand recluses went one way, and the Bodhisat went another way.

Now there arose in the mind of Gotama the Bodhisat, when he had gone to his place and was meditating in seclusion, this thought: Verily, this world has fallen upon trouble—one is born, and grows old, and dies, and falls from one state, and springs up in another. And from the suffering, moreover, no one knows of any way of escape, even from decay and death. O, when shall a way of escape from this suffering be made known—from decay and from death?'

> From Clarence H. Hamilton, *Buddhism* (New York, 1952), pp. 6-11, quoting translation by E. H. Brewster, in his *Life of Gotama the Buddha*, pp. 15-19. See also Rhys Davids, *Dialogues of the Buddha*, part 2 (Oxford, 1910), pp. 18 ff., which follows Brewster translation closely

226. GOTAMA'S FIRST MASTERS: KĀLĀMA AND RĀMAPUTTA

('Majjhima-nikāya,' XXVI ['Ariya-pariyesana-sutta'])

Yes, I myself too, in the days before my full enlightenment, when I was but a Bodhisatta, and not yet fully enlightened,—I too, being subject in myself to rebirth, decay and the rest of it, pursued what was no less subject thereto. But the thought came to me:—Why do I pursue what, like myself, is subject to rebirth and the rest? Why, being myself subject thereto, should I not, with my eyes open to the perils which these things entail, pursue instead the consummate peace of Nirvāna,—which knows neither rebirth nor decay, neither disease nor death, neither sorrow nor impurity?

There came a time when I, being young, with a wealth of coal-black hair untouched by grey and in all the beauty of my early prime— despite the wishes of my parents, who wept and lamented—cut off my hair and beard, donned the yellow robes and went forth from home to homelessness on Pilgrimage. A pilgrim now, in search of the right, and in quest of the excellent road to peace beyond compare, I came to Ālāra Kālāma and said:—It is my wish, reverend Kālāma, to lead the higher life in this your Doctrine and Rule. Stay with us, venerable sir, was his answer; my Doctrine is such that ere long an intelligent man can for himself discern, realize, enter on, and abide in, the full scope of his master's teaching. Before long, indeed very soon, I had his Doctrine by heart. So far as regards mere lip-recital and oral repetition, I could say off the (founder's) original message and the elders' exposition of it, and could profess, with others, that I knew and saw it to the full. Then it struck me that it was no Doctrine merely accepted by him on trust that Ālāra Kālāma, preached, but one which he professed to have entered on and to abide in after having discerned and realized it for himself; and assuredly he had real knowledge and vision thereof. So I went to him and asked him up to what point he had for himself discerned and realized the Doctrine he had entered on and now abode in.

Up to the plane of Naught, answered he.

Hereupon, I reflected that Ālāra Kālāma was not alone in possessing faith, perseverance, mindfulness, rapt concentration, and intellectual insight; for, all these were mine too. Why, I asked myself, should not I strive to realize the Doctrine which he claims to have entered on and to abide in after discerning and realizing it for himself? Before long, indeed very soon, I had discerned and realized his Doctrine for myself and had entered on it and abode therein. Then I went to him and asked him whether this was the point up to which he had discerned and realized for himself the Doctrine which he professed. He said yes; and I said that I had reached the same point for myself. It is a great thing, said he, a very great thing for us, that in you, reverend sir, we find such a fellow in the higher life. That same Doctrine which I for myself have discerned, realized, entered on, and profess,—that have you for yourself discerned, realized, entered on and abide in; and that same Doctrine which you have for yourself discerned, realized, entered on and profess,—that have I for myself discerned, realized, entered on, and profess. The Doctrine which I know, you too know; and the Doctrine which you know, I too know. As I am, so are you; and as you are, so am I. Pray, sir, let us be joint wardens of this company! In such wise did Ālāra Kālāma, being my master, set me, his pupil, on precisely the same footing as himself and show me great worship. But, as I bethought me that his Doctrine merely led to attaining the plane of Naught and not to Renunciation, passionlessness, cessation, peace, discernment, enlightenment and Nirvāna,—I was not taken with his Doctrine but turned away from it to go my way.

Still in search of the right, and in quest of the excellent road to peace beyond compare, I came to Uddaka Rāmaputta and said;—It is my wish, reverend sir, to lead the higher life in this your Doctrine and Rule. Stay with us . . . vision thereof. So I went to Uddaka Rāmaputta and asked him up to what point he had for himself discerned and realized the Doctrine he had entered on and now abode in.

Up to the plane of neither perception or non-perception, answered he.

Hereupon, I reflected that Uddaka Rāmaputta was not alone in possessing faith . . . show me great worship. But, as I bethought me that his Doctrine merely led to attaining the plane of neither perception nor non-perception, and not to Renunciation, passionlessness, cessation, peace, discernment, enlightenment and Nirvāna,—I was not taken with his Doctrine but turned away from it to go my way.

Still in search of the right, and in quest of the excellent road to peace beyond compare, I came, in the course of an alms-pilgrimage through Magadha, to the Camp township at Uruvelā and there took up my abode. Said I to myself on surveying the place:—Truly a delightful spot, with its goodly groves and clear flowing river with ghāts and amenities, hard by a village for sustenance. What more for his striving can a young man need whose heart is set on striving? So there I sat me down, needing nothing further for my striving.

Subject in myself to rebirth—decay—disease—death—sorrow—and impurity, and seeing peril in what is subject thereto, I sought after the consummate peace of Nirvāna, which knows neither sorrow nor decay, neither disease nor death, neither sorrow nor impurity;—this I pursued, and this I won; and there arose within me the conviction, the insight, that now my Deliverance was assured, that this was my last birth, nor should I ever be reborn again.

Translation by Lord Chalmers, *Further Dialogues of the Buddha*, 1 (London, 1926), pp. 115-18

227. AFTER THE ILLUMINATION THE BUDDHA PROCLAIMS:
'I AM THE HOLY ONE IN THIS WORLD, I AM THE HIGHEST
TEACHER . . .'

('Mahāvagga,' I, 7-9)

Now Upaka, a man belonging to the Ājīvaka sect (i.e. the sect of naked ascetics), saw the Blessed One travelling on the road, between Gayā and the Bodhi tree; and when he saw him, he said to the Blessed One: 'Your countenance, friend, is serene; your complexion is pure and bright. In whose name, friend, have you retired from the world? Who is your teacher? Whose doctrine do you profess?'

When Upaka the Ājīvaka had spoken thus, the Blessed One addressed him in the following stanzas: 'I have overcome all foes; I am all-wise; I am free from stains in every way; I have left everything; and have obtained emancipation by the destruction of desire. Having myself gained knowledge, whom should I call my master? I have no teacher; no one is equal to me; in the world of men and of gods no being is like me. I am the holy One in this world, I am the highest teacher, I alone am the Absolute Sambuddha; I have gained coolness (by the extinction of all passion) and have obtained Nirvāna. To found the Kingdom of Truth I go to the city of the Kāsis (Benares); I will beat the drum of the Immortal in the darkness of this world.'

(Upaka replied): 'You profess then, friend, to be the holy, absolute Jina.[1]

(Buddha said): 'Like me are all Jinas who have reached extinction of the Āsavas;[2] I have overcome all states of sinfulness; therefore, Upaka, am I the Jina.'

When he had spoken thus, Upaka, the Ājīvaka replied: 'It may be so, friend': shook his head, took another road, and went away.

Notes

1 *Jina*, or the victorious One, is one of the many appellations common to the founders of Buddhism and Jainism.
2 *Āsava*,—sensuality, individuality, delusion, and ignorance.

Translation and notes by T. W. Rhys Davids and Hermann Oldenberg, *Vinaya Texts*, part I, in *Sacred Books of the East*, XIII, (Oxford, 1881), pp. 90-1

228. GOTAMA BUDDHA PONDERS: 'MUST I NOW PREACH
WHAT I SO HARDLY WON?'

(*'Majjhima-nikāya,'* XXVI [*'Āriya-pariyesana-sutta'*])

I have attained, thought I, to this Doctrine profound, recondite, hard
to comprhend, serene, excellent, beyond dialectic, abstruse, and only
to be perceived by the learned. But mankind delights, takes delight,
and is happy in what it clings on to, so that for it, being thus minded
it is hard to understand causal relations and the chain of causation,—
hard to understand the stilling of all plastic forces, or the renunciation
of all worldly ties, the extirpation of craving, passionlessness, peace
and Nirvāna. Were I to preach the Doctrine, and were others not to
understand it, that would be labour and annoyance to me! Yes, and
on the instant there flashed across my mind these verses, which no
man had heard before:—

> *Must I now preach what I so hardly won?*
> *Men sunk in sin and lusts would find it hard*
> *to plumb this Doctrine,—up stream all the way,*
> *abstruse, profound, most subtle, hard to grasp.*
> *Dear lusts will blind them that they shall not see,*
> *—in densest mists of ignorance befogged.*

As thus I pondered, my heart inclined to rest quiet and not to preach
my Doctrine. But, Brahmā Sahāmpati's mind came to know what
thoughts were passing within my mind, and he thought to himself:—
The world is undone, quite undone, inasmuch as the heart of the
Truth-finder inclines to rest quiet and not to preach his Doctrine!
Hereupon, as swiftly as a strong man might stretch out his arm or
might draw back his outstretched arm, Brahmā Sahāmpati vanished
from the Brahmā-world and appeared before me. Towards me he came
with his right shoulder bared, and with his clasped hands stretched
out to me in reverence, saying:—May it please the Lord, may it
please the Blessed One, to preach his doctrine! Beings there are whose
vision is but little dimmed, who are perishing because they do not
hear the Doctrine;—these will understand it!

Translation by Lord Chalmers, *Further Dialogues of
the Buddha,* I (London, 1926), pp. 118-19

229. GOTAMA BUDDHA REMEMBERS HIS EARLIER
EXISTENCES

('Majjhima-nikāya,' IV ['Bhaya-bherava-sutta])

With heart thus steadfast, thus clarified and purified, clean and
cleansed of things impure, tempered and apt to serve, stablished and
immutable,—it was thus that I applied my heart to the knowledge
which recalled my earlier existences. I called to mind my divers existences in the past,—a single birth, then two . . . [and so on to] . . .
a hundred thousand births, many an aeon of disintegration of the
world, many an aeon of its redintegration, and again many an aeon
both of its disintegration and of its redintegration. In this or that
former existence, I remembered, such and such was my name, my
sept, my class, my diet, my joys and sorrows, and my term of life.
When I passed thence, I came by such and such subsequent existence,
wherein such and such was my name and so forth. Thence I passed to
my life here. Thus did I call to mind my divers existences of the past
in all their details and features.—This, brahmin, was the first knowledge attained by me, in the first watch of that night,—ignorance dispelled and knowledge won, darkness dispelled and illumination won,
as befitted my strenuous and ardent life, purged of self.

That same steadfast heart I now applied to knowledge of the passage
hence, and re-appearance elsewhere, of other beings. With the Eye
Celestial, which is pure and far surpasses the human eye, I saw things
in the act of passing hence and of re-appearing elsewhere,—being high
and low, fair or foul to view, in bliss or woe; I saw them all faring
according to their past. Here were beings given over to evil in act,
word and thought, who decried the Noble and had a wrong outlook
and became what results from such wrong outlook;—these, at the
body's dissolution after death, made their appearance in states of
suffering, misery and tribulation and in purgatory. Here again were
beings given to good in act, word and thought, who did not decry the
Noble, who had the right outlook and became what results from right
outlook;—these, at the body's dissolution after death, made their
appearance in states of bliss in heaven. All this did I see with the Eye
Celestial; and this, brahmin, was the second knowledge attained by
me, in the second watch of that night,—ignorance dispelled and
knowledge won, darkness dispelled and illumination won, as befitted
my strenuous and ardent life, purged of self.

That same steadfast heart I next applied to knowledge of the eradication of Cankers. I comprehended, aright and to the full, Ill, the origin of Ill, the cessation of Ill, and the course that leads to the cessation of Ill. I comprehend, aright and to the full, what the Cankers were, with their origin, cessation, and the course that leads to their cessation. When I knew this and when I saw this, then my heart was delivered from the Canker of sensuous pleasure, from the Canker of continuing existence, and from the Canker of ignorance; and to me thus delivered came the knowledge of my Deliverance in the conviction—Rebirth is no more; I have lived the highest life; my task is done; and now for me there is no more of what I have been. This, Brahmin, was the third knowledge attained by me, in the third watch of that night,—ignorance dispelled and knowledge won, darkness dispelled and illumination won, as befitted my strenuous and ardent life, purged of self.

Translation by Lord Chalmers, *Further Dialogues of the Buddha*, I (London, 1926), pp. 15-17

230. THE BUDDHA ENTERS NIRVĀNA

(Ashvagosha, 'Buddhacarita,' XXVI, 83-6, 88-106)

Thereupon the Buddha turned to his Disciples, and said to them: 'Everything comes to an end, though it may last for an aeon. The hour of parting is bound to come in the end. Now I have done what I could do, both for myself and for others. To stay here would from now on be without any purpose. I have disciplined, in heaven and on earth, all those whom I could discipline, and I have set them in the stream. Hereafter this my Dharma, O monks, shall abide for generations and generations among living beings. Therefore, recognize the true nature of the living world, and do not be anxious; for separation cannot possibly be avoided. Recognize that all that lives is subject to this law; and strive from today onwards that it shall be thus no more! When the light of gnosis has dispelled the darkness of ignorance, when all existence has been seen as without substance, peace ensues when life draws to an end, which seems to cure a long sickness at last. Everything, whether stationary or moveable, is bound to perish in the end. Be ye therefore mindful and vigilant! The time for my entry into Nirvāna has now arrived. These are my last words!'

Thereupon, supreme in his mastery of the trances, He at that moment entered into the first trance, emerged from it and went on to the second, and so in due order he entered all of them without omitting one. And then, when he had ascended through all the nine stages of meditational attainment, the great Seer reversed the process, and returned again to the first trance. Again he emerged from that, and once more he ascended step by step to the fourth trance. When he emerged from the practice of that, he came face to face with everlasting Peace.

And when the Sage entered Nirvāna, the earth quivered like a ship struck by a squall, and firebrands fell from the sky. The heavens were lit up by a preternatural fire, which burned without fuel, without smoke, without being fanned by the wind. Fearsome thunderbolts crashed down on the earth, and violent winds raged in the sky. The moon's light waned, and, in spite of a cloudless sky, an uncanny darkness spread everywhere. The rivers, as if overcome with grief, were filled with boiling water. Beautiful flowers grew out of season on the Sal trees above the Buddha's couch, and the trees bent down over him and showered his golden body with their flowers. Like as many gods the five-headed Nāgas stood motionless in the sky, their eyes reddened with grief, their hoods closed and their bodies kept in restraint, and with deep devotion they gazed upon the body of the Sage. But, well-established in the practice of the supreme Dharma, the gathering of the gods round king Vaishravana was not grieved and shed no tears, so great was their attachment to the Dharma. The Gods of the Pure Abode, though they had great reverence for the Great Seer, remained composed, and their minds were unaffected; for they hold the things of this world in the utmost contempt. The Kings of the Gandharvas and Nāgas, as well as the Yakshas and the Devas who rejoice in the true Dharma—they all stood in the sky, mourning and absorbed in the utmost grief. But Mara's hosts felt that they had obtained their heart's desire. Overjoyed they uttered loud laughs, danced about, hissed like snakes, and triumphantly made a frightful din by beating drums, gongs and tom-toms. And the world, when the Prince of Seers had passed beyond, became like a mountain whose peak has been shattered by a thunderbolt; it became like the sky without the moon, like a pond whose lotuses the frost has withered, or like learning rendered ineffective by lack of wealth.

Translation by Edward Conze, in Conze (ed.), *Buddhist Scriptures* (Penguin Books, 1959), pp. 62-4

231. MUHAMMAD'S CALL (AT-TABARĪ)

Ahmad b. 'Uthman, who is known as Abu'l-jawza', has related to me on the authority of Wahb b. Jarir, who heard his father say that he had heard from an-Nu'man b. Rashid, on the authority of az-Zuhri from 'Urwa, from 'A'isha, who said: The way revelation (*wahy*) first began to come to the Apostle of Allah—on whom be Allah's blessing and peace—was by means of true dreams which would come like the morning dawn. Then he came to love solitude, so he used to go off to a cave in Hira[1] where he would practise *tahannuth*[2] certain nights before returning to his family. Then he would come back to his family and take provisions for the like number [of nights] until unexpectedly the truth came to him.

He (i.e., Gabriel) came to him saying: 'O Muhammad, thou art Allah's Apostle (*rasūl*[3]).' Said the Apostle of Allah—upon whom be Allah's blessing and peace: 'Thereat I fell to my knees where I had been standing, and then with trembling limbs dragged myself along till I came in to Khadija,[4] saying: "Wrap ye me up! Wrap ye me up!"[5] till the terror passed from me. Then [on another occasion] he came to me again and said: "O Muhammad, thou art Allah's Apostle," [which so disturbed me] that I was about to cast myself down from some high mountain cliff. But he appeared before me as I was about to do this, and said: "O Muhammad, I am Gabriel, and thou art Allah's Apostle." Then he said to me: "Recite!"; but I answered: "What should I recite?"; whereat he seized me and grievously treated me three times, till he wore me out. Then he said: "Recite, in the name of thy Lord who has created" (Sūra XCVI, 1). So I recited it and then went to Khadija, to whom I said: "I am worried about myself." Then I told her the whole story. She said: "Rejoice, for by Allah, Allah will never put thee to shame. By Allah, thou art mindful of thy kinsfolk, speakest truthfully, renderest what is given thee in trust, bearest burdens, art ever hospitable to the guest, and dost always uphold the right against any wrong." Then she took me to Waraqua b. Naufal b. Asad [to whom] she said: "Give ear to what the son of thy brother [has to report]." So he questioned me, and I told him [the whole] story. Said he: "This is the *nāmūs*[6] which was sent down upon Moses the son of Amram. Would that I might be a stalwart youth [again to take part] in it. Would that I might still be alive when your people turn you out." "And will they turn me out?" I asked. "Yes," said he, "never yet has a man come with that with which you come but has been turned away. Should I be there when your day comes I will lend you mighty assistance." '

Notes

1 A mountain in the environs of Mecca.
2 This is probably intended to represent the Hebrew word *tihinnōth* 'prayers.'
3 *Rasūl* is literally 'messenger,' but like the New Testament *apostolos*, as a messenger of God it technically means an Apostle.
4 His first wife, an elderly and wealthy Meccan widow who had married him some years earlier.
5 See Sūra LXXIII, 1.
6 This is from the Syriac transliteration of the Greek word *nomos*, 'law,' which is used in the Septuagint and the New Testament for the Mosaic law, i.e., the Torah.

> Translation and notes by Arthur Jeffery, *Islam. Muhammad and His Religion* (New York: Liberal Arts Press, 1958), pp. 15-17; from at-Tabarī, *Ta'rīkh ar-rusul wa'l-mulūk* (Leiden, 1881), I, 1147-52

232. MUHAMMAD IS THE MESSENGER OF GOD

('Koran,' XLVIII, 30-3)

> Muhammad is the Messenger of God,
> and those who are with him are hard
> against the unbelievers, merciful
> one to another. Thou seest them
> bowing, prostrating, seeking bounty
> from God and good pleasure. Their
> mark is on their faces, the trace of
> prostration. That is their likeness
> in the Torah, and their likeness
> in the Gospel: as a seed that puts
> forth its shoot, and strengthens it,
> and it grows stout and rises straight
> upon its stalk, pleasing the sowers,
> that through them He may enrage
> the unbelievers. God has promised
> those of them who believe and do deeds
> of righteousness forgiveness and
> a mighty wage.

> Translation by A. J. Arberry

233. MUHAMMAD PROCLAIMS THE KORAN, 'THE BOOK WHEREIN IS NO DOUBT . . .'

('Koran,' II, 1-23)

That is the book, wherein is no doubt,
  a guidance to the godfearing
who believe in the Unseen, and perform the prayer,
and expend of that We have provided them;
who believe in what has been sent down to thee
  and what has been sent down before thee,
  and have faith in the Hereafter;
those are upon guidance from their Lord,
  those are the ones who prosper.

As for the unbelievers, alike it is to them
whether thou hast warned them or hast not warned them,
  they do not believe.
God has set a seal on their hearts and on their hearing,
  and on their eyes is a covering,
and there awaits them a mighty chastisement.

  And some men there are who say,
'We believe in God and the Last Day';
  but they are not believers.
They would trick God and the believers,
  and only themselves they deceive,
    and they are not aware.
  In their hearts is a sickness,
  and God has increased their sickness,
and there awaits them a painful chastisement
  for that they have cried lies.
When it is said to them, 'Do not corruption in the land,'
they say, 'We are only ones that put things right.'
  Truly, they are the workers of corruption
    but they are not aware.
When it is said to them, 'Believe as the people believe,'
they say, 'Shall we believe, as fools believe?'
  Truly, they are the foolish ones,
    but they do not know.
When they meet those who believe, they say, 'We believe';

but when they go privily to their Satans, they say,
　‘We are with you; we were only mocking.’
　God shall mock them, and shall lead them on
　blindly wandering in their insolence.
　Those are they that have bought error
　　at the price of guidance,
　and their commerce has not profited them,
　　and they are not right-guided.
The likeness of them is as the likeness of a man
who kindled a fire, and when it lit all about him
God took away their light, and left them in darkness
　　　unseeing,
　　deaf, dumb, blind—
　　so they shall not return;
　or as a cloudburst out of heaven
in which is darkness, and thunder, and lightning—
　they put their fingers in their ears
　against the thunderclaps, fearful of death;
　　and God encompasses the unbelievers;
the lightning wellnigh snatches away their sight;
whensoever it gives them light, they walk in it,
and when the darkness is over them, they halt;
　had God willed, He would have taken away
　　their hearing and their sight.
Truly, God is powerful over everything.

O you men, serve your Lord Who created you,
and those that were before you; haply so
　you will be godfearing;
who assigned to you the earth for a couch,
and heaven for an edifice, and sent down
out of heaven water, wherewith He brought forth
fruits for your provision; so set not up
　compeers to God wittingly.
And if you are in doubt concerning that We have
sent down on Our servant, then bring a sura
like it, and call your witnesses, apart from
　God, if you are truthful.
And if you do not—and you will not—then
fear the Fire, whose fuel is men and stones,
　prepared for unbelievers.

*Give thou good tidings to those who believe
and do deeds of righteousness, that for them
await gardens underneath which rivers flow;
whensoever they are provided with fruits therefrom
they shall say, 'This is that wherewithal
we were provided before'; that they shall be
given in perfect semblance; and there
for them shall be spouses purified; therein
  they shall dwell forever.*

Translation by A. J. Arberry

234. ALLAH TELLS MUHAMMAD THE STORY OF ABRAHAM

('Koran,' XIX, 42-52)

*And mention in the Book Abraham;
surely he was a true man, a Prophet.
When he said to his father, 'Father,
why worshippest thou that which neither
hears nor sees, nor avails thee anything?
Father, there has come to me knowledge
such as came not to thee; so follow me,
And I will guide thee on a level path.
Father, serve not Satan; surely Satan
is a rebel against the All-merciful.
Father, I fear that some chastisement
from the All-merciful will smite thee,
so that thou becomest a friend to Satan.'
Said he, 'What, art thou shrinking
from my gods, Abraham? Surely, if thou
givest not over, I shall stone thee;
so forsake me now for some while.'
He said, 'Peace be upon thee!
I will ask my Lord to forgive thee;
surely He is ever gracious to me.
Now I will go apart from you
and that you call upon, apart from*

67

God; I will call upon my Lord,
and haply I shall not be, in calling
upon my Lord, unprosperous.'
So, when he went apart from them
and that they were serving, apart
from God, We gave him Isaac and
Jacob, and each We made a Prophet
and We gave them of Our mercy,
and We appointed unto them
a tongue of truthfulness, sublime.

Translation by A. J. Arberry

235. ALLAH REVEALS TO MUHAMMAD HOW HE SAVED
THE CHILDREN OF ISRAEL

('Koran,' XVII, 104-9)

And We gave Moses nine signs,
clear signs. Ask the Children of Israel
when he came to them, and Pharaoh
said to him, 'Moses, I think thou art bewitched.'
He said, 'Indeed thou knowest that none
sent these down, except the Lord
of the heavens and earth, as clear
proofs; and, Pharaoh, I think thou art accursed.'
He desired to startle them from the land;
and We drowned him and those with him, all together.
And We said to the Children of Israel
after him, 'Dwell in the land; and
when the promise of the world to come
comes to pass, we shall bring you a rabble.'

With the truth We have sent it down,
and with the truth it has come down;
and We have sent thee not, except
good tidings to bear, and warning;
and a Koran We have divided,
for thee to recite it to mankind

at intervals, and We have sent it down successively.
Say: 'Believe in it, or believe not';
those who were given the knowledge before it
when it is recited to them, fall down
upon their faces prostrating, and say,
'Glory be to our Lord! Our Lord's promise is performed.'

Translation by A. J. Arberry

236. ALLAH SENT THE TORAH, THE PROPHETS, AND JESUS, SON OF MARY

('Koran,' V, 50-3)

And We sent, following
in their footsteps, Jesus
son of Mary, confirming
the Torah before him;
and We gave to him
the Gospel, wherein
is guidance and light,
and confirming the Torah
before it, as a guidance
and an admonition
unto the godfearing.
So let the People of the Gospel judge
according to what God has sent down
therein. Whosoever judges not
according to what God has sent down—
they are the ungodly.

And We have sent down to thee the Book
with the truth, confirming the Book
that was before it, and assuring it.
So judge between them according to what
God has sent down, and do not follow
their caprices, to forsake the truth
that has come to thee. To every one
of you We have appointed a right way
and an open road.

Translation by A. J. Arberry

237. MUHAMMAD SPEAKS BY REVELATION

('Koran,' XLII, 50-4)

It belongs not to any mortal that
God should speak to him, except
by revelation, or from behind a veil,
or that He should send a messenger
and He reveal whatsoever He will
by His leave; surely He is
    All-high, All-wise.
Even so We have revealed to thee a
Spirit of Our bidding. Thou knewest
not what the Book was, nor belief;
but We made it a light, whereby We
guide whom We will of Our servants. And thou,
surely thou shalt guide unto a straight path—
the path of God, to whom belongs whatsoever is in
the heavens and whatsoever is in the earth. Surely
    unto God all things come home.

Translation by A. J. Arberry

See also nos. 43, 252, 268, 269

E. SPIRITUAL TECHNIQUES AND MYSTICAL EXPERIENCES

238. A NEOPLATONIST PHILOSOPHER ON THE ARTS AND EFFECTS OF ECSTASY

(Iamblichus, 'On the Mysteries,' III, 4-6)

Iamblichus was born in Syria and lived from ca. 250 to 325 A.D. His book On the Mysteries *is in the form of a reply by a certain Abammon to a letter by Porphyry addressed 'To Anebo' and is a defence of ritualistic magic or theurgy. Iamblichus' presentation of Neoplatonism fell far below the high teaching of Plotinus and incorporated much popular superstition.*

(4) Among the signs by which those who are truly possessed by the gods may be known, the greatest is the fact that many [of those who experience ecstasy] are not burned, though fire is applied to them, since the deity breathing within them does not permit the fire to touch them; many, though burned, are unaware of it, since at that moment they are not dwelling in the body [literally, not living an animal life]. Many have daggers thrust through their bodies without feeling it; others have their backs cut [open] with hatchets, or cut their arms with knives, without taking any notice. The activities in which they are engaged are not of a human kind, and since they are borne by God they can reach places which are inaccessible to men; they pass through fire unharmed; they tread upon fire and cross over streams, like the priestess in Castabala [who walked barefoot on snow and hot coals]. This proves that in their enthusiasm [i.e., their state of inspiration] they are not aware of what they are doing and are not living a human or bodily existence as far as sensation and volition are concerned, but live instead another and diviner kind, which fills them and takes complete possession of them.

(5) There are many different kinds of divine possession, and there are different ways of awakening the divine spirit; consequently there are many different indications of this state. For one thing, there are

different gods from whom we receive the spirit [i.e., are inspired], and this results in a variety of forms in which the inspiration manifests itself; further, the kinds of influence exerted are different, and so there are various ways in which the divine seizure takes place. For either the god takes possession of us, or else we are entirely absorbed in him, or else [thirdly] we co-operate with him. At times we partake of the lowest power of God, at others of the middle [power], at still others of the highest [i.e., first]. Sometimes it is a mere participation, again it is a communion [fellowship or sharing], or again it becomes a union of these [two] kinds. Now the soul enjoys complete separation; again it is still involved in the body, or [else] the whole nature is laid hold of [and controlled].

Hence the signs of possession are manifold: either movement of the body and its parts, or complete relaxation; [either] singing choirs, round dances, and harmonious voices, or the opposite of these. [The] bodies have been seen to rise up, grow, or move freely in the air, and the opposite has also been observed. They have been heard to utter [different] voices of equal strength, or with great diversity and inequality, in tones that alternated with silence; and again in other cases harmonious crescendo or diminuendo of tone, and in still other cases other kinds of utterance.

(6) But the greatest thing [about this experience] is that the one who thus draws down a deity beholds the greatness and the nature of the invading spirit; and he is secretly guided and directed by him. So too he who receives a god sees also a fire before he takes it into himself. Now and then the god manifests himself to all who are present, either as he comes or as he goes. From this it is made known, to those who have the knowledge, wherein his truth and his power chiefly consist and his place [in the divine hierarchy], and what qualifies him by his nature to make known the truth; and also what power he is able to grant or to maintain. Those, however, who without this beatifying view invoke the spirits are merely reaching out and touching things in the dark, and do not know what they are doing, save for certain minor signs in the body of the possessed person and other indubitable, visible symptoms; but the full understanding of divine possession is denied them, being hid in the invisible.

Translation and introduction by Frederick C. Grant, in his *Hellenistic Religions* (New York, 1953), pp. 173-5

TECHNIQUES OF YOGA

239. CONCENTRATION 'ON A SINGLE POINT'

The point of departure of Yoga meditation is concentration on a single object; whether this is a physical object (the space between the eyebrows, the tip of the nose, something luminous, etc.), or a thought (a metaphysical truth), or God (Ishvara) makes no difference. This determined and continuous concentration, called *ekāgratā* ('on a single point'), is obtained by integrating the psychomental flux (*sarvārthatā*, 'variously directed, discontinuous, diffused attention'). This is precisely the definition of yogic technique: *yogah cittavritti-nirodhyah*, i.e., the yoga is the suppression of psychomental states (*Yoga-sūtras*, I, 2).

The immediate result of *ekāgratā*, concentration on a single point, is prompt and lucid censorship of all the distractions and automatisms that dominate—or, properly speaking, compose—profane consciousness. Completely at the mercy of associations (themselves produced by sensations and the *vāsanās*), man passes his days allowing himself to be swept hither and thither by an infinity of disparate moments that are, as it were, external to himself. The senses or the subconscious continually introduce into consciousness objects that dominate and change it, according to their form and intensity. Associations disperse consciousness, passions do it violence, the 'thirst for life' betrays it by projecting it *outward*. Even in his intellectual efforts, man is passive, for the fate of secular thoughts (controlled not by *ekāgratā* but only by fluctuating moments of concentration, *kshiptavikshiptas*) is to be thought by objects. Under the appearance of thought, there is really an indefinite and disordered flickering, fed by sensations, words, and memory. The first duty of the yogin is to think—that is, not to let *himself* think. This is why Yoga practice begins with *ekāgratā*, which dams the mental stream and thus constitutes a 'psychic mass,' a solid and unified continuum.

The practice of *ekāgratā* tends to control the two generators of mental fluidity: sense activity (*indriya*) and the activity of the subconscious (*samskāra*). Control is the ability to intervene, at will and directly, in the functioning of these two sources of mental 'whirlwinds' (*cittavritti*). A yogin can obtain discontinuity of consciousness at will;

in other words, he can, at any time and any place, bring about concentration of his attention on a 'single point' and become insensible to any other sensory or mnemonic stimulus. Through *ekāgratā* one gains a genuine will—that is, the power freely to regulate an important sector of biomental activity. It goes without saying that *ekāgratā* can be obtained only through the practice of numerous exercises and techniques, in which physiology plays a role of primary importance. One cannot obtain *ekāgratā* if, for example, the body is in a tiring or even uncomfortable posture, or if the respiration is disorganized, unrhythmical. This is why, according to Patañjali, yogic technique implies several categories of physiological practices and spiritual exercises (called *angas*, 'members'), which one must have learned if one seeks to obtain *ekāgratā* and, ultimately, the highest concentration, *samādhi*. These 'members' of Yoga can be regarded both as forming a group of techniques and as being stages of the mental ascetic itinerary whose end is final liberation. They are: (1) restraints (*yama*), (2) disciplines (*niyama*); (3) bodily attitudes and postures (*āsana*); (4) rhythm of respiration (*prānāyāma*); (5) emancipation of sensory activity from the domination of exterior objects (*pratyāhāra*); (6) concentration (*dhāranā*); (7) yogic meditation (*dhyāna*); (8) *samādhi* (Yoga-sūtras, II, 29).

Each class (*anga*) of practices and disciplines has a definite purpose. Patañjali hierarchizes these 'members of Yoga' in such a way that the yogin cannot omit any of them, except in certain cases. The first two groups, *yama* and *niyama*, obviously constitute the necessary preliminaries for any type of asceticism, hence there is nothing specifically yogic in them. The restraints (*yama*) purify from certain sins that all systems of morality disapprove but that social life tolerates. Now, the moral law can no longer be infringed here—as it is in secular life—without immediate danger to the seeker for deliverance. In Yoga, every sin produces its consequences immediately. The five restraints are *ahimsā*, 'not to kill,' *satya*, 'not to lie,' *asteya*, 'not to steal,' *brahmacarya*, 'sexual abstinence,' *aparigraha*, 'not to be avaricious.'

Together with these restraints, the yogin must practise the *niyamas* —that is, a series of bodily and psychic 'disciplines.' 'Cleanliness, serenity "*samtosha*," asceticism "*tapas*," the study of Yoga metaphysics, and the effort to make God "*Īshvara*," the motive of all one's actions constitute the disciplines.' (Y.S., II, 32.)

M. Eliade, *Yoga: Immortality and Freedom*, trans. Willard R. Trask (New York: Bollingen Series LVI, 1958), pp. 47-50

240. YOGIC POSTURES (ĀSANA) AND RESPIRATORY
DISCIPLINE (PRĀNĀYĀMA)

It is only with the third 'member of Yoga' (yogānga) that yogic technique, properly speaking, begins. This third 'member' is āsana, a word
designating the well-known yogic posture that the Yoga-sūtras (11, 46)
define as sthirasukham, 'stable and agreeable.' Āsana is described in
numerous Hatha Yoga treatises; Patañjali defines it only in outline,
for āsana is learned from a guru and not from descriptions. The important thing is that āsana gives the body a stable rigidity, at the same
time reducing physical effort to a minimum. Thus, one avoids the
irritating feeling of fatigue, of enervation in certain parts of the body,
one regulates the physical processes, and so allows the attention to
devote itself solely to the fluid part of consciousness. At first an āsana
is uncomfortable and even unbearable. But after some practice, the
effort of maintaining the body in the same position becomes incon-
siderable. Now (and this is of the highest importance), effort must
disappear, the position of meditation must become natural; only then
does it further concentration. 'Posture becomes perfect when the effort
to attain it disappears, so that there are no more movements in the
body. In the same way, its perfection is achieved when the mind is
transformed into infinity—that is, when it makes the idea of its infinity
its own content' (Vyāsa, ad Y.S. 11, 47.) And Vācaspatimishra, com-
menting on Vyāsa's interpretation, writes: 'He who practises āsana
must employ an effort that consists in suppressing the natural efforts
of the body. Otherwise this kind of ascetic posture cannot be realized.'
As for 'the mind transformed into infinity,' this means a complete
suspension of attention to the presence of one's own body.

Āsana is one of the characteristic techniques of Indian asceticism.
It is found in the Upanishads and even in Vedic literature, but allusions
to it are more numerous in the Mahābhārata and in the Purānas.
Naturally, it is in the literature of Hatha Yoga that the āsanas play
an increasingly important part; the Gheranda Samhitā describes thirty-
two varieties of them. Here, for example, is how one assumes one of
the easiest and most common of the meditational positions, the
padmāsana: 'Place the right foot on the left thigh and similarly the
left one on the right thigh, also cross the hands behind the back and
firmly catch the great toes of the feet so crossed (the right hand on
the right great toe and the left hand on the left). Place the chin on the
chest and fix the gaze on the tip of the nose.' (11, 8.) Lists and descrip-

tions of *āsanas* are to be found in most of the tantric and Hatha-yogic treatises. The purpose of these meditational positions is always the same; 'absolute cessation of trouble from the pairs of opposites' (*Yoga-sūtras*, II, 48.) In this way one realizes a certain 'neutrality' of the senses; consciousness is no longer troubled by the 'presence of the body.' One realizes that first stage towards isolation of consciousness; the bridges that permit communication with sensory activity begin to be raised.

On the plane of the 'body,' *āsana* is an *ekāgratā*, a concentration on a single point; the body is 'tense,' concentrated in a single position. Just as *ekāgratā* puts an end to the fluctuation and dispersion of the states of consciousness, so *āsana* puts an end to the mobility and dis-posability of the body, by reducing the infinity of possible positions to a single archetypal, iconographic posture. Refusal to move (*āsana*), to let oneself be carried along on the rushing stream of states of conscious-ness (*ekāgratā*) will be continued by a long series of refusals of every kind.

The most important—and, certainly, the most specifically yogic—of these various refusals is the disciplining of respiration (*prāṇāyāma*)—in other words, the 'refusal' to breathe like the majority of mankind, that is, nonrhythmically. Patañjali defines this refusal as follows: '*Prāṇāyāma* is the arrest [*viccheda*] of the movements of inhalation and exhalation and it is obtained after *āsana* has been realized. (Y.S., II, 49.) Patañjali speaks of the 'arrest,' the suspension, of respiration; however, *prāṇāyāma* begins with making the respiratory rhythm as slow as possible; and this is its first objective. There are a number of texts that treat of this Indian ascetic technique, but most of them do no more than repeat the traditional formulas. Although *prāṇāyāma* is a specifically yogic exercise, and one of great importance, Patañjali devotes only three *sūtras* to it. He is primarily concerned with the theoretical bases of ascetic practices; technical details are found in the commentaries by Vyāsa, Bhoja, and Vācaspatimishra, but especially in the Hatha-yogic treatises.

A remark of Bhoja's reveals the deeper meaning of *prāṇāyāma*: 'All the functions of the organs being preceded by that of respiration—there being always a connection between respiration and conscious-ness in their respective functions—respiration, when all the functions of the organs are suspended, realizes concentration of consciousness on a single object' (ad Y.S. I, 34.). The statement that a connection always exists between respiration and mental states seems to us highly important. It contains far more than mere observation of the bare fact, for example, the respiration of a man in anger is agitated, while that of one who is concentrating (even if only provisionally and without any yogic purpose) becomes rhythmical and automatically slows down, etc. The relation connecting the rhythm of respiration with the states of consciousness mentioned by Bhoja, which has undoubtedly been observed and experienced by yogins from the earliest times—this relation has served them as an instrument for 'unifying' consciousness. The 'unification' here under consideration must be understood in the sense that, by making his respiration rhythmical and progressively slower, the yogin can 'penetrate'—that is, he can experience, in perfect lucidity—certain states of consciousness that are inaccessible in a waking condition, particularly the states of consciousness that are peculiar to sleep. For there is no doubt that the respiratory system of a man asleep is slower than that of a man awake. By reaching this rhythm of sleep through the practice of *prānāyāma*, the yogin, without renouncing his lucidity, penetrates the states of consciousness that accompany sleep.

The Indian ascetics recognize four modalites of consciousness (beside the enstatic 'state'): diurnal consciousness, consciousness in sleep with dreams, consciousness in sleep without dreams, and 'cataleptic consciousness.' By means of *prānāyāma*—that is, by increasingly prolonging inhalation and exhalation (the goal of this practice being to allow as long an interval as possible to pass between the two moments of respiration)—the yogin can, then, penetrate all the modalities of consciousness. For the noninitiate, there is discontinuity between these several modalities; thus he passes from the state of waking to the state of sleep unconsciously. The yogin must preserve continuity of consciousness—that is, he must penetrate each of these states with determination and lucidity.

But experience of the four modalities of consciousness (to which a particular respiratory rhythm naturally corresponds), together with *unification* of consciousness (resulting from the yogin's getting rid of the discontinuity between these four modalities), can only be realized after long practice. The immediate goal of *prānāyāma* is more modest. Through it one first of all acquires a 'continuous consciousness,' which alone can make yogic meditation possible. The respiration of the ordinary man is generally arhythmic; it varies in accordance with external circumstances or with mental tension. This irregularity produces a dangerous psychic fluidity, with consequent instability and diffusion of attention. One can become attentive by making an effort to do so. But, for Yoga, effort is an exteriorization. Respiration must be made rhythmical, if not in such a way that it can be 'forgotten' entirely, at least in such a way that it no longer troubles us by discontinuity. Hence, through *prāṇāyāma*, one attempts to do away with the effort of respiration, rhythmic breathing must become something so automatic that the yogin can forget it.

Rhythmic respiration is obtained by harmonizing the three 'moments'; inhalation *(pūraka)*, exhalation *(recaka)*, and retention of the inhaled air *(kumbhaka)*. These three moments must each fill an equal space of time. Through practice the yogin becomes able to prolong them considerably, for the goal of *prāṇāyāma* is, as Patañjali says, to suspend respiration as long as possible; one arrives at this by progressively retarding the rhythm.

M. Eliade, *Yoga, op. cit.,* pp. 53-8

241. YOGIC CONCENTRATION AND MEDITATION

Āsana, prāṇāyāma and *ekāgratā* succeed—if only for the short time the respective exercise continues—in abolishing the human condition. Motionless. breathing rhythmically, eyes and attention fixed on a single point, the yogin experiences a passing beyond the secular modality of existence. He begins to become autonomous in respect to the cosmos: external tensions no longer trouble him (having passed beyond 'the opposites,' he is equally insensible to heat and cold, to light and darkness, etc.); sensory activity no longer carries him outward, toward the objects of the senses;. the psychomental stream is no longer either invaded or directed by distractions, automatisms, and memory: it is 'concentrated,' 'unified.' This retreat outside the cosmos is accompanied by a sinking into the self, progress in which is directly proportional to progress in the retreat. The yogin returns to himself, takes, so to speak, possession of himself, surrounds himself with increasingly stronger 'defences' to protect him against invasion from without—in a word, he becomes invulnerable. . . .

Making respiration rhythmical and, as far as possible, suspending it greatly promote concentration *(dhāraṇā)*. For, Patañjali tells us (Y.S., II, 52, 53), through *prāṇāyāma* the veil of darkness is rent and the intellect becomes capable *(yogyata)* of concentration *(dhāraṇā)*. The yogin can test the quality of his concentration by *pratyāhāra* (a term usually translated 'withdrawal of the senses' or 'abstraction,' which we prefer to translate 'ability to free sense activity from the domination of external objects'). According to the *Yoga-sūtras* (II, 54), *pratyāhāra* could be understood as the faculty through which the intellect (*citta*) possesses sensations as if the contact were real.

This withdrawal of sensory activity from the domination of exterior objects (*pratyāhāra*) is the final stage of psychophysiological *ascesis*. Thenceforth the yogin will no longer be 'distracted' or 'troubled' by the senses, by sensory activity, by memory, etc. All activity is suspended. The *citta*—being the psychic mass that orders and illuminates sensations coming from without—can serve as a mirror for objects, without the senses interposing between it and its object. The non-initiate is incapable of gaining this freedom, because his mind, instead of being stable is constantly violated by the activity of the senses, by the subconscious, and by the 'thirst for life.' By realizing *cittavritti nirodhyah* (i.e., the suppression of psychomental states), the *citta* abides in itself *(svarūpamātre)*. But this 'autonomy' of the intellect does not result in the suppression of phenomena. Even though detached from phenomena, the yogin continues to contemplate them. Instead of knowing through forms (*rūpa*) and mental states (*cittavritti*), as formerly, the yogin now contemplates the essence *(tattva)* of all objects directly.

Autonomy with respect to stimuli from the outer world and to the dynamism of the subconscious—an autonomy that he realizes through *pratyāhāra*—allows the yogin to practise a threefold technique, which the texts call *samyama*. The term designates the last stages of yogic meditation, the last three 'members of Yoga' *(yoganga)*. These are concentration (*dhāranā*), meditation properly speaking (*dhyāna*), and stasis *(samādhi)*.

Concentration (*dhāranā*, from the root *dhrī*, 'to hold fast') is in fact an *ekāgratā*, a 'fixing on a single point,' but its content is strictly notional. In other words, *dhāranā*—and this is what distinguishes it from *ekāgratā*, whose sole purpose is to arrest the psychomental flux and 'fix it on a single point'—realizes such a 'fixation' for the purpose of *comprehension*. Patañjali's definition of it is: 'fixation of thought on a single point' (*deshabandhashcittasya dhāranā*; Y.S. III, 1); Vyāsa adds that the concentration is usually on 'the centre [*cakra*] of the navel, on the lotus of the heart, on the light within the head, on the tip of the nose, on the tip of the tongue, or on any external place or object.' Vācaspatimishra further adds that one cannot obtain *dhāranā* without the aid of an object on which to fix one's thought.

In his *Yogasāra-samgraha*, Vijñānabhikshu quotes a passage from the

Ishvara Gītā according to which a *dhāraṇā* takes the time of twelve *prāṇāyāmas*. 'The time necessary for concentration of the mind on an object [*dhāraṇā*] is equal to the time taken by twelve *prāṇāyāmas*' (i.e., by twelve controlled, equal, and retarded respirations). By prolonging this concentration on an object twelve times, one obtains 'yogic meditation,' *dhyāna*. Patañjali defines *dhyāna* as 'a current of unified thought' (Y.S., III, 2), and Vyāsa adds the following gloss to the definition: 'Continuum of mental effort to assimilate other objects.' Vijñānabhikshu explains this process as follows: when, after achieving *dhāraṇā* on some point, one's mind has succeeded for a sufficient time in holding itself before itself under the form of the object of meditation, without any interruption caused by the intrusion of any other function, one attains *dhyāna*.

M. Eliade, *Yoga, op. cit.,* pp. 66-72

242. SAMĀDHI

The passage from 'concentration' to 'meditation' does not require the application of any new technique. Similarly, no supplementary yogic exercise is needed to realize *samādhi*, once the yogin has succeeded in 'concentrating' and 'meditating.' *Samādhi*, yogic 'enstasis,' is the final result of the crown of all the ascetic's spiritual efforts and exercises. The meanings of the term *samādhi* are union, totality; absorption in, complete concentration of mind; conjunction. The usual translation is 'concentration,' but this embarks the risk of confusion with *dhāraṇā*. Hence we have preferred to translate it 'entasis,' 'stasis,' and conjunction.

. . . Patañjali and his commentators distinguish several kinds or stages of supreme concentration. When *samādhi* is obtained with the help of an object or idea (that is, by fixing one's thought on a point in space or on an idea), the stasis is called *samprajñāta samādhi* ('enstasis with support,' or 'differentiated enstasis'). When, on the other hand, *samādhi* is obtained apart from any 'relation' (whether external or mental)—that is, when one obtains a 'conjunction' into which no 'otherness' enters, but which is simply a full comprehension of being—one has realized *asamprajñāta samādhi* ('undifferentiated stasis'). Vijñānabhikshu adds that *samprajñāta samādhi* is a means of liberation in so far as it makes possible the comprehension of truth and ends every kind of suffering. But *asamprajñāta samādhi* destroys the 'impressions [*samskāra*] of all antecedent mental functions' and even succeeds in arresting the karmic forces already set in motion by the yogin's past activity. During 'differentiated stasis,' Vijñābhikshu continues, all the mental functions are 'arrested' ('inhibited'), except that which 'meditates on the object'; whereas in *asamprajñāta samādhi* all 'consciousness' vanishes, the entire series of mental functions are blocked. 'During this stasis, there is no other trace of the mind [*citta*] save the impressions [*samskāra*] left behind (by its past functioning). If these impressions were not present, there would be no possibility of returning to consciousness.'

We are, then, confronted with two sharply differentiated classes of 'states.' The first class is acquired through the yogic technique of concentration (*dhāranā*) and meditation (*dhyāna*); the second class comprises only a single 'state'—that is, unprovoked enstasis, 'raptus.' No doubt, even this *asamprajñāta samādhi* is always owing to prolonged efforts on the yogin's part. It is not a gift or a state of grace. One can hardly reach it before having sufficiently experienced the kinds of *samādhi* included in the first class. It is the crown of the innumerable 'concentrations' and 'meditations' that have preceded it. But it comes without being summoned, without being provoked, without special preparation for it. That is why it can be called a 'raptus.'

Obviously, 'differentiated enstasis,' *samprajñāta samādhi*, comprises several stages. This is because it is perfectible and does not realize an absolute and irreducible 'state.' Four stages or kinds are generally distinguished: 'argumentative' (*savitarka*), 'nonargumentative' (*nirvitarka*), 'reflective' (*savicāra*), 'super-reflective' (*nirvicāra*). Patañjali also employs another set of terms: *vitarka, vicāra, ānanda, asmitā.* (Y.S., 1, 17). But, as Vijñānabhikshu, who reproduces this list, remarks, 'the four terms are purely technical, they are applied conventionally to different forms of realization.' These four forms or stages of *samprajñāta samādhi*, he continues, represent an ascent; in certain cases the grace of God (Īshvara) permits direct attainment of the higher states, and in such cases the yogin need not go back and realize the preliminary states. But when this divine grace does not intervene, he must realize the four states gradually, always adhering to the same object of meditation (for example, Vishnu). These four grades or stages are also known as *samāpattis*, 'coalescences.' (Y.S., 1, 41.)

All these four stages of *samprajñāta samādhi* are called *bīja samādhi* ('*samādhi* with seed') or *sālambana samādhi* ('with support'); for Vijñānabhikshu tells us, they are in relation with a 'substratum' (support) and produce tendencies that are like 'seeds' for the future functions of consciousness. *Asamprajñāta samādhi*, on the contrary, is *nirbīja*, 'without seed,' without support. By realizing the four stages of *samprajñāta*, one obtains the 'faculty of absolute knowledge' (Y.S., I, 48). This is already an opening towards *samādhi* 'without seed,' for absolute knowledge discovers the ontological completeness in which *being* and *knowing* are no longer separated. Fixed in *samādhi*, consciousness *(citta)* can now have direct revelation of the Self *(purusha)*. Through the fact that this contemplation (which is actually a 'participation') is realized, the pain of existence is abolished.

Vyāsa (ad Y.S., III, 55) summarizes the passage from *samprajñāta* to *asamprajñāta samādhi* as follows: through the illumination *(prajñā*, 'wisdom') spontaneously obtained when he reaches the stage of *dharma-megha-samādhi*, the yogin realizes 'absolute isolation' *(kaivalya)*—that is, liberation of *purusha* from the dominance of *prakriti*. For his part, Vācaspatimishra says that the 'fruit' of *samprajñāta samādhi* is *asamprajñāta samādhi*, and the 'fruit' of the latter is *kaivalya*, liberation. It would be wrong to regard this mode of being of the Spirit as a simple 'trance' in which consciousness was emptied of all content. Nondifferentiated enstasis is not absolute emptiness.' The 'state' and the 'knowledge' simultaneously expressed by this term refer to a total absence of objects in consciousness, not to a consciousness absolutely empty. For, on the contrary, at such a moment consciousness is saturated with a direct and total intuition of being. As Mādhava says, '*nirodha* [final arrest of all psychomental experience] must not be imagined as a nonexistence, but rather as the support of a particular condition of the Spirit.' It is the enstasis of total emptiness, without sensory content or intellectual structure, an unconditioned state that is no longer 'experience' (for there is no further relation between consciousness and the world) but 'revelation.' Intellect *(buddhi)*, having accomplished its mission, withdraws, detaching itself from the Self *(purusha)* and returning into *prakriti*. The Self remains free, autonomous: it contemplates itself. 'Human' consciousness is suppressed; that is, it no longer functions, its constituent elements being reabsorbed into the primordial substance. The yogin attains deliverance; like a dead man, he has no more relation with life; he is 'dead in life.' He is the *jīvan-mukta*, the 'liberated in life.' He no longer lives in time and under the domination of time, but in an eternal present, in the *nunc stans* by which Boethius defined eternity.

M. Eliade, *Yoga, op. cit.*, pp. 77, 79-81, 83-4, 93-4

JAPANESE BUDDHISM

243. KŪYA, 'THE SAINT OF THE STREETS': A PIONEER OF THE PURE LAND BUDDHISM

The rise of Pure Land Buddhism was not merely an outgrowth of the new feudal society, translating into religious terms the profound social changes which then took place. Already in the late Heian period we find individual monks who sensed the need for bringing Buddhist faith within the reach of the ordinary man, and thus anticipated the mass religious movements of medieval times. Kūya (903-72), a monk on Mt. Hiei, was one of these. The meditation on the Buddha Amida, which had long been accepted as an aid to the religious life, he promoted as a pedestrian devotion. Dancing through the city streets with a tinkling bell hanging from around his neck, Kūya called out the name of Amida and sang simple ditties of his own composition, such as:

> He never fails
> To reach the Lotus Land of Bliss
> Who calls,
> If only once,
> The name of Amida.

> A far, far distant land
> Is Paradise,
> I've heard them say;
> But those who want to go
> Can reach there in a day.

In the market places all kinds of people joined him in his dance and sang out the invocation to Amida, 'Namu Amida Butsu.' When a great epidemic struck the capital, he proposed that these same people join him in building an image of Amida in a public square, saying that common folk could equal the achievement of their rulers, who had built the Great Buddha of Nara, if they cared to try. In country districts he built bridges and dug wells for the people where these were needed, and to show that no one was to be excluded from the blessings of

Paradise, he travelled into regions inhabited by the Ainu and for the first time brought to many of them the evangel of Buddhism.

Wm. Theodore de Bary (ed.), *Sources of Japanese Tradition* (New York: Columbia University Press, 1958), pp. 193-4

244. HŌNEN AND THE INVOCATION OF AMIDA, THE BUDDHA OF BOUNDLESS LIGHT

Hōnen (1133-1212) believed that the invocation of Amida's name, Namu Amida Butsu, was the only sure hope of salvation. This invocation became known as the Nembutsu, *a term which originally signified meditation on the name of Amida, but later meant simply the fervent repetition of his name.*

The wife of the ex-Regent, Kanezane Tsukinowa, already converted to Hōnen's faith, asked him some questions regarding the practice of Nembutsu. *Hōnen replied as follows:*

I have the honour of addressing you regarding your inquiry about the *Nembutsu*. I am delighted to know that you are invoking the sacred name. Indeed the practice of the *Nembutsu* is the best of all for bringing us to Ōjō,[1] because it is the discipline prescribed in Amida's Original Vow. The discipline required in the Shingon, and the meditation of the Tendai, are indeed excellent, but they are not in the Vow. This *Nembutsu* is the very thing that Shākya himself entrusted[2] to his disciple, Ānanda. As to all other forms of religious practice belonging to either the meditative or non-meditative classes, however excellent they may be in themselves, the great Master did not specially entrust them to Ānanda to be handed down to posterity. Moreover, the *Nembutsu* has the endorsation of all the Buddhas of the six quarters; and, while the disciples of the exoteric and esoteric schools, whether in relation to the phenomenal or noumenal worlds, are indeed most excellent, the Buddhas do not give them their final approval. And so, although there are many kinds of religious exercise, the *Nembutsu* far excels them all in its way of Attaining Ōjō. Now there are some people who are unacquainted with the way of birth into the Pure Land, who say, that because the *Nembutsu* is so easy, it is all right for those who are incapable of keeping up the practices required in the Shingon, and the meditation of the Tendai sects, but such a cavil is absurd. What I mean is, that I throw aside those practices not included in Amida's Vow, nor prescribed by Shākyamuni, nor having the endorsement of the Buddhas of all quarters of the universe, and now only throw myself upon the Original Vow of Amida, according to the authoritative teaching of Shākyamuni, and in harmony with what the many Buddhas of the six quarters have definitely approved. I give up my own foolish plans of salvation, and devote myself exclusively to the practice of that mightily effective discipline of the Nembutsu, with earnest prayer for birth into the Pure Land. This is the reason why the abbot of the Eshin-in Temple in his work *Essentials of Salvation (Ōjōyōshū)* makes the Nembutsu the most fundamental of all. And so you should now cease from all other religious practices, apply yourself to the Nembutsu alone, and in this it is all-important to do it with undivided attention. Zendō,[3] who himself attained to that perfect insight (*samādhi*) which apprehends the truth, clearly expounds the full meaning of this in his Commentary on the *Meditation Sūtra*, and in the *Two-volumed Sūtra* the Buddha (Shākya) says, 'Give yourself with undivided mind to the repetition of the name of the Buddha who is in Himself endless life.' And by 'undivided mind' he means to present a contrast to a mind which is broken up into two or three sections, each pursuing its own separate object, and to exhort to the laying aside of everything but this one thing only. In the prayers which you offer for your loved ones, you will find that the Nembutsu is the one most conducive to happiness. In the *Essentials of Salvation*, it says that the Nembutsu is superior to all other works. Also Dengyō Daishi, when telling how to put an end to the misfortunes which result from the seven evils, exhorts to the practice of the Nembutsu. Is there indeed anything anywhere that is superior to it for bringing happiness in the present or the future life? You ought by all means to give yourself up to it alone.'

Notes

1 Rebirth in the Pure Land.
2 This refers to the passage in the *Meditation Sūtra* which says: 'Buddha said to Ānanda, "Preserve well these words. I mean to preserve well the name of the Buddha of Endless Life."'
3 Chinese Patriarch of Pure Land Sect.

Translation and notes by Rev. Harper Havelock Coates and Rev. Ryugaku Ishizuka, *Hōnen, the Buddhist Saint*, III (Kyoto, 1925), pp. 371-3

245. SHINRAN: 'THE NEMBUTSU ALONE IS TRUE'

('Tannishō,' selections)

Shinran (1173-1262), who claimed to be Hōnen's true disciple, is regarded as the founder of the most important of all 'Pure Land' sects. Shinran's utter reliance on the power of Amida is emphasized by his reinterpretation of the Nembutsu. A single, sincere invocation is enough, said Shinran, and any additional recitation of the Name should merely be an expression of thanksgiving to Amida.

The collection of Shinran's sayings is said to have been made by his disciple Yuiembō, who was concerned over heresies and schisms developing among Shinran's followers and wished to compile a definitive statement of his master's beliefs.

Your aim in coming here, travelling at the risk of your lives through more than ten provinces, was simply to learn the way of rebirth in the Pure Land. Yet you would be mistaken if you thought I knew of some way to obtain rebirth other than by saying the *Nembutsu*, or if you thought I had some special knowledge of religious texts not open to others. Should this be your belief, it is better for you to go to Nara or Mt. Hiei, for there you will find many scholars learned in Buddhism and from them you can get detailed instruction in the essential means of obtaining rebirth in the Pure Land. As far as I, Shinran, am concerned, it is only because the worthy Hōnen taught me so that I believe salvation comes from Amida by saying the *Nembutsu*. Whether the *Nembutsu* brings rebirth in the Pure Land or leads one to Hell, I myself have no way of knowing. But even if I had been misled by Hōnen and went to Hell for saying the *Nembutsu*, I would have no regrets. If I were capable of attaining Buddhahood on my own through the practice of some other discipline, and yet went down to Hell for saying the *Nembutsu*, then I might regret having been misled. But since I am incapable of practising such disciplines, there can be no doubt that I would be doomed to Hell anyway.

If the Original Vow of Amida is true, the teaching of Shākyamuni cannot be false. If the teaching of the Buddha is true, Zendō's commentary on the *Meditation Sūtra* cannot be wrong. And if Zendō is right, what Hōnen says cannot be wrong. So if Hōnen is right, what I, Shinran, have to say may not be empty talk.

Such, in short, is my humble faith. Beyond this I can only say that, whether you are to accept this faith in the *Nembutsu* or reject it, the choice is for each of you to make. . . .

'If even a good man can be reborn in the Pure Land, how much more so a wicked man.'

People generally think, however, that if even a wicked man can be reborn in the Pure Land, how much more so a good man! This latter view may at first sight seem reasonable, but it is not in accord with the purpose of the Original Vow, with faith in the Power of Another. The reason for this is that he who, relying on his own power, undertakes to perform meritorious deeds, has no intention of relying on the Power of Another and is not the object of the Original Vow of Amida. Should he, however, abandon his reliance on his own power and put his trust in the Power of Another, he can be born in the True Land of Recompense. We who are caught in the net of our own passions cannot free ourselves from bondage to birth and death, no matter what kind of austerities or good deeds we try to perform. Seeing this and pitying our condition, Amida made his Vow with the intention of bringing wicked men to Buddhahood. Therefore the wicked man who depends on the Power of Another is the prime object of salvation. This is the reason why Shinran said, 'If even a good man can be reborn in the Pure Land, how much more so a wicked man!' . . .

It is regrettable that among the followers of the *Nembutsu* there are some who quarrel, saying 'These are my disciples, those are not.' There is no one whom I, Shinran, can call my own disciple. The reason is that, if a man by his own efforts persuaded others to say the *Nembutsu*, he might call them his disciples, but it is most presumptuous to call those 'my disciples' who say the *Nembutsu* because they have been moved by the grace of Amida. If it is his karma to follow a teacher, a man will follow him; if it is his karma to forsake a teacher, a man will forsake him. It is quite wrong to say that the man who leaves one teacher to join another will not be saved by saying the *Nembutsu*. To claim as one's own and attempt to take back that faith which is truly the gift of Amida—such a view is wholly mistaken. In the normal course of things a person will spontaneously recognize both what he owes to the grace of Amida and what he owes to his teacher [without the teacher having to assert any claims]. . . .

The Master was wont to say, 'When I ponder over the Vow which Amida made after meditating for five kalpas, it seems as if the Vow were made for my salvation alone. How grateful I am to Amida, who thought to provide for the salvation of one so helplessly lost in sin!'

When I now reflect upon this saying of the Master, I find that it is

fully in accordance with the golden words of Zendō. 'We must realize
that each of us is an ordinary mortal, immersed in sin and crime,
subject to birth and death, ceaselessly migrating from all eternity and
ever sinking deeper into Hell, without any means of delivering ourselves from it.'

It was on this account that Shinran most graciously used himself as
an example, in order to make us realize how lost every single one of us
is and how we fail to appreciate our personal indebtedness to the
grace of Amida. In truth, none of us mentions the great love of
Amida, but we continually talk about what is good and what is bad.
Shinran said, however, 'Of good and evil I am totally ignorant. If I
understood good as Buddha understands it, then I could say I knew
what was good. If I understood evil as Buddha understands it, then
I could say I knew what was bad. But I am an ordinary mortal, full
of passion and desire, living in this transient world like the dweller in
a house on fire. Every judgment of mine, whatever I say, is nonsense
and gibberish. The *Nembutsu* alone is true.'

Translation in Wm. Theodore de Bary (ed.), *Sources
of Japanese Tradition* (New York: Columbia University Press, 1958), pp. 216-18. Introductory note based
on De Bary

246. NICHIREN AND THE 'ADORATION TO THE LOTUS OF THE PERFECT TRUTH'

*Nichiren (1222-82) held that the Lotus Sūtra represents the final
and supreme teaching of the Buddha Shākyamuni, revealing the one
and only way of salvation. While the prevailing schools of Japanese
Buddhism emphasize one form of Buddha at the expense of the others,
the Lotus Sūtra alone upholds the truth of the triune Buddha (i.e.,
Dharmakāya, Sambhogakāya, and Nirmānakāya). For Nichiren, only
in this trinity is the salvation of all assured. So it is the name of the
Lotus Sūtra, not the name of Amida Buddha, which should be on the
lips of every Buddhist.*

If you desire to attain Buddhahood immediately, lay down the banner
of pride, cast away the club of resentment, and trust yourselves to the
unique Truth. Fame and profit are nothing more than vanity of this
life; pride and obstinacy are simply fetters to the coming life. . . .

When you fall into an abyss and some one has lowered a rope to pull you out, should you hesitate to grasp the rope because you doubt the power of the helper? Has not Buddha declared, 'I alone am the protector and saviour'? There is the power! Is it not taught that faith is the only entrance [to salvation]? There is the rope! One who hesitates to seize it, and will not utter the Sacred Truth, will never be able to climb the precipice of Bodhi (Enlightenment). . . . Our hearts ache and our sleeves are wet [with tears], until we see face to face the tender figure of the One, who says to us, 'I am thy Father.' At this thought our hearts beat, even as when we behold the brilliant clouds in the evening sky or the pale moonlight of the fast-falling night. . . . Should any season be passed without thinking of the compassionate promise, 'Constantly I am thinking of you'? Should any month or day be spent without revering the teaching that there is none who cannot attain Buddhahood? . . . Devote yourself wholeheartedly to the 'Adoration to the Lotus of the Perfect Truth,' and utter it yourself as well as admonish others to do the same. Such is your task in this human life.

Masaharu Anesaki, *Nichiren, the Buddhist Prophet* (Cambridge, Mass., 1916), pp. 46-7; as quoted in Wm. Theodore de Bary (ed.), *Sources of Japanese Tradition* (New York: Columbia University Press, 1958), pp. 222-23

See also nos. 193, 216, 217

ZEN BUDDHISM

To bring salvation within the reach of ordinary men—this was the common aim of the Buddhist sects which spread abroad in medieval Japan. Yet to achieve this same end, and to guide men through the uncertainties, turmoil and suffering of that difficult age, these new movements sometimes employed quite different means. The Pure Land and Nichiren sects stressed the need for complete faith in something beyond oneself: the saving power of Amida or of the *Lotus Sūtra.* To find rest and security, they said, man had to turn himself and this world to the Other World. By contrast Zen Buddhism, which first rose to prominence in these same times, firmly opposed the idea that

Buddhahood is something to be sought outside oneself or in another world. Every man has a Buddha-nature, and to realize it he need only look within. Self-understanding and self-reliance are the keynote of Zen.

The means by which this inner realization may be achieved is indicated by the term Zen, meaning 'meditation' or 'concentration.' To speak of it as a 'means,' however, is appropriate only with reference to the specific procedure involved in the practice of meditation: sitting erect, cross-legged and motionless, with the mind concentrated so as to achieve, first, tranquility, and then active insight. But in the light of this insight the method and realization are seen to be one; no 'means' is employed, no 'end' is attained.

> Wm. Theodore de Bary (ed.), *Sources of Japanese Tradition* (New York: Columbia University Press, 1958), p. 232

247. REALIZING THE SOLUTION (GENJŌ KŌAN)

[Against the notion that enlightenment is a single, momentary experience.]

To study the way of the Buddha is to study your own self. To study your own self is to forget yourself. To forget yourself is to have the objective world prevail in you. To have the objective world prevail in you, is to let go of your 'own' body and mind as well as the body and mind of 'others.' The enlightenment thus attained may seem to come to an end, but though it appears to have stopped this momentary enlightenment should be prolonged and prolonged.

[Against the notion that the objective world is merely a projection of one's own mind.]

When you go out on a boat and look around, you feel as if the shore were moving. But if you fix your eyes on the rim of the boat, you become aware that the boat is moving. It is exactly the same when you try to know the objective world while still in a state of confusion in regard to your own body and mind; you are under the misapprehension that your own mind, your own nature, is something real and enduring [while the external world is transitory]. Only when you sit straight and look into yourself, does it become clear that [you yourself are changing and] the objective world has a reality apart from you.

[The fullness of enlightenment.]

Our attainment of enlightenment is something like the reflection of the moon in water. The moon does not get wet, nor is the water cleft apart. Though the light of the moon is vast and immense, it finds a home in water only a foot long and an inch wide. The whole moon and the whole sky find room enough in a single dewdrop, a single drop of water. And just as the moon does not cleave the water apart, so enlightenment does not tear man apart. Just as a dewdrop or drop of water offers no resistance to the moon in heaven, so man offers no obstacle to the full penetration of enlightenment. Height is always the measure of depth. [The higher the object, the deeper will seem its reflection in the water.]

> From Hashida, *Shōbō genzō shakui*, I, 142-64, selections translated in De Bary (ed.), *Sources of Japanese Tradition*, op. cit., pp. 251-2

248. SITTING AND THE KŌAN

In the pursuit of the Way [Buddhism] the prime essential is sitting (*zazen*). . . . By reflecting upon various 'public-cases' (*kōan*) and dialogues of the patriarchs, one may perhaps get the sense of them but it will only result in one's being led astray from the way of the Buddha, our founder. Just to pass the time in sitting straight, without any thought of acquisition, without any sense of achieving enlightenment —this is the way of the Founder. It is true that our predecessors recommended both the *kōan* and sitting, but it was the sitting that they particularly insisted upon. There have been some who attained enlightenment through the test of the *kōan*, but the true cause of their enlightenment was the merit and effectiveness of sitting. Truly the merit lies in the sitting.

> From the *Shōbō genzō zuimonki*, pp. 98-9, translated in De Bary (ed.), *Sources of Japanese Tradition*, op. cit., p. 253

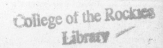

249. THE IMPORTANCE OF SITTING

When I stayed at the Zen lodge in T'ien-t'ung [China], the venerable Ching used to stay up sitting until the small hours of the morning and then after only a little rest would rise early to start sitting again. In the meditation hall we went on sitting with the other elders, without letting up for even a single night. Meanwhile many of the monks went off to sleep. The elder would go around among them and hit the sleepers with his fist or a slipper, yelling at them to wake up. If their sleepiness persisted, he would go out to the hallway and ring the bell to summon the monks to a room apart, where he would lecture to them by the light of a candle.

'What use is there in your assembling together in the hall only to go to sleep? Is this all that you left the world and joined holy orders for? Even among laymen, whether they be emperors, princes, or officials, are there any who live a life of ease? The ruler must fulfill the duties of the sovereign, his ministers must serve with loyalty and devotion, and commoners must work to reclaim land and till the soil —no one lives a life of ease. To escape from such burdens and idly while away the time in a monastery—what does this accomplish? Great is the problem of life and death; fleeting indeed is our transitory existence. Upon these truths both the scriptural and meditation schools agree. What sort of illness awaits us tonight, what sort of death tomorrow? While we have life, not to practise Buddha's Law, but to spend the time in sleep is the height of foolishness. Because of such foolishness Buddhism today is in a state of decline. When it was at its zenith monks devoted themselves to the practice of sitting in meditation (*zazen*), but nowadays sitting is not generally insisted upon and consequently Buddhism is losing ground.' . . .

Upon another occasion his attendants said to him, 'The monks are getting overtired or falling ill, and some are thinking of leaving the monastery, all because they are required to sit too long in meditation. Shouldn't the length of the sitting period be shortened?' The master became highly indignant. 'That would be quite wrong. A monk who is not really devoted to the religious life may very well fall asleep in a half hour or an hour. But one truly devoted to it who has resolved to persevere in his religious discipline will eventually come to enjoy the practice of sitting, no matter how long it lasts. When I was young I used to visit the heads of various monasteries, and one of them explained to me, "Formerly I used to hit sleeping monks so hard that my fist just about broke. Now I am old and weak, so I can't hit them hard enough. Therefore it is difficult to produce good monks. In many monasteries today the superiors do not emphasize sitting strongly enough, and so Buddhism is declining. The more you hit them the better," he advised me.'

From the *Shōbō genzō zuimonki*, pp. 50-2, translated by Wm. Theodore de Bary, in De Bary (ed.), *Sources of Japanese Tradition, op. cit.*, pp. 253-4

250. CONTEMPT FOR THE SCRIPTURES

There are Zen masters of a certain type who join in a chorus to deny that the sūtras contain the true teaching of the Buddha. 'Only in the personal transmission from one patriarch to another is the essential truth conveyed; only in the transmission of the patriarchs can the exquisite and profound secrets of Buddha be found.' Such statements represent the height of folly, they are the words of madmen. In the genuine tradition of the patriarchs there is nothing secret or special, not even a single word or phrase, at variance with the Buddhist sūtras. Both the sūtras and the transmission of the patriarchs alike represent the genuine tradition deriving from Shākyamuni Buddha. The only difference between them is that the patriarchs' transmission is a direct one from person to person. Who dares, then, to ignore the Buddha's sūtras? Who can refuse to study them, who can refuse to recite them? Wisely it has been said of old, 'It is you who get lost in the sūtras, not the sūtras that lead you astray.' Among our worthy predecessors there were many who studied the Scriptures. Therefore these loose-tongued individuals should be told, 'To discard the sūtras of the Buddha, as you say, is to reject the mind of the Buddha, to reject the body of the Buddha. To reject the mind and body of the Buddha is to reject the children [followers] of the Buddha. To reject children of the Buddha is to reject the teaching of the Buddha. And if the teaching of the Buddha itself is to be rejected, why should not the teaching of the patriarchs be rejected? And when you have abandoned the teaching of the Buddha and the patriarchs, what will be left except a lot of bald-headed monks? Then you will certainly deserve to be chastised by the rod. Not only would you deserve to be enslaved by the rulers of the world, but to be cast into Hell for punishment.'

From Etō, *Shūso to shite no Dōgen Zenji*, p. 246, translated by Wm. Theodore de Bary, in De Bary (ed.), *Sources of Japanese Tradition, op, cit.*, pp. 255-6

ISLAM

251. MUHAMMAD'S ASCENSION

Each year throughout the Muslim world, on the night of the 27th day of the month Rajah, is celebrated the festical called *Lailat al-Mi'raj*, i.e., the Night of the Prophet's Ascension. The Qur'anic basis for this is Sura XVII, 1: 'Glory be to Him Who took His servant by night from the sacred temple [at Mecca] to the more remote temple, whose precincts We have blessed, to show him some of Our signs.' On this night mosques are lit up and special services of celebration held at which it is customary to read certain little chapbooks which give more or less elaborate accounts of the famous Night Journey. The brief account of the *Mi'raj* given here is that found in the well-known compendium of Traditions, al-Baghawi's *Masabih as-Sunna* (Khairiyya edition: Cairo, A.H. 1318=A.D. 1900) II, 169-72.

[It is related] from Quatada, quoting from Anas b. Malik—with whom may Allah be pleased—from Malik b. Sa'sa'a, who said that the Prophet of Allah—on whom be Allah's blessing and peace—related to them [the story of] the night on which he was taken on his heavenly journey, saying: While I was in al-Hatim[1]—or maybe he said, While I was in al-Hijr—lying at rest, one came to me,[2] split all between here and here—i.e., from the hollow of his throat to his pubic hair—and drew out my heart. Then there was brought a golden basin filled with faith in which he washed my heart and my bowels and then they were returned [to their place]. According to another line of transmission [the Prophet] said: Then he washed my stomach with water of Zazam,[3] and filled it with faith and wisdom. Then a white riding beast was brought, somewhat smaller than a mule yet bigger than an ass, whose every bound carried him as far as his eye could reach. Him I mounted and Gabriel set off with me till we came to the lowest heaven, which he asked should be opened. 'Who is this?' he was asked. 'Gabriel,' he replied. 'And who is that with you?' 'Muhammad,' said he. 'And has he had revelation sent him?' 'Assuredly,' said he. 'Then welcome to him. How blessed a coming.' Thereat [the gate] was opened, and when I had cleared it, lo! there was Adam. [Gabriel] said: 'This is your father Adam, greet him.' So I gave him greeting, which he returned, saying: 'Welcome to you, O righteous son, righteous prophet.' Then Gabriel mounted up with me till we came to the second heaven, which he asked should be opened. 'Who is this?' he was asked. 'Gabriel,' he replied. 'And who is that with you?' 'Muhammad,' said he. 'And has he had revelation sent him?' 'Assuredly,' said he. 'Then welcome to him. How blessed a coming.' Thereat [the gate] was opened, and when I had cleared it, lo! there was John [the Baptist] and Jesus, who were cousins on their mothers' side. Said [Gabriel]: 'These are John and Jesus, give them greeting.' So I greeted them and they returned it saying: 'Welcome to the righteous brother, the righteous prophet.' Then he ascended with me to the third heaven, which he asked should be opened. 'Who is this?' he was asked. 'Gabriel,' he replied. 'And who is that with you?' 'Muhammad,' said he. 'And has he had revelation sent him?' 'Assuredly,' said he. 'Then welcome to him. How blessed a coming.' Thereat [the gate] was opened, and when I had cleared it, lo! there was Joseph. [Gabriel] said: 'This is Joseph, greet him.' So I gave him greeting, which he returned, saying, 'Welcome to the righteous brother, the righteous prophet.' Then he ascended with me till we came to the fourth heaven, which he asked should be opened. 'Who is this?' he was asked. 'Gabriel,' he replied. 'And who is that with you?' 'Muhammad,' said he. 'And has he had revelation sent him?' 'Assuredly,' said he. 'Then welcome to him. How blessed a coming.' Thereat [the gate] was opened, and when I had cleared it, lo! there was Idris (Enoch). Said [Gabriel]: 'This is Idris, give him greeting.' So I greeted him, and he returned it, saying: 'Welcome to the righteous brother, the righteous prophet.' Then he ascended with me to the fifth heaven, which he asked should be opened. 'Who is this?' he was asked. 'Gabriel,' he replied. 'And who is that with you?' 'Muhammad,' said he. 'And has he had revelation sent him?' 'Assuredly,' said he. 'Then welcome to him. How blessed a coming.' When I had cleared [the gate], lo! there was Aaron. Said [Gabriel]: 'This is Aaron, give him greeting.' So I greeted him, and he returned it, saying: 'Welcome to the righteous brother, the righteous prophet.' Then he ascended with me to the sixth heaven, which he asked should be opened. 'Who is this?' he was asked. 'Gabriel,' he replied. 'And who is that with you?' 'Muhammad,' said he. 'And has he had revelation sent him?' 'Assuredly,' said he. 'Then welcome to him. How blessed a coming.' When I had cleared [the gate] lo! there was Moses. Said [Gabriel]: 'This is Moses, give him greeting.' So I greeted him, and he returned it saying: 'Welcome to the righteous brother, the righteous prophet.' When I passed on he wept, and one asked him why he wept. 'I weep,' said he, because of a youth who has been sent [as an Apostle] after me, more of whose community will enter Paradise than my community.' Then [Gabriel] ascended with me till we reached the seventh heaven, which he asked should be opened. 'Who is this?' he was asked. 'Gabriel,' he replied. 'And who is that with you?' 'Muhammad,' said he. 'And has he had revelation sent him?' 'Assuredly,' said he. 'Then welcome to him. How blessed a coming.' When I had cleared [the gate], lo! there was Abraham. Said [Gabriel]: 'This is your father Abraham, so greet him.' I gave him greeting, which he returned, saying: 'Welcome to the righteous son, the righteous prophet.'

Then I ascended to the Sidrat al-Muntaha, whose fruits were the size of Hajar[4] waterpots and its leaves like elephants' ears. Said [Gabriel]: 'This is the Sidrat al-Muntaha.'[5] There I beheld four streams, two within and two without, so I asked: 'What are these, O Gabriel?' 'The two within,' he answered, are the two rivers of Paradise, but the two without are the Nile and the Euphrates.' Then I was taken up to the Frequented Fane, where a vessel of wine, a vessel of milk, and a vessel of honey were brought to me. I took the milk, whereat he said: 'This is the *fitra*[6] of you and your community.' Then there was laid on me the religious duty of performing fifty prayer services daily, and I departed. As I passed by Moses he asked: 'With what have you been commanded?' 'With fifty prayer services each day,' I replied. 'But your community,' said he, 'will never be able to perform fifty prayer services a day. By Allah, I have had experience with people before you, and I had to strive hard with the Children of Israel. Return to your Lord and ask Him to lighten it for your community.' So I went back and He remitted ten. Then I returned to Moses, but he said the like [of what he had said before], so I went back and He remitted ten more. When, however, I got back to Moses he said the like again, so I returned and He remitted another ten. When I returned to Moses he again said the like, so I went back and was commanded ten prayer services each day and night. When I got back to Moses he said as he had said before, so I went back and was bidden perform five prayer services daily. When I got back to Moses, he said: 'And with what are you commanded now?' 'I am bidden,' I replied, 'perform five prayer services day and night.' 'Your community,' said he, 'will never be able to perform five prayer services daily. I have had experience with people before you, and have had to strive hard with the Children of Israel. Go back to your Lord and ask Him to lighten it for your community.' 'I have been asking of my Lord,' I replied, 'till I am ashamed, I am content and I submit.' Then as I passed on a Crier cried: 'I have settled my ordinance, and have made things easy for My servants.'

Notes

1 The Hatim is a semi-circular, low, and thick wall to the northwest of the Ka'ba at Mecca. The Hijr is the space between this wall and the Ka'ba itself.
2 Lit. 'a comer came,' a common way of expressing the coming of some supernatural visitor. From what follows we may assume that it was the archangel Gabriel.
3 This is the sacred well in the precincts of the shrine of Mecca from which the pilgrims drink as an act of piety and thereby partake of its blessedness.
4 Hajar is the district of Arabia which includes Bahrain over on the Persian Gulf. The *Sidrat al-Muntaha*, i.e., 'lote tree of the boundary,' is said to be a celestial tree which marks the boundary beyond which creatures may not ascend. It is mentioned in Sura LIII, 14.
5 This is the celestial Ka'ba, the navel of the celestial world, situated directly above the earthly Ka'ba.
6 A *fifra* is a natural, inborn disposition. The meaning here is that the Muslim community will be a 'middler' community, like milk, which has neither the intoxicating qualities of wine nor the cloying sweetness of honey.

Translation, introductory comment, and notes by Arthur Jeffery, *Islam. Muhammad and His Religion* (New York: Liberal Arts Press, 1958) pp. 35-9

252. MUHAMMAD'S MEETING WITH HIS LORD

A favourite episode in the account of Muhammad's Ascension is that which tells of the Prophet being taken into the presence of Allah. As Enoch walked with God, as Abraham was the friend of God, as Moses spoke with God face to face on Mt. Sinai, as Jesus had a son's relationship with his Father, so this story is intended to show how Muhammad had an equally intimate acquaintance with his Lord. There are many versions of the story. That given here is from *as-Suyūti's al-La'ālī al-masnū'sa* (Cairo, 1317 A.H.=A.D. 1899), I, 39.

Now when I was brought on my Night Journey to the [place of the] Throne and drew near to it, a green *rafraf*[1] was let down to me, a thing too beautiful for me to describe to you, whereat Gabriel advanced and seated me on it. Then he had to withdraw from me, placing his hands over his eyes, fearing lest his sight be destroyed by the scintillating light of the Throne, and he began to weep aloud, uttering *tasbih*, *tahmid* and *tathniya* to Allah. By Allah's leave, as a sign of His mercy towards me and the perfection of His favour to me, that *rafraf* floated me into the [presence of the] Lord of the Throne, a thing too stupendous for the tongue to tell of or the imagination to picture. My sight was so dazzled by it that I feared blindness. Therefore I shut my eyes, which was by Allah's good favour. When I thus veiled my sight Allah shifted my sight [from my eyes] to my heart, so with my heart I began to look at what I had been looking at with my eyes. It was a light so bright in its scintillation that I despair of ever describing to you what I saw of His majesty. Then I besought my Lord to complete His favour to me by granting me the boon of having a steadfast vision of Him with my heart. This my Lord did, giving me that favour, so I gazed at Him with my heart till it was steady and I had a steady vision of Him.

There He was, when the veil had been lifted from Him, seated on His Throne, in His dignity, His might, His glory, His exaltedness, but beyond that it is not permitted me to describe Him to you. Glory be to Him! How majestic is He. How bountiful are His works! How exalted is His position! How brilliant is His light! Then He lowered somewhat for me His dignity and drew me near to Him, which is as He has said in His book, informing you of how He would deal with me and honour me: 'One possessed of strength. He stood erect when He was at the highest point of the horizon. Then He drew near and descended, so that He was two bows' lengths off, or even nearer' (LIII, 6-9). This means that when He inclined to me He drew me as near to Him as the distance between the two ends of a bow, nay, rather, nearer than the distance between the crotch of the bow and its curved ends. 'Then He revealed to His servant what He revealed' (v. 10), i.e., what matters He had decided to enjoin upon me. 'His heart did not falsify what it saw' (v. 11), i.e., my vision of him with my heart. 'Indeed he was seeing one of the greatest signs of his Lord.' (v. 18).

Now when He—glory be to Him—lowered His dignity for me He placed one of His hands between my shoulders and I felt the coldness of his finger tips for a while on my heart, whereat I experienced such a sweetness, so pleasant a perfume, so delightful a coolness, such a sense of honour in [being granted this] vision of Him, that all my terrors melted away and my fears departed from me, so my heart became tranquil. Then was I filled with joy, my eyes were refreshed, and such delight and happiness took hold of me that I began to bend and sway to right and left like one overtaken by slumber. Indeed, it seemed to me as though everyone in heaven and earth had died, for I heard no voices of angels, nor during the vision of my Lord did I see any dark bodies. My Lord left me there such time as He willed, then brought me back to my senses, and it was as though I had been asleep and had awakened. My mind returned to me and I was tranquil, realizing where I was and how I was enjoying surpassing favour and being shown manifest preference.

Then my Lord, glorified and praised be He, spoke to me, saying: 'O Muhammad, do you know about what the Highest Council is disputing?' I answered: 'O Lord, Thou knowest best about that, as about all things, for Thou art the One who knows the unseen' (cf. v. 109/108). 'They are disputing,' He said, 'about the degrees *(darajat)* and the excellences *(hasanat)*. Do you know, O Muhammad, what the degrees and the excellences are?' 'Thou, O Lord,' I answered, 'knowest better and art more wise.' Then He said: 'The degrees are concerned with performing one's ablutions at times when that is disagreeable, walking on foot to religious assemblies, watching expectantly for the next hour of prayer when one time of prayer is over. As for the excellences, they consist of feeding the hungry, spreading peace, and performing the *Tahajjud* prayer at night when other folk are sleeping.' Never have I heard anything sweeter or more pleasant than the melodious sound of His voice.

Such was the sweetness of His melodious voice that it gave me confidence, and so I spoke to Him of my need. I said: 'O Lord, Thou didst take Abraham as a friend, Thou didst speak with Moses face to face, Thou didst raise Enoch to a high place, Thou didst give Solomon a kingdom such as none after him might attain, and didst give to David the Psalter. What then is there for me, O Lord?' He replied: 'O Muhammad, I take you as a friend just as I took Abraham as a friend. I am speaking to you just as I spoke face to face with Moses. I am giving you the *Fatiha* (*Sūra* 1) and the closing verses of *al-Baqara* (11, 284-6), both of which are from the treasuries of My Throne and which I have given to no prophet before you. I am sending you as a prophet to the white folk of the earth and the black folk and the red folk, to jinn and to men thereon, though never before you have I sent a prophet to the whole of them. I am appointing the earth, its dry land and its sea, for you and for your community as a place for purification and for worship. I am giving your community the right to booty which I have given as provision to no community before them. I shall aid you with such terrors as will make your enemies flee before you while you are still a month's journey away. I shall send down to you the Master of all Books and the guardian of them, a Qur'an which We Ourselves have parcelled out (XVII, 106/107). I shall exalt your name for you (XCIV, 4), even to the extent of conjoining it with My name, so that none of the regulations of My religion will ever be mentioned without you being mentioned along with Me.'

Then after this He communicated to me matters which I am not permitted to tell you, and when He had made His covenant with me and had left me there such time as He willed, He took His seat again upon His Throne. Glory be to Him in His majesty, his dignity, His might. Then I looked, and behold, something passed between us and a veil of light was drawn in front of Him, blazing ardently to a distance that none knows save Allah, and so intense that were it to be rent at any point it would burn up all Allah's creation. Then the green *rafraf* on which I was desecended with me, gently rising and falling with me in 'Illiyun² . . . till it brought me back to Gabriel, who took me from it. Then the *rafraf* mounted up till it disappeared from my sight.

Notes

1 The lexicons give as one meaning of *rafraf* 'a narrow piece of silk brocade.' It was an ancient idea that a human must be accompanied during ascent to celestial places. Gabriel had accompanied Muhammad so far, but now he can go no further, so a kind of magic carpet is sent down to bring the Prophet the rest of the way into the Divine Presence.

2 'Illiyun is said to be the highest of all celestial regions. It is mentioned in *Sura* LXXXIII, 18-21.

Translation, introductory comment, and notes by Arthur Jeffery, *Islam. Muhammad and His Religion* (New York: Liberal Arts Press, 1958) pp. 42-6

See also nos. 43, 237, 268, 269

Spiritual Techniques

253. A SUFI MYSTIC SPEAKS TO HIS GOD

The following is from the writing of Dhu 'l-Nūn, the Egyptian, who died A.D. 861 *(246* A.H.*).*

O God, I never hearken to the voices of the beasts or the rustle of the trees, the splashing of waters or the song of birds, the whistling of the wind or the rumble of thunder, but I sense in them a testimony to Thy Unity (*wahdānīya*), and a proof of Thy Incomparableness; that Thou art the All-prevailing, the All-knowing, the All-wise, the All-just, the All-true, and that in Thee is neither overthrow nor ignorance nor folly nor injusice nor lying. O God, I acknowledge Thee in the proof of Thy handiwork and the evidence of Thy acts; grant me, O God, to seek Thy Satisfaction with my satisfaction, and the Delight of a Father in His child, remembering Thee in my love for Thee, with serene tranquility and firm resolve.

[In his poetry Dhu 'l-Nūn uses the passionate language of the devoted lover, as Rābi'a of Basra had done before him, and so helped to fix a tradition that is thereafter so prominent a characteristic of Sufi literature:]

> *I die, and yet not dies in me*
> *The ardour of my love for Thee,*
> *Nor hath Thy Love, my only goal,*
> *Assuaged the fever of my soul.*
>
> *To Thee alone my spirit cries;*
> *In Thee my whole ambition lies,*
> *And still Thy Wealth is far above*
> *The poverty of my small love.*
>
> *I turn to Thee in my request,*
> *And seek in Thee my final rest;*
> *To Thee my loud lament is brought,*
> *Thou dwellest in my secret thought.*
>
> *However long my sickness be,*
> *This wearisome infirmity,*
> *Never to men will I declare*
> *The burden Thou hast made me bear.*

To Thee alone is manifest
The heavy labour of my breast,
Else never kin nor neighbours know
The brimming measure of my woe.

A fever burns below my heart
And ravages my every part;
It hath destroyed my strength and stay,
And smouldered all my soul away.

Guidest Thou not upon the road
The rider wearied by his load,
Delivering from the steeps of death
The traveller as he wandereth?

Didst Thou not light a Beacon too
For them that found the Guidance true
But carried not within their hand
The faintest glimmer of its brand?

O then to me Thy Favour give
That, so attended, I may live
And overwhelm with ease from Thee
The rigour of my poverty.

Translation and parenthetical note by A. J. Arberry,
in his *Sufism, An Account of the Mystics of Islam*
(London, 1950), pp. 52-4.)

245. ABŪ YAZĪD'S MYSTICAL ASCENSION

Abū Yazīd (Bāyazīd) of Bistam, the Persian (d. 261/875), was the
first to take the Prophet's Ascension (mi'rāj) as a theme for expressing
his own mystical experience, thereby setting a fashion which others
later followed.

I saw that my spirit was borne to the heavens. It looked at nothing and
gave no heed, though Paradise and Hell were displayed to it, for it was
freed of phenomena and veils. Then I became a bird, whose body was of
Oneness and whose wings were of Everlastingness, and I continued to
fly in the air of the Absolute, until I passed into the sphere of Purification, and gazed upon the field of Eternity and beheld there the tree

of Oneness. When I looked I myself was all those. I cried: 'O Lord, with my egoism I cannot attain Thee, and I cannot escape from my selfhood. What am I to do?' God spake: 'O Abū Yazīd, thou must win release from thy thou-ness by following my Beloved (sc. Muhammad). Smear thine eyes with the dust of his feet and follow him continually.'

Translation and introductory note by A. J. Arberry,
Sufism, op. cit., pp. 54-5

255. AL-JUNAID ON UNION AND SEPARATION

Al-Junaid of Baghdad (d. 298/910), called in later times 'the Shaikh of the Order,' was the most original and penetrating intellect among the Sufis of his time. He elaborated a consistent system of Islam's theosophy.

> Now I have known, O Lord,
> What lies within my heart;
> In secret, from the world apart,
> My tongue hath talked with my Adored.
>
> So in a manner we
> United are, and One;
> Yet otherwise disunion
> Is our estate eternally.
>
> Though from my gaze profound
> Deep awe hath hid Thy Face,
> In wondrous and ecstatic Grace
> I feel Thee touch my inmost ground.

Translation and introductory note by A. J. Arberry,
Sufism, op. cit., p. 59

256. AL-HALLĀJ SPEAKS OF GOD: 'I AM HE WHOM I LOVE . . .'

Husayn ibn Mausūr al-Hallāj (d. 309/922) chose Jesus as his model and claimed: 'I am the Truth' (Ana al-Haqq) (cf. John 14:6). Since al-Haqq, the Truth, is one of the names of God, he was accused of claiming divinity and finally was publicly scourged and crucified.

Betwixt me and Thee there lingers an 'it is I' that torments me.
Ah, of Thy grace, take this 'I' from between us!

I am He whom I love, and He whom I love is I,
We are two spirits dwelling in one body.
If thou seest me, thou seest Him,
And if thou seest Him, thou seest us both.

Ibrāhim ibn Fātik, his servant, said: 'When al-Hallāj was brought to be crucified and saw the cross and the nails . . . he prayed a prayer of two inclinations, and I was standing near him. He recited in the first the Opening of the Qur'an and the verse 'And we shall try you with something of fear and of hunger' (Sūra 21:35). In the second he recited the Opening and the verse beginning 'Every soul shall taste of death' (Sūra 29:57). When he was finished he said some words I do not remember, but of what I remember was: '. . . Oh my God, who art revealed in every place and who art not in any place, I beseech Thee by the truth of Thy Divine word which declared that I am, and by the truth of my weak human word which declares that Thou art, sustain me in gratitude for this Thy grace, that Thou didst hide from others what Thou didst reveal to me of the glory of Thy countenance, and didst forbid to them what thou didst permit to me: the sight of things hidden by Thy mystery.

'And these Thy servants, who are gathered together to slay me in zeal for Thy religion, seeking Thy favour, forgive them. For if Thou hadst revealed to them that which Thou hast revealed to me, they would not have done that which they have done; hadst Thou withheld from me what Thou hast withheld from them, I should never have been tried with this tribulation. To Thee be praise in all Thou doest; to Thee be praise in whatsoever Thou willest.'

Then he was silent. The Herdsman stepped up and dealt him a smashing blow which broke his nose, and the blood ran onto his white robe. The mystic al-Shiblī, who was in the crowd, cried aloud and rent his garment, and Abū Husayn al-Wasitī fell fainting, and so did other famous Sufis who were there, so that a riot nearly broke out. Then the executioners did their work.

Translation and introduction by John Alden Williams, *Islam* (New York, 1961), pp. 148-9, from L. Massignon and Kraus (eds.), *Akhbār al-Hallāj* (Paris, 1936), pp. 7-8. The poem quoted at the beginning was translated by R. A. Nicholson, *The Legacy of Islam* (London, 1939), p. 218

257. THE 'REVELATION' OF AL-NIFFARI

The following is from Kitāb al-Mawāqif by Muhammad b. Abd al-Jabbār al-Niffari (fl. 350/961).

The writer pictures himself as standing before God (mauqif—a term perhaps originally borrowed from the descriptions of the Last Day) in a spiritual state, and hears God speaking to him.

He stayed me in Death; and I saw the acts, every one of them, to be evil. And I saw Fear holding sway over Hope; and I saw Riches turned to fire and cleaving to the fire; and I saw Poverty an adversary adducing proofs; and I saw every thing, that it had no power over any other thing; and I saw this world to be a delusion, and I saw the heavens to be a deception. And I cried out, 'O Knowledge!' and it answered me not. Then I cried out, 'O Gnosis!'; and it answered me not. And I saw every thing, that it had deserted me, and I saw every created thing, that it had fled from me; and I remained alone. And the act came to me, and I saw in it secret imagination, and the secret part was that which persisted; and naught availed me, save the Mercy of my Lord. And he said to me, 'Where is thy knowledge?' And I saw the Fire. And he said to me, 'Where is thy act?' and I saw the Fire. And he said to me, 'Where is thy gnosis?' And I saw the Fire. And He unveiled for me His Gnoses of Uniqueness, and the Fire died down. And He said to me, 'I am thy Friend.' And I was stablished. And He said to me, 'I am thy Gnosis.' And I spoke. And He said to me, 'I am thy Seeker.' And I went forth.

> Translation and comment on it by A. J. Arberry, *Sufism, op. cit.,* pp. 64-5

258. AL-GHAZĀLĪ'S CONVERSION TO SUFISM

Abū Hāmid Muhammad b. Muhammad al-Ghazālī (451/1059-505/ 1111) was a leading orthodox theologian and lawyer; yet he was dissatisfied with the intellectual and legalistic approach to religion and felt a yearning for a more personal experience of God. He tells about his conversion to Sufism in an autobiographical work.

Then I turned my attention to the Way of the Sufis. I knew that it could not be traversed to the end without both doctrine and practice,

and that the gist of the doctrine lies in overcoming the appetites of
the flesh and getting rid of its evil dispositions and vile qualities, so
that the heart may be cleared of all but God; and the means of clearing
it is *dhikr Allah,* i.e., commemoration of God and concentration of
every thought upon Him. Now, the doctrine was easier to me than
the practice, so I began by learning their doctrine from the books and
sayings of their Shaykhs, until I acquired as much of their Way as it
is possible to acquire by learning and hearing, and saw plainly that
what is most peculiar to them cannot be learned, but can only be
reached by immediate experience and ecstasy and inward transformation. I became convinced that I had now acquired all the knowledge
of Sufism that could possibly be obtained by means of study; as for
the rest, there was no way of coming to it except by leading the mystical life. I looked on myself as I then was. Worldly interests encom-
passed me on every side. Even my work as a teacher—the best thing
I was engaged in—seemed unimportant and useless in view of the life
hereafter. When I considered the intention of my teaching, I perceived that instead of doing it for God's sake alone I had no motive but
the desire for glory and reputation. I realized that I stood on the edge
of a precipice and would fall into Hell-fire unless I set about to mend
my ways. . . . Conscious of my helplessness and having surrendered
my will entirely, I took refuge with God as a man in sore trouble who
has no resource left. God answered my prayer and made it easy to
turn my back on reputation and wealth and wife and children and
friends.

Translation by A. J. Arberry, *Sufism, op. cit.,* p. 80.
Introduction adapted from Arberry

259. RŪMĪ DOES NOT RECOGNIZE HIMSELF

*Jalāl al-Dīn Rūmī (d. 1273) came under the influence of the Sufi Shams
al-Dīn Tabrizi, who was killed by an angry mob. In acknowledgment
of the influence of his master, Rūmī called his collection of poems
(Diwān) The Diwān of Shams-i-Tabrīz.*

What is to be done, O Moslems? for I do not recognize myself.
I am neither Christian nor Jew nor Gabr nor Moslem.
I am not of the East, nor of the West, nor of the land, nor of the sea;

Spiritual Techniques

I am not of Nature's mint, nor of the circling heavens.
I am not of earth, nor of water, nor of air, nor of fire;
I am not of the empyrean, nor of the dust, nor of existence, nor of
    entity.
I am not of the Kingdom of 'Iraquain, nor of the country of Khorāsān,
I am not of this world, nor of the next, nor of Paradise, nor of hell.
My place is the Placeless, my trace is the Traceless;
'Tis neither body nor soul, for I belong to the soul of the Beloved.
I have put duality away, I have seen that the two worlds are one;
One I seek, One I know, One I see, One I call.
He is the first, He is the last, He is the outward, He is the inward.
I know none other except 'Yā Hū' [O He!] and 'Yā man Hū.'
I am intoxicated with Love's cup; the two worlds have passed out of
    my ken.
I have no business save in carouse and revelry.
If once in my life I spent a moment without thee,
From that time and from that hour I repent of my life.
If once in this world I win a moment with thee,
I will trample on both worlds, I will dance in triumph forever.
Oh Shamsi Tabrīz, I am drunken in this world,
That except of drunkenness and revelry I have no tale to tell.

Translation by R. A. Nicholson, Dīvānī Shamsi Tabrīz
(Cambridge, 1898), p. 125. Introduction adapted from
Nicholson

CHAPTER II

Speculations on Man and God

A. DIFFERENT UNDERSTANDINGS
OF THE HUMAN CONDITION

260. EGYPTIAN PESSIMISM: A DISPUTE OVER
SUICIDE

*The name of the author of 'A Dispute over Suicide' has not survived.
The text is written in hieratic on a papyrus in the Berlin Museum:
no other copies are known. The handwriting dates the papyrus to the
Middle Kingdom (ca. 2000-1740 B.C.). It seems probable that the work
was composed a few hundred years previously in the First Intermediate
Period (ca. 2280-2000 B.C.), like the Instruction for King Meri-ka-re,
when the troubled times caused men to reassess religious and ethical
beliefs.*

*The 'Dispute' is in the form of a dialogue between an unnamed
man, who is weary of his life, and his soul. The man speaks in the first
person and tries to convince his soul of the desirability of suicide and
death. The course of the argument is difficult to follow and the text is
very obscure in places, especially the first half where there are parables
and metaphors, the point of which often escapes the modern reader. It
seems not improbable that the man consistently argues in favour of
suicide while his soul attempts throughout to dissuade him, but such
is the difficulty of the text that sometimes the attitude of the soul
is not clear and scholars hold varying views on the tenor of some of
its speeches.*

My soul opened its mouth to me that it might answer what I had
said. If thou recallest burial, it is a sad matter. It is the bringing of
tears, making a man sad. It is dragging a man from his house and
casting him on the hillside. Thou shalt never go up that thou mayest
see the sun. Those who built in granite[1] and who hewed chambers in
fine pyramid(s) with good work, when the builders became gods their
offering stelae[2] were destroyed like (those of) the weary ones that died
on the dyke, through lack of a survivor, the water having taken its
toll, and the sun likewise to whom the fishes of the river banks talk.
Listen to me.

Behold it is good for men to listen. Follow pleasure and forget care. . . .
I opened my mouth to my soul that I might answer what it had said.

> Behold my name stinks
>> Behold more than the stench of fish
>> On a summer's day when the sky is hot. . . .
> Behold my name stinks
>> Behold more than a woman
>> About whom a lie has been told to a man.
> Behold my name stinks
>> Behold more than a sturdy lad
>> About whom it is said 'He belongs to his rival.'[3]

> To whom shall I speak today?
>> Brothers are evil,
>> The companions of yesterday do not love.
> To whom shall I speak today?
>> Hearts are rapacious,
>> Every man seizes the goods of his neighbour . . .
> To whom shall I speak today?
>> Men are contented with evil,
>> Goodness is neglected everywhere.
> To whom shall I speak today?
>> One who should make a man enraged by his evil behaviour
>> Makes everyone laugh, though his iniquity is grievous. . . .
> To whom shall I speak today?
>> The wrongdoer is an intimate,
>> The brother with whom one should act is become an enemy.
> To whom shall I speak today?
>> Yesterday is not remembered,
>> No one now helps him that hath done (good).
> To whom shall I speak today?
>> Faces are averted,
>> Every man has (his) face downcast towards his brethren.
> To whom shall I speak today?
>> Hearts are rapacious,
>> No man has a heart upon which one can rely.
> To whom shall I speak today?
>> There are no righteous men.
>> The land is left over to workers of iniquity. . . .
> To whom shall I speak today?
>> I am laden with misery

Through lack of an intimate.
To whom shall I speak today?
The sin that roams the land,
It has no end.
Death is in my sight today
(Like) the recovery of a sick man,
Like going abroad after detention.
Death is in my sight today
Like the smell of myrrh,
Like sitting under an awning on a windy day.
Death is in my sight today
Like the scent of lotus flowers,
Like sitting on the bank of drunkenness.
Death is in my sight today
Like a well trodden way,
As when a man returns home from an expedition.
Death is in my sight today
Like the clearing of the sky,
Like a man attracted thereby to what he knows not.
Death is in my sight today
Like the longing of a man to see home,
When he has spent many years held in capitvity.
Surely he who is yonder[4] shall
Be a living god,
Punishing the sin of him who commits it.
Surely he who is yonder shall
Stand in the barque of the sun,
Causing the choicest things to be given therefrom to the
temples.
Surely he who is yonder shall
Be a man of knowledge,
Who cannot be prevented from petitioning Re when he
speaks.

What my soul said to me. Put care aside, my comrade and brother. Make an offering on the brazier and cling to life, according as I (?) have said.[5] Desire me here and reject the West, but desire to reach the West when thy body goes into the earth, that I may alight after thou hast grown weary.[6] Then let us make an abode together.

IT IS FINISHED FROM ITS BEGINNING TO ITS END, AS IT WAS FOUND IN WRITING.

Notes

1 *Those who built in granite* refers to the kings and nobles of the Old Kingdom who built the great pyramids and who erected fine tombs for themselves in order that their mortal remains should be preserved for ever. Preservation of the physical body was essential for life after death. The sense of the passage is that these kings and nobles are now no better off than poor men who died in the open, without shelter and without relatives to perform the mortuary rites for them. Soon after the great ones *became gods* (i.e., died), their pyramids and tombs were plundered and their offering stelae were destroyed, thus reducing them to the level of the paupers.

2 *offering stelae* were necessary for the mortuary cult. It was believed that the deceased needed food and drink after death. Stelae were erected on the outside of the tomb, at which such offerings were made. The wealthy endowed mortuary priests to make the offerings daily while the less fortunate relied on relatives and friends.

3 *his rival*, i.e., the lad's father's rival for his mother's affections. The imputation levelled against the lad is that he is a bastard.

4 *he who is yonder* is a euphemism for 'the dead.'

5 *as I (?) have said.* The original has 'as you have said.' The pronoun of the second person is emended to that of the first person.

6 *grown weary* is a euphemism for 'died'; cp. earlier in the text *like (those of) the weary ones that died on the dyke.*

Translation, introduction, and notes by T. W. Thacker, in D. Winton Thomas (ed.), *Documents from Old Testament Times* (London: Thomas Nelson, 1958)

261. THE EGYPTIAN SONG OF THE HARPIST: 'NONE RETURNETH AGAIN THAT IS GONE THITHER'

How prosperous is this good prince![1]
It is a goodly destiny, that the bodies diminish,
Passing away while others remain,
Since the time of the ancestors,
The gods who were aforetime,
Who rest in their pyramids,
Nobles and the glorious departed likewise,
Entombed in their pyramids.
Those who built their (tomb)-temples,
Their place is no more.
Behold what is done therein.
I have heard the words of Imhotep and Hardedef,[2]
(Words) greatly celebrated as their utterances.

Different Understandings

Behold the places thereof;
Their walls are dismantled,
Their places are no more,
As if they had never been.

None cometh from thence
That he may tell (us) how they fare;
That he may tell (us) of their fortunes,
That he may content our heart,
Until we (too) depart
To the place whither they have gone.

Encourage thy heart to forget it,
Making it pleasant for thee to follow thy desire,
While thou livest.
Put myrrh upon thy head,
And garments on thee of fine linen,
Imbued with marvellous luxuries,
The genuine things of the gods.

Increase yet more thy delights,
And let (not) thy heart languish.
Follow thy desire and thy good,
Fashion thine affairs on earth
After the mandates of thine (own) heart.
(Till) that day of lamentation cometh to thee,
Then the silent-hearted hears not their lamentation,
Nor he that is in the tomb attends the mourning.

Celebrate the glad day,
Be not weary therein.
Lo, no man taketh his goods with him.
Yea, none returneth again that is gone thither.

Notes

1 Meaning the dead king in whose tomb the song was written.
2 Imhotep was grand vizier, chief architect, and famous wise man under king
Zoser of the Third Dynasty (thirtieth century B.C.). Hardedef was a royal
prince, son of Khufu of Gizeh, and hence connected with the greatest pyramid.
He lived about a century after Imhotep. Both of them had thus become
proverbial wise men a thousand years after they passed away.

Translation and notes by J. H. Breasted, in his
*Development of Religion and Thought in Ancient
Egypt*, 1912, pp. 182-3. Cf. translation by John A.
Wilson, in ANET, p. 467

262. EGYPTIAN DISILLUSION AND DESPAIR: THE ADMONITIONS OF IPU

The Admonitions *date originally from the twenty-second century* B.C.

It used to be said that he was every man's shepherd, that there was no evil in his heart, that however insignificant his flock he would spend the whole day caring for them. . . . Ah! Had he understood the character of men in the first generation he would have launched his curse and raised his arm against them. He would have destroyed their heirs, although they were his own seed. But he wished that birth should continue . . . it could not come to an end as long as these gods (the righteous kings of the past) were there. Progeny still comes forth from the wombs of the women of Egypt but one does not find it [playing?] in the road. It is rapine and violence against the weak that these gods (the recent kings) have wrought. There has been no true pilot in their time. Where is he? Does he sleep perchance? Behold, one sees no sign of his almighty power!

> A. H. Gardiner, *The Admonitions of an Egyptian Sage* (Leipzig, 1909), as printed in R. T. Rundle Clark, *Myth and Symbol in Ancient Egypt* (New York, 1960), pp. 68-9

See also nos. 18-20, 166-70, 272, 273

263. A JAIN PARABLE: THE MAN IN THE WELL

(Haribhadra, 'Samarādityakathā,' II, 55-88)

A certain man, much oppressed by the woes of poverty,
Left his own home, and set out for another country.
He passed through the land, with its villages, cities, and harbours,
And after a few days he lost his way.

And he came to a forest, thick with trees . . . and full of wild beasts.
There, while he was stumbling over the rugged paths, . . . a prey to
thirst and hunger, he saw a mad elephant, fiercely trumpeting, charg-

Different Understandings

ing him with upraised trunk. At the same time there appeared before him a most evil demoness, holding a sharp sword, dreadful in face and form, and laughing with loud and shrill laughter. Seeing them he trembled in all his limbs with deathly fear, and looked in all directions. There, to the east of him, he saw a great banyan tree. . . .

And he ran quickly, and reached the mighty tree.
But his spirits fell, for it was so high that even the birds could not
    fly over it,
And he could not climb its high unscalable trunk. . . .
All his limbs trembled with terrible fear,
Until, looking round, he saw nearby an old well covered with grass.
Afraid of death, craving to live if only a moment longer,
He flung himself into the well at the foot of the banyan tree.
A clump of reeds grew from its deep wall, and to this he clung,
While below him he saw terrible snakes, enraged at the sound of
    his falling;
And at the very bottom, known from the hiss of its breath, was a
    black and mighty python
With mouth agape, its body thick as the trunk of a heavenly elephant,
    with terrible red eyes.
He thought, 'My life will only last as long as these reeds hold fast,'
And he raised his head; and there, on the clump of reeds, he saw two
    large mice,
One white, one black, their sharp teeth ever gnawing at the roots of
    the reed-clump.
Then up came the wild elephant, and, enraged the more at not catching
    him,
Charged time and again at the trunk of the banyan tree.
At the shock of his charge a honeycomb on a large branch
Which hung over the old well, shook loose and fell.
The man's whole body was stung by a swarm of angry bees,
But, just by chance, a drop of honey fell on his head,
Rolled down his brow, and somehow reached his lips,
And gave him a moment's sweetness. He longed for other drops,
And he thought nothing of the python, the snakes, the elephant, the
    mice, the well, or the bees,
In his excited craving for yet more drops of honey.
This parable is powerful to clear the minds of those on the way to
    freedom.
Now hear its sure interpretation.

The man is the soul, his wandering in the forest the four types of
existence.
The wild elephant is death, the demoness old age.
The banyan tree is salvation, where there is no fear of death, the
elephant,
But which no sensual man can climb.
The well is human life, the snakes are passions,
Which so overcome a man that he does not know what he should do.
The tuft of reed is man's allotted span, during which the soul exists
embodied;
The mice which steadily gnaw it are the dark and bright fortnights.
The stinging bees are manifold diseases,
Which torment a man until he has not a moment's joy.
The awful python is hell, seizing the man bemused by sensual pleasure,
Fallen in which the soul suffers pains by the thousand.
The drops of honey are trivial pleasures, terrible at the last.
How can a wise man want them, in the midst of such peril and hard-
ship?

Translation by A. L. Basham, in Wm. Theodore de
Bary (ed.), *Sources of Indian Tradition* (New York:
Columbia University Press, 1958), pp. 56-8

264. THE INDESTRUCTIBLE, ETERNAL SELF: KRISHNA'S TEACHING TO ARJUNA

('Bhagavad Gītā,' II, 16-26, 47)

16. Of what is not, no coming to be occurs;
   No coming not to be occurs of what is;
But the dividing-line of both is seen,
   Of these two, by those who see the truth.

17. But know that that is indestructible,
   By which this all is pervaded;
Destruction of this imperishable one
   No one can cause.

18. These bodies come to an end,
   It is declared, of the eternal embodied (soul),
Which is indestructible and unfathomable.
   Therefore fight, son of Bharata!

19. Who believes him a slayer,
    And who thinks him slain,
    Both these understand not:
    He slays not, is not slain.

20. He is not born, nor does he ever die;
    Nor, having come to be, will he ever more come not to be.
    Unborn, eternal, everlasting, this ancient one
    Is not slain when the body is slain.

21. He knows as indestructible and eternal
    This unborn, imperishable one,
    That man, son of Prithā, how
    Can he slay or cause to slay—whom?

22. As leaving aside worn-out garments
    A man takes other, new ones,
    So leaving aside worn-out bodies
    To other, new ones goes the embodied (soul).

23. Swords cut him not,
    Fire burns him not,
    Water wets him not,
    Wind dries him not.

24. Not to be cut is he, not to be burnt is he,
    Not to be wet nor yet dried;
    Eternal, omnipresent, fixed,
    Immovable, everlasting is he.

25. Unmanifest he, unthinkable he,
    Unchangeable he is declared to be;
    Therefore knowing him thus
    Thou shouldst not mourn him.

26. Moreover, even if constantly born
    Or constantly dying thou con_idered him,
    Even so, great-armed one, thou
    Shouldst not mourn him. . . .

47. On action alone be thy interest,
    Never on its fruits;
    Let not the fruits of action be thy motive,
    Nor be thy attachment to inaction.

Translation by Franklin Edgerton, *The Bhagavad Gītā*
(Vol. I, Harvard Oriental Series, Vol. 38 (Cambridge:
Harvard University Press, 1944)

265. GREEK PESSIMISM

What life is there, what pleasure without golden Aphrodite? May I die, as soon as I have no part in her ways. Stealthy wooing, lovers' gifts and lovers' unions—these alone are flowers of youth worth plucking for man or woman. Once let old age come on, making a man evil and ugly at once, and heavy cares gnaw at the heart continually. No joy has he in seeing the sun's light, unhonoured by the young and despised by womankind. Thus bitter is old age, as the god hath willed.

Like are we to the leaves that flowery springtime bears, when swiftly they wax strong beneath the rays of the sun. Like them we enjoy for a span the flowers of youth, knowing from the gods neither good nor evil. But the black fates stand by, and one holds in her hand the goal of bitter old age, the other that of death. Brief is the fruit of youth, no longer than the daily spread of the sunshine over the earth; but when once that springtime of life is past, then verily to die is better than life, for many are the ills that invade the heart.

Mimnermos of Kolophon, seventh century B.C.

Honourable it is and glorious for a man to fight with foes for his country, his children and his wedded wife. As for death, it will come whenever the Fates with their spindle decide. . . . For in no way is it decreed that a man may escape death, though he have the Immortals themselves for forebears. He may retire and shun the fray and the javelin's blow, but in his house the Fate of death finds him out. Then is he less loved and less regretted by the people, but the warrior if aught befall him is mourned by low and high, and in life is the equal of the demi-gods.

Kallinos, seventh century B.C.

My son, the end of all things is in the hand of Zeus the heavy thunderer. There is no wit in man. Creatures of a day, we live like cattle, knowing nothing of how the god will bring each one to his end. Hope and self-persuasion are the nourishment of us all as we seek the unattainable. [One man, he continues, is caught up by old age before he reaches his goal, others have wasting diseases, are taken off by war or shipwreck or commit suicide; and so it goes on.] Thus evil is with

Different Understandings

everything. Yea ten thousand dooms, woes and grief beyond speaking are the lot of mankind.

Semonides, seventh century B.C.

Men? Small is their strength, fruitless their cares, brief their life, toil upon toil. Death unescapable hangs over all alike, dealing impartially with good and bad.

All wisdom is with God. In mortal life nothing is free from woe.

Simonides of Keos, seventh century B.C.

Translation by W. K. C. Guthrie, in his *The Greeks and Their Gods* (London, 1950), pp. 129-31

266. A PAGAN PHILOSOPHER ON THE USE OF IMAGES

(Maximus of Tyre, 'Oration,' VIII, 10)

Maximus of Tyre (ca. A.D. 125-185) was a Sophist and eclectic philosopher who travelled widely and lectured both at Athens and at Rome.

For the God who is the Father and Creator of all that is, older than the sun, older than the sky, greater than time and eternity and the whole continual flow of nature, is not to be named by any lawgiver, is not to be uttered by any voice, is not to be seen by any eye. But we, being unable to grasp his essence, make use of sounds and names and pictures, of beaten gold and ivory and silver, of plants and rivers, of mountain peaks and torrents, yearning for the knowledge of him, and in our weakness naming all that is beautiful in this world after his nature. The same thing happens to those who love others; to them the sweetest sight will be the actual figures of their children, but sweet also will be their memory—they will be happy at [the sight of] a lyre, a little spear, or a chair, perhaps, or a running ground, or anything whatever that wakens the memory of the beloved. Why should I go any further in examining and passing judgment about images? Let all men know what is divine; let them know, that is all. If Greeks are stirred to the remembrance of God by the art of Phidias, or the Egyptians by paying worship to animals, or others by a river, or others by fire, I will not quarrel with their differences. Only let them know, let them love, let them remember.

Translation by Frederick C. Grant, in his *Hellenistic Religions* (New York, 1953), p. 168

121

Speculations on Man and God

267. RELIGIOUS SKEPTICISM IN CICERO'S TIME

(Cicero, 'The Nature of the Gods,' III, 79-95)

This work of Cicero's was one of the most important writings in the history of ancient religious thought and in the philosophy of religion. It marked a summation and turning point in the perennial discussion, for Cicero recognized the difficulties which educated men faced in his time, viz., the decline of confidence in the traditional gods and in divine providence (i.e., the divine rule of the world) while at the same time having a half-conscious longing for a rational and defensible belief in divine purpose.

The Nature of the Gods was written in the summer of 45 B.C. The arrangement of the dialogue is simple. Cotta and his friends have gathered at his villa during the Latin Festival in the summer of the year 76 B.C. They are Gaius Velleius, the leading Roman expert in Epicureanism, Balbus, the renowned Stoic, and Cotta, the host, an acute and eminent exponent of the New Academy. Cicero is present. In book I, Velleius sets forth the main principles of Epicurean teachings on the existence and nature of gods (§§ 18-56). The remainder of book I is the reply made by Cotta the Academic, who completely demolishes Epicurean theology and shows that philosophy to be wholly destructive of religion (§§ 57-124).

Book II sets forth in detail the positive teachings of the Stoic theology as expounded by Balbus under four main headings: (1) the existence of the gods, proved by many arguments (§§ 4-44); (2) their nature (§§ 45-72); and their providential government of the world (§§ 73-153); and (3) their providential care for man (§§ 154-168). Book III contains Cotta's criticism, from the Academic point of view, of Balbus' exposition of Stoicism.

'However, we need say nothing more on a point that is already perfectly clear. Telamon dismisses the whole subject, viz., that the gods pay no attention to man, in a single line [of Ennius' play]:

> *If they cared [for us], the good would prosper*
> *and the evil suffer:*
> *But this does not happen.*
> (Frag. 330)

Indeed, the gods should have made all men good, if they were really

concerned over the welfare of the human race; (80) or at the very least
they should certainly have taken care of the good. But why, then, were
the two Scipios, the bravest and best of men, defeated in Spain by the
Carthaginians? Why did Maximus have to bury his son, a consul?
Why was Hannibal permitted to kill Marcellus? Why was Paulus
overwhelmed at Cannae? Why was Regulus handed over to be tortured
by the Carthaginians? Why was not Africanus protected by his own
walls? [He was murdered in bed by an unknown assassin.] But these
instances and many others belong to the past; let us look at more recent
ones. Why is my uncle, Publius Rutilius, a man of unsullied character
and of the greatest learning, now in exile? Why was my colleague
Drusus murdered in his own house? Why was that model of tem-
perance and prudence, Quintus Scaevola, the Pontifex Maximus,
assassinated in the very presence of the statue of Vesta? And before
that, why were so many of the foremost citizens put to death by
Cinna? Why was the most treacherous man of all, Gaius Marius, given
the power to order the death of that noblest of men, Quintus Catulus?
(81) The day would be too short if I set out to make a list of the good
men who have been overwhelmed by adversity, or, equally, the wicked
who have prospered. Why did Marius die comfortably at home, an
old man, and a consul for the seventh time? Why did that utterly
cruel man Cinna rule for so long? "But," you say, "he was punished."
It would have been far better had he been prevented from murdering
all those eminent men, rather than himself eventually punished. . . .
Further, we are told that Anaxarchus, the follower of Democritus, was
slaughtered by the tyrant of Cyprus, and that Zeno of Elea was
tortured to death. Why should I mention Socrates, of whose death I can
never read, in Plato [in the *Phaedo*], without weeping? Do you not
see, then, that the judgment of the gods, supposing they pay any
attention to human affairs, has obliterated all distinctions? [i.e.,
between good and evil, or between the upright and the wicked. Cf.
§ 84 *ad fin.*]

(83) 'Diogenes the Cynic used to say that Harpalus, a bandit in
those days who was looked upon as a happy man, was the standing
witness against the gods, since he lived and prospered for so long.
Dionysius, whom I have just mentioned, after plundering the temple
of Proserpine at Locri, was sailing back to Syracuse, and as he held his
course with a strong following wind, smiled and said, "Do you see, my
friends, what a fine voyage the immortal gods provide those who
commit sacrilege?" He was a very clever fellow, and he caught hold of
the truth so thoroughly and so clearly that he persevered in this view.

When his fleet touched the coast of the Peloponnese and he arrived at the temple of Olympian Zeus, he stripped off the immensely heavy gold mantle of the god which the tyrant Celo had devoted to Jove out of the spoils taken from the Carthaginians; and he actually joked about it, saying that a golden mantle was much too heavy for summer and too cold for winter and tossing him a woollen mantle, which was good for any time of year.

'He also ordered the removal of the gold beard of Aesculapius at Epidaurus, saying it was not proper for the son to wear a beard when his father [Apollo] in all his temples appeared without one. (84) He even ordered the silver tables removed from the shrines, since in accordance with ancient Greek custom they were inscribed, "The property of the good gods"; for he said he wished to benefit by their goodness. . . .

(86) ' "But," it may be urged, "the gods pay no attention to little matters (cf. II, 167), and are not concerned with the tiny farms and poor vines of individual persons, so that any small damage done by blight or hail can scarcely have come to Jupiter's attention. In kingdoms the rulers do not look after every last detail of affairs." This is your argument. As if it were Publius Rutilius' estate at Formiae about which I was complaining [§ 80], and not his total loss of safety! But this is a way mortals have: their external commodities ["the good things of life"], vineyards, grain, fields, olive groves, abundant harvests of fruit and grain—in short, all the comforts and prosperity which enrich their life—these, they say, are derived from the gods; but no one ever looked upon virtue as the gift of a god! (87) And no doubt with good reason, since our virtue entitles us to receive praise from others, and in virtue we have a right to take pride, which we could not do if it came as a gift from God, and not from ourselves. On the other hand, when we gain new honours, or are blessed with some increase in our property, or when we receive any other of the good things that come by fortune or luckily escape any of the evils, we then return thanks to the gods, and do not assume that any praise is due to ourselves. But who ever thanked the gods that he was a good man? No, but we thank them that we are rich, honoured, safe and sound. . . .

(89) ' "But good men sometimes end their lives happily." Yes, and so we seize their examples and without the least show of reason attribute their success to the gods. Diagoras, who was called the Atheist, once visited Samothrace, where one of his friends showed him several pictures of people who had survived very dangerous storms. "You assume," he said, "that the gods pay no attention to human affairs. Do you

not recognize from these painted tablets how many persons through their vows to the gods have escaped the violence of tempests and reached ports in safety?" "Sure enough," replied Diagoras, "but there are no pictures of those who were shipwrecked and lost at sea." On another voyage he himself ran into a storm, and the sailors, alarmed and terrified, told him they justly deserved their misfortune for admitting him on board their ship. But he pointed out to them several other ships labouring through the storm and asked if they thought these ships also had a Diagoras on board. And so with regard to good or bad fortune, it makes not the slightest difference what you are or how you have lived.

(90) ' "The gods, like kings, do not pay attention to everything," it is said [cf. § 86]. But what is the parallel here? If kings knowingly overlook anything [for which they are responsible], they are very guilty; but a god cannot be plead ignorance as an excuse. Yet what an extraordinary defence you make for his case when you say that even if a wicked man escapes his punishment by dying, the penalty is inflicted on his children, his children's children, and all his posterity. What a marvellous example of divine justice! Would any city tolerate the proposal of a law like that, which sentenced a son or a grandson for the crime committed by a father or a grandfather? . . .

(93) ' "Providence," you say, "does not concern itself with individual men" (cf. II, 164). No wonder!—since it does not care for cities. Not even for cities? No, nor for whole nations of peoples. If, therefore, it even despises whole nations, what wonder is there if it scorns the whole human race? But how can you assert that the gods do not concern themselves with all the petty circumstances of life, and at the same time hold that specific, individual dreams are distributed to men by the immortal gods! I take up this question with you because your school believes in the truth of dreams. And do you also maintain that men ought to obligate themselves with vows? But vows are taken by individuals; hence it appears that the divine mind listens even to private matters, and can you not see, accordingly, that it is not so heavily engrossed [with public affairs] as you supposed? Assume that it is busily engaged in moving the heavens and looking after the earth and controlling the seas: why does it permit so many gods to be idle and do nothing? Why is not the management of human affairs handed over to some of those idle deities, which you, Balbus, described as innumerable?

'This is about what I have to say concerning the nature of the gods; not with a desire to destroy [the idea], but merely to let you see how obscure a subject it is, and how difficult to explain' [cf. I, 1].

(94) When he had said this, Cotta ceased speaking. But Lucilius replied, 'You have been very severe in your attack upon divine providence, that doctrine established by the Stoics with the greatest piety and wisdom! But as it is growing late, please set another day for our answer to your views. For it is my duty to challenge you in defence of our altars and hearths, the temples and shrines of the gods, nay, even the walls of the City, which you pontiffs declare to be sacred— for you surround the City with religion [ceremonies] even more carefully than you do with walls. This is something which, as long as I am able to breathe, I think it utterly wrong for me to abandon.'

(95) To which Cotta replied, 'I really wish that you would refute me, Balbus! What I have set forth was intended not to decide this debate, but to discuss it; and I am sure that you can easily defeat me.'

'No doubt of that,' said Velleius, 'when he even believes that our dreams are sent from Jupiter, which, unsubstantial as they are, still have more weight than a Stoic discourse on the nature of the gods!'

Translation by Frederick C. Grant, in his *Ancient Roman Religion*, Library of Religion paperbook series (New York, 1957), pp. 140 ff.; introduction adapted from Grant

268. ALLAH IS NEARER TO MAN THAN THE JUGULAR VEIN

('Koran,' L, 1-15)

Nay, but they marvel that a warner has come to
them from among them; and the unbelievers say,
   'This is a marvellous thing!
What, when we are dead and become dust? That
   is a far returning!'
We know what the earth diminishes of them;
   with Us is a book recording.
  Nay, but they cried lies to the truth
  when it came to them, and so they are
  in a case confused.
What, have they not beheld heaven above them,
how We have built it, and decked it out fair,
   and it has no cracks?

And the earth—We stretched it forth, and cast on it
    firm mountains,
and We caused to grow therein of every joyous kind
    for an insight
    and a reminder to every penitent servant.
    And We sent down out of heaven
        water blessed,
    and caused to grow thereby gardens
        and grain of harvest
and tall palm-trees with spathes compact,
    a provision for the servants,
and thereby We revived a land that was dead.
    Even so is the coming forth.

Cried lies before them the people of Noah
    and the men of Er-Rass, and Thamood, and
    Ad and Pharaoh, the brothers of Lot, the
    men of the Thicket, the people of Tubba',
    Every one cried lies to the Messengers,
        and My threat came true.
What, were We wearied by the first creation?
    No indeed; but they are in uncertainty
        as to the new creation.

We indeed created man; and We know
what his soul whispers within him,
and We are nearer to him than the
    jugular vein.

Translation by A. J. Arberry

269. GOD 'KNOWS THE THOUGHTS WITHIN THE BREASTS'

('Koran,' XXXIX, 5-10)

Surely God guides not him who is a liar,
        unthankful.
    Had God desired to take to Him a son,
He would have chosen whatever He willed of that
He has created. Glory be to Him! He is God,
        the One, the Omnipotent.

He created the heavens and the earth in truth,
  wrapping night about the day, and
  wrapping the day about the night;
and He has subjected the sun and the moon, each of them running
  to a stated term.

Is not He the All-mighty, the All-forgiving?
  He created you of a single soul, then
  from it He appointed its mate;
and He sent down to you of the cattle eight couples.
  He creates you in your mothers' wombs
    creation after creation
    in threefold shadows.
    That then is God, your Lord;
    to Him belongs the Kingdom;
    there is no god but He;
    so how are you turned about?
If you are unthankful, God is independent of you,
yet He approves not unthankfulness in His servants;
but if you are thankful, He will approve it in you.
And no soul laden bears the load of another. Then
to your Lord shall you return, and He will tell you
    what you have been doing.
    He knows the thoughts within the breasts.

Translation by A. J. Arberry

See also nos. 73, 237, 252

270. 'WHERE IS THE LAND IN WHICH ONE DOES NOT DIE?' (NAHUATL)

The Nahuatl were an ancient people in Mexico.

The more I weep, the more I am afflicted,
the more my heart may not desire it,
have I not, when all is said, to go to the Land of the Mystery?

Here on earth our hearts say:
'Oh my friends, would that we were immortal,
oh friends, where is the land in which one does not die?

128

Shall it be that I go? Does my mother live there? Does my
  father live there?

In the Land of the Mystery ... my heart shudders:
if only I had not to die, had not to perish. ...
I suffer and feel pain.

Thou hast left thy fame already well-founded,
O Prince Tlacahuepantzin.
The fact is that here we are but slaves.
Men are simply standing
before him through whom everything lives.
Birth comes, life comes upon earth.
For a short while it is lent us,
the glory of that by which everything lives.
Birth comes, life comes upon earth.

We come only to sleep,
We come only to dream:
It is not true, not true we come to live on the earth:

Spring grass are we become:
It comes, gloriously trailing, it puts out buds, our heart,
the flower of our bodies opens a few petals, then withers!

Nahuatl poem quoted by Laurette Séjourné, *Burning
Water*, trans. Irene Nicholson (London, 1957), pp.
63-4

271. A MEXICAN LAMENT (NAHUATL)

1. Weeping, I, the singer, weave my song of flowers of sadness; I call
to memory the youths, the shards, the fragments, gone to the land
of the dead; once noble and powerful here on earth, the youths were
dried up like feathers, were split into fragments like an emerald, before
the face and in the sight of those who saw them on earth, and with
the knowledge of the Cause of All.

2. Alas! Alas! I sing in grief as I recall the children. Would that I
could turn back again; would that I could grasp their hands once more;
would that I could call them forth from the land of the dead; would
that we could bring them again on earth, that they might rejoice and
delight the Giver of Life; is it possible that we His servants should reject

him or should be ungrateful? Thus I weep in my heart as I, the singer, review my memories, recalling things sad and grievous.

3. Would only that I knew they could hear me, there in the land of the dead, were I to sing some worthy song. Would that I could gladden them, that I could console the suffering and the torment of the children. How can it be learned? Whence can I draw the inspiration? They are not where I may follow them; neither can I reach them with my calling as one here on earth.

Daniel G. Brinton, *Ancient Nahuatl Poetry* (Philadelphia, 1890), p. 73; as quoted in Charles Samuel Braden, *The Scriptures of Mankind* (New York, 1952), pp. 30-1

B. HUMILITY, WISDOM, TOLERANCE

EGYPTIAN TEACHING

272. AN EGYPTIAN RELIGIOUS THINKER:
THE INSTRUCTION FOR KING MERI-KA-RE

The extract which follows is taken from a work composed by an Egyptian king for the benefit of his son Meri-ka-re, who succeeded him on the throne. They lived in the period of confusion and anarchy known as the First Intermediate Period, which followed the downfall of the Old Kingdom (ca. 2280 B.C.) and which preceded the rise of the Middle Kingdom (ca. 2000 B.C.). The Instruction for King Meri-ka-re was thus composed in times of violence and intrigue, and it is in this setting that it must be interpreted and understood. . . .

In the Leningrad Papyrus (the only one in which this portion of the text is fully preserved), the first sentence of each of the two paragraphs is written in red. Capitals are used here to reproduce these headings.

DO JUSTICE SO LONG AS THOU ABIDEST ON EARTH. Calm the weeper and oppress not the widow. Do not oust a man from the property of his father. Do not harm officials in respect of their posts.[1] Beware of punishing wrongfully. Do not kill: it shall not profit thee. Punish with caution[2] by beating—so shall this country[3] be peaceful—except (for) the rebel when his plans have been discovered, for God knows the treacherous of heart and God requiteth his sins in blood. It is the mild man who . . . a lifetime. Do not slay a man whose good qualities thou knowest, one with whom thou didst chant the writings[4] and read in the inventory. . . . God, bold of thy step in difficult places. The soul cometh to the place it knoweth: it cannot stray from the paths of yesterday and no magic can oppose it. It cometh to those that give it water.

THE JUDGES[5] WHO JUDGE THE DEFICIENT, thou knowest that

they are not lenient on that day of judging the miserable, in the hour of performing (their) duty. It is hard when the accuser is possessed of knowledge.[6] Put not thy trust in length of years:[7] they regard a lifetime as an hour. A man surviveth after death and his deeds are placed beside him in heaps. Eternal is the existence yonder. He who makes light of it is a fool. As for him who reaches it without doing wrong, he shall exist yonder like a god, striding forth like the Lords of Eternity.

Notes

1 *posts*. The Egyptian word is of uncertain meaning and the translation is a guess.

2 *caution*. The meaning of the Egyptian word is uncertain.

3 *this country* is a common expression for Egypt, exactly as 'this country' is used by Englishmen in speaking of England.

4 *with whom thou didst chant the writings*. This expression seems to mean 'with whom you were at school.'

5 The *Judges* are a tribunal of gods who judge the dead and decide their fate on the basis of their behaviour whilst on earth.

6 *It is hard when the accuser is possessed of knowledge*, i.e., when the accuser is armed with facts detrimental to the dead person appearing before the divine judges it goes ill with him.

7 *Put not thy trust in length of years*. However long it may be since a sin was committed, the accuser and the judges will remember.

Translation, introduction, and notes by T. W. Thacker, in D. Winton Thomas (ed..), *Documents from Old Testament Times* (London: Thomas Nelson, 1958)

273. THE TEACHING OF AMENEMOPE

The literary remains of the ancient Egyptians reveal that didactic treatises containing wise maxims and proverbial truths were very greatly to their taste. It had long been suspected that for some, at least, of the Hebrew proverbs, models had been provided by this Wisdom Literature, but it was not until the publication of the 'Teaching of Amenemope' that definite evidence to support this conjecture was forthcoming. A number of passages in the Egyptian text were then seen to be so remarkable in resemblance to passages in the book of Proverbs that, even if it could not be proved that the Hebrew borrowed directly from the Egyptian, or *vice-versa*, nevertheless there could be little doubt that both were essentially related. It has been suggested that an international, pan-oriental, common stock of proverbial literature existed in the ancient Near East. Certainly the resemblances between Amenemope's work and the book of Proverbs indicate that the proverbial literature of O.T. times knew no national boundaries.

The papyrus roll containing the 'Teaching of Amenemope' was secured for the British Museum in 1888. . . . The date of the British Museum text is open to question. Suggested dates range from ca. 1000 B.C. to *ca.* 600 B.C. . . . Possibly the original work was written at the end of the Eighteenth or the beginning of the Nineteenth Dynasty (*ca.* 1300 B.C.), when contact between Egypt and Syria was particularly close.

Second Chapter

Guard thyself against robbing the wretched
And against being puissant over the man of broken arm.
Stretch not forth thy hand to repel an old man,
Nor anticipate the aged.
5. *Let not thyself be sent on a wicked mission,*
Nor love him who hath performed it.
Cry not out against him whom thou hast injured,
Nor answer him back to justify thyself.
He who hath done evil, the river-bank abandons him,
10. *And his flooded land carries him away.*
The north wind cometh down that it may end his hour;
It is united to the tempest;
The thunder is loud, and the crocodiles are evil.
O hot-head, what is thy condition?
15. *He is crying out, his voice to heaven.*
O Moon, arraign his crime!
Steer that we may ferry the wicked man across,
For we shall not act like him—
Lift him up, give him thy hand;
20. *Leave him (in) the hands of the god;*
Fill his belly with bread that thou hast,
So that he may be sated and may cast down his eye.

Notes

Lines 1 f. Cp. Prov. xxii, 22. *The man of broken arm,* i.e., helpless; cp. a similar use in Hebrew in reference to the weakness of Pharaoh (Ezek. xxx, 21 f., 24) and of Moab (Jer. xlviii, 25).
Line 4. *anticipate,* i.e., not allowing the aged to speak.

Line 9. *the river-bank abandons him.* Perhaps the meaning is that it crumbles away under his feet because it has been weakened by the inundation.

Line 16. O Moon. The moon was the symbol of Thoth, the Ibis-headed god who presided at the Judgment of the Dead when a man's heart was weighed against the feather of Truth. The scene is often depicted in copies of the Book of the Dead.

Lines 17-22. This remarkable passage is in striking contrast to the *lex talionis* of ancient times.

Line 18. Cp. Prov. xxiv, 29.

Line 20. Cp. Deut. xxxiii, 27.

Lines 21 f. Cp. Prov. xxv, 21. *cast down his eye,* i.e., to be ashamed.

Sixth Chapter

Remove not the landmark at the boundaries of the arable land,
Nor disturb the position of the measuring-cord;
Covet not a cubit of land,
Nor throw down the boundaries of a widow. . . .
5. Beware of throwing down the boundaries of the fields,
Lest a terror carry thee off. . . .
Better is poverty in the land of the god
Than riches in a storehouse;
Better is bread, when the heart is happy,
10. Than riches with vexation.

Notes

Lines 1-4. Cp. Prov. xxiii, 10 (also xxii, 28).
Lines 5 f. Cp. Prov. xxiii, 11.
Lines 7-10. Cp. Prov. xv, 16 f., xviii, 1.

Seventh Chapter

Cast not thy heart after riches;
There is no ignoring Shay and Renent.
Place not thy heart upon externals;
Every man belongeth to his hour.
5. Labour not to seek for increase;
Thy needs are safe for thee.
If riches are brought to thee by robbery,
They will not spend the night with thee;
At daybreak they are not in thy house:
10. Their places may be seen, but they are not.
The ground has opened its mouth—'Let him enter that it may swallow,'
They sink into the underworld.

They have made for themselves a great breach suitable to their
size
And are sunken down in the storehouse.
15. They have made themselves wings like geese
And are flown away to heaven.
Rejoice not thyself (over) riches (gained) by robbery.
Nor groan because of poverty.

Notes

Line 2. *Shay* and *Renent* were deities of fortune. Perhaps 'Fate and Fortune' is
the best translation.
Line 4. *his hour.* This is possibly a reference to a man's horoscope.
Lines 5-16. Cp. the remarkable parallel in Prov. xxiii, 4 f.
Line 11. 'Let him enter . . . swallow' is a descriptive epithet of the devouring
mouth of the earth.
Line 15. *geese.* In the book of Proverbs it is the soaring eagle which is the
simile of the flight of wealth (xxiii, 5).

Thirteenth Chapter

Injure not a man, [with] pen upon papyrus—
O abomination of the god!
Bear not witness with lying words,
Nor seek another's reverse with thy tongue.
5. Make not a reckoning with him who hath nothing,
Nor falsify thy pen.
If thou hast found a large debt against a poor man,
Make it into three parts,
Forgive two, and let one remain,
10. In order that thou shalt find thereby the ways of life.
Thou wilt lie down—the night hasteneth away—(lo!) thou art
in the morning;
Thou has found it like good news.
Better is praise for one who loves men
Than riches in a storehouse;
15. Better is bread, when the heart is happy,
Than riches with contention.

Notes

Line 6. Cp. Jer. viii, 8.
Lines 7-10. It has been suggested that the difficult parable of the Unjust Steward,
recorded in St. Luke's Gospel, but absent from the other Gospels, may be a
reminiscence of these lines (Luke xvi, 1 *ff.*).
Lines 13 f. Cp. Prov. xvi, 8. Lines 13 f. Cp. Prov. xvii, 1.

Thirtieth Chapter

See for thyself these thirty chapters:
They give pleasure; they instruct;
They are the foremost of all books;
They instruct the ignorant.
5. If they are read out in the presence of the ignorant,
Then he will be cleansed by reason of them.
Fill thyself with them; put them in thy heart,
And be a man who can explain them,
Interpreting them as a teacher.
10. As for the scribe who is experienced in his office,
He shall find himself worthy to be a courtier.

Colophon

It has come to its end
In the writing of Senu, son of the God's Father Pa-miu

Notes

Line 1. Cp. Prov. xxii, 20.
Lines 10 f. Cp. Prov. xxii, 29.
Lines 12 f. The colophon records the successful completion of the copying of the text and gives the name of the copyist. Egyptian books were normally concluded in this way. the God's Father was a title given to a class of elder temple priests.

Translation, introduction, and notes by J. M. Plumley, in D. Winton Thomas (ed.), Documents from Old Testament Times (London: Thomas Nelson, 1958)

GREEK THOUGHT

274. 'I AM A MORTAL, A MAN'

(Aeschylus, 'Agamemnon,' 914-30)

Clytaemnestra's handmaidens spread a bright carpet between the chariot and the door, and Agamemnon speaks.

Daughter of Leda, you who kept my house for me,
there is one way your welcome matched my absence well.

You strained it to great length. Yet properly to praise
me thus belongs by right to other lips, not yours.
And all this—do not try in women's ways to make
me delicate, nor, as if I were some Asiatic
bow down to earth and with wide mouth cry out to me,
nor cross my path with jealousy by strewing the ground
with robes. Such state becomes the gods, and none beside.
I am a mortal, a man; I cannot trample upon
these tinted splendours without fear thrown in my path.
I tell you, as a man, not god, to reverence me.
Discordant is the murmur at such treading down
of lovely things; while God's most lordly gift to man
is decency of mind. Call that man only blest
who has in sweet tranquillity brought his life to close.
If you could only act as such, my hope is good.

Translation by Richmond Lattimore. Published by
University of Chicago Press, 1959

JAIN BELIEF

275. THE JAIN CONCEPTION OF KARMAN

('Sūtrakritānga,' I, 2, 1)

The Jain believe that the essentials of their doctrine were revealed in
the most ancient times (as a matter of fact, in mythical time) by
a series of prophets or founders of religion, called Tīrthamkara.
Rishabha, the supposed inspirer of the following text, was the first
Tīrthamkara.

(Rishabha said to his sons):
   Acquire perfect knowledge of the Law! Why do you not study it?
It is difficult to obtain instruction in it after this life. The days (that
are gone by) will never return, nor is it easy a second time to obtain
human birth.
   See, young and old men, even children in the mother's womb die.
As a hawk catches a quail, so (life) will end when its time is spent.
   (A man) may suffer for the sake of his parents; he will not easily

obtain happiness after this life. A pious man should consider these causes of danger and cease to act.

For in this world living beings suffer individually for their deeds; for the deed they have done themselves, they obtain (punishment), and will not get over it before they have felt it.

Even gods, Gandharvas, Rākshasas, and Asuras; animals who live on earth, and snakes; kings, common people, merchants, and Brāhmanas; they all must leave their rank and suffer.

Notwithstanding their pleasures and relations, all men must suffer in due time the fruit of their works; as a cocoa-nut detaching itself from its stalk (falls down), so (life) will end when its time is spent.

Even a very learned or virtuous man, or a Brāhmana or an ascetic, will be severely punished for his deed when he is given to actions of deceit.

See, those (heretics) who search for the knowledge of truth, but who do not cross the Samsāra, talk only about the highest good (without reaching it).

How will you understand what is near you and what is beyond? In the meanwhile you suffer for your deeds.

He who walks about naked and lean, he who eats only once after a month, if he is filled with deceit, will be born an endless number of times.

Man, cease from sins! For the life of men will come to an end. Men who are drowned (in lust, as it were), and addicted to pleasure will, for want of control, be deluded.

Exert and control yourself! For it is not easy to walk on ways where there are minutely small animals. Follow the commandments which the Arhats have well proclaimed.

Heroes (of faith) who desist (from sins) and exert themselves aright, who subdue wrath, fear, etc., will never kill living beings; they desist from sins and are entirely happy.

It is not myself alone who suffers, all creatures in the world suffer; this a wise man should consider, and he should patiently bear (such calamities) as befall him, without giving way to his passions.

As a wall covered with a plastering (of dried cowdung) is by a shock made thin, so (a monk) should make his body lean by fasting, etc. He should abstain from slaughter of living beings. This is the Law proclaimed by the Sage.

As a bird covered with dust removes the grey powder by shaking itself, so a worthy and austere Brāhmana, who does penance, annihilates his Karman.

Humility, Wisdom, Tolerance

Young and old people claim a houseless Shrāmana as their own, though he begs according to the Law, observes the rules of conduct, and performs austerities. People will ever cry themselves hoarse, but will not captivate him.

Whatever they will do to move his pity, however they will cry about their son, they will not captivate a worthy and virtuous monk or make him return to domestic life.

Though they tempt him with pleasures, and though they should bind him and carry him home, if he does not care for a (worldly) life, they will not captivate him or make him return to domestic life.

His father and mother, his children and wife who claim him, will admonish him; 'See, you are our supporter; care not for the next world in order to support us.'

Some people are (foolishly) attached to others, and are thereby deluded; the unrighteous make them adopt unrighteousness, and they exult in their wickedness.

Therefore a worthy and wise man should be careful, ceasing from sin and being entirely happy. The virtuous heroes of faith (have chosen) the great road, the right and certain path to perfection.

He who has entered the road leading to the destruction (of Karman), who controls his mind, speech, and body, who has given up his possessions and relations and all undertakings, should walk about subduing his senses.

Translation from prakrit by Herman Jacobi, *Jaina Sūtras*, Part II, in *Sacred Books of the East*, XLV (Oxford, 1895), pp. 249-53

A BUDDHIST EMPEROR AND PHILOSOPHER: ASHOKA

The Edicts of Ashoka.

Ashoka (*ca.* 274-232 B.C.) was an emperor and conqueror who was afflicted by repentance after the short and sanguinary Kalinga war. He revealed himself a philosopher in the consequences he draws from his repentance—a political philosopher who expressed himself in proclamations and laws, bounding his country with Rock Edicts to publish his ideals and aims to his neighbours and to his subjects along the frontiers, erecting Pillar Edicts in the important places of his empire to express his moral and social objectives, and dedicating in the Cave Edicts places for religious observance; and a moral philosopher who found a substitute for conquests by arms in conquest by Dharma, by righteousness and morality. He was a religious leader who turned from external observances to internal meditations, from temporal possessions to eternal truths. But above all he was a teacher and, in particular, a teacher of understanding and tolerance.

Ashoka sums up his teaching in a single word, 'Dharma.' His Edicts make it clear that he conceived his mission to consist in defining, publishing and propagating Dharma; and the strength and originality of his teaching are underlined by the meaning he gave to that ambiguous term. 'Dharma' means the insights and percepts of religion and piety; it also means the principles and prescriptions of ethics and morality. With remarkable clarity, Ashoka recognized the interplay of the various dimensions of the moral life: it reflects a man's duties as determined by his station in life; it reflects a basic order in the universe and a truth discerned in that order; it is a bond uniting people in their associations in families, communities, religions, and nations; it is a fundamental insight, differently expressed in different cultures and religions, which serves as a basis for mutual understanding and peace; it is a guide to action and to self-realization and happiness; it is achieved by action, advanced by instruction, and protected by sanctions, and in turn it provides a basis for policy, education, and justice; it is discovered by self-scrutiny, meditation, and conversion, and it entails renunciation of whatever is inconsistent with it.

Ashoka attributes his own interest in Dharma to repentance for the violence and cruelty of the Kalinga war. The change of heart brought about by his reflections on war inspired him to the promulgation of his Edicts by providing an insight for moral reform. His interest throughout is practical in its orientation. He devoted himself to study of Dharma, to action according to Dharma, and to inculcation of Dharma, but the three are inseparable—the study of Dharma translates Dharma into concrete action; action according to Dharma provides examples to guide inculcation; inculcation of Dharma, although it depends on instruction, supervision, administration, and institutions, is achieved finally only by meditation and study.

The Edicts of Asoka, edited and translated by N. A. Vicam and Richard McKeon (Chicago: University of Chicago Press, 1959), pp. ix-xii

276. KING ASHOKA DISCRIMINATES BETWEEN MEANINGLESS CEREMONIES AND THE 'CEREMONIES OF DHARMA'

('Rock Edict' IX)

King Priyadarshī, the Beloved of the Gods, says: People perform various ceremonies. Among the occasions on which ceremonies are performed are sicknesses, marriages of sons or daughters, children's births, and departures on journeys. Women in particular have recourse to many diverse, trivial, and meaningless ceremonies.

It is right that ceremonies be performed. But this kind bears little fruit. The ceremony of Dharma (*Dharma-mangala*), on the contrary, is very fruitful. It consists in proper treatment of slaves and servants, reverence to teachers, restraint of violence towards living creatures, and liberality to priests and ascetics. These and like actions are called the ceremonies of Dharma.

Therefore, a father, son, brother, master, friend, acquaintance, or even a neighbour ought to say about such actions, 'They are good; they should be performed until their purpose is achieved. I shall observe them.'

Other ceremonies are of doubtful value. They may achieve their purpose, or they may not. Moreover, the purposes for which they are performed are limited to this world.

The ceremony of Dharma, on the other hand, is not limited to time. Even if it does not achieve its object in this world, it produced unlimited merit in the next world. But if it produces its object in this world, it achieves both effects; the purpose desired in this world and unlimited merit in the next.

It has also been said that liberality is commendable. But there is no greater liberality than the gift of Dharma or the benefit of Dharma. Therefore, a friend, well-wisher, relative, or companion should urge one when the occasion arises, saying, 'You should do this; this is commendable. By doing this you may attain heaven.' And what is more worth doing than attaining heaven?

Translation by N. A. Nikam and Richard McKeon,
The Edicts of Asoka, op. cit., pp. 46-7

277. ASHOKA'S CHANGE OF HEART AND THE IDEAL
OF CONQUEST BY DHARMA

(*'Rock Edict'* XIII)

The Kalinga country was conquered by King Priyadarshī, Beloved of the Gods, in the eighth year of his reign. One hundred and fifty thousand persons were carried away captive, one hundred thousand were slain, and many times that number died.

Immediately after the Kalingas had been conquered, King Priyadarshī became intensely devoted to the study of Dharma, to the love of Dharma, and to the inculcation of Dharma.

The Beloved of the Gods, conqueror of the Kalingas, is moved to remorse now. For he has felt profound sorrow and regret because the conquest of a people previously unconquered involves slaughter, death, and deportation.

But there is a more important reason for the King's remorse. The Brāhmanas and Shramanas [the priestly and ascetic orders] as well as the followers of other religions and the householders—who all practised obedience to superiors, parents, and teachers, and proper courtesy and firm devotion to friends, acquaintances, companions, relatives, slaves, and servants—all suffer from the injury, slaughter and deportation inflicted on their loved ones. Even those who escaped calamity themselves are deeply afflicted by the misfortunes suffered by those friends, acquaintances, companions, and relatives for whom they feel an undiminished affection. Thus all men share in the misfortune, and this weighs on King Priyadarshī's mind.

[Moreover, there is no country except that of the Yōnas (that is, the Greeks) where Brahmin and Buddhist ascetics do not exist] and there is no place where men are not attached to one faith or another.

Therefore, even if the number of people who were killed or who died or who were carried away in the Kalinga war had been only one one-hundredth or one one-thousandth of what it actually was, this would still have weighed on the King's mind.

King Priyadarshī now thinks that even a person who wrongs him must be forgiven for wrongs that can be forgiven.

King Priyadarshī seeks to induce even the forest peoples who have come under his dominion [that is, primitive peoples in the remote sections of the conquered territory] to adopt this way of life and this ideal. He reminds them, however, that he exercises the power to punish, despite his repentance, in order to induce them to desist from their crimes and escape execution.

For King Priyadarshī desires security, self-control, impartiality, and cheerfulness for all living creatures.

King Priyadarshī considers moral conquest [that is, conquest by Dharma, Dharma-vijaya] the most important conquest. He has achieved this moral conquest repeatedly both here and among the peoples living beyond the borders of his kingdom, even as far away as six hundred yojanas [about three thousand miles], where the Yōna [Greek] king Antiyoka rules, and even beyond Antiyoka in the realms of the four kings named Turamaya, Antikini, Maka, and Alikasudara[1] and to the south among the Cholas and Pandyas [in the southern tip of the Indian peninsula] as far as Ceylon.

Here in the King's dominion also, among the Yōnas [inhabitants of a northwest frontier province, probably Greeks] and the Kambōjas [neighbours of the Yōnas], among the Nābhakas and Nābhapanktis [who probably lived along the Himalayan frontier], among the Bhojas and Paitryanikas, among the Andhras and Paulindas [all peoples of the Indian peninsula], everywhere people heed his instructions in Dharma.

Even in countries which King Priyadarshī's envoys have not reached, people have heard about Dharma and about his Majesty's ordinances and instructions in Dharma, and they themselves conform to Dharma and will continue to do so.

Wherever conquest is achieved by Dharma, it produces satisfaction. Satisfaction is firmly established by conquest by Dharma [since it generates no opposition of conquered and conqueror]. Even satisfaction, however, is of little importance. King Priyadarshī attaches value ultimately only to consequences of action in the other world.

This edict on Dharma has been inscribed so that my sons and great-grandsons who may come after me should not think new conquests worth achieving. If they do conquer, let them take pleasure in moderation and mild punishments. Let them consider moral conquest the only true conquest.

That is good, here and hereafter. Let their pleasure be pleasure in morality [Dharma-rati]. For this alone is good, here and hereafter.

Note

1 The five kings referred to have been identified as follows: Antiyoka—Antiochus II Theos of Syria (261-246 B.C.); Turamaya—Ptolemy II Philadelphos of Egypt (285-247 B.C.); Antikini—Antigonos Gonatas of Macedonia (278-239

B.C.); Maka—Magas of Cyrene (300-258 B.C.); and Alikasudra—Alexander of Epirus (272?-258 B.C.). The passage is of extreme importance not only for dating the events of Ashoka's reign but also for judging the extent of communications in his times. It indicates, moreover, the date 258 B.C., as the latest date at which all five could be referred to simultaneously and therefore fixes the approximate date of the edict.

Translation and note by N. A. Nikam and Richard McKeon, *The Edicts of Asoka, op. cit.*, pp. 27-30

278: KING ASHOKA AGAINST RELIGIOUS INTOLERANCE

('Rock Edict' XII)

King Priyadarshī honours men of all faith, members of religious orders and laymen alike, with gifts and various marks of esteem. Yet he does not value either gifts or honours as much as growth in the qualities essential to religion in men of all faiths.

This growth may take many forms, but its root is in guarding one's speech to avoid extolling one's own faith and disparaging the faith of others improperly or, when the occasion is appropriate, immoderately.

The faiths of others all deserve to be honoured for one reason or another. By honouring them, one exalts one's own faith and at the same time performs a service to the faith of others. By acting otherwise, one injures one's own faith and also does disservice to that of others. For if a man extols his own faith and disparages another because of devotion to his own and because he wants to glorify it, he seriously injures his own faith.

Therefore concord alone is commendable, for through concord men may learn and respect the conception of Dharma accepted by others.

King Priyadarshī desires men of all faiths to know each other's doctrines and to acquire sound doctrines. Those who are attached to their particular faiths should be told that King Priyadarshī does not value gifts or honours as much as growth in the qualities essential to religion in men of all faiths.

Many officials are assigned to tasks bearing on this purpose—the officers in charge of spreading Dharma, the superintendents of women in the royal households, the inspectors of cattle and pasture lands, and other officials.

The objective of these measures is the promotion of each man's particular faith and the glorification of Dharma.

Translation by N. A. Nikam and Richard McKeon, *The Edicts of Asoka, op. cit.*, pp. 51-2

279. ASHOKA AGAINST AGGRESSION AND TENSION BETWEEN STATES

('*Kalinga Edict*' II)

King Priyadarshī says:

I command that the following instructions be communicated to my official at Samāpā:

Whenever something right comes to my attention, I want it put into practice and I want effective means devised to achieve it. My principal means to do this is to transmit my instructions to you.

All men are my children. Just as I seek the welfare and happiness of my own children in this world and the next, I seek the same things for all men.

Unconquered peoples along the borders of my dominions may wonder what my disposition is towards them. My only wish with respect to them is that they should not fear me, but trust me; that they should expect only happiness from me, not misery; that they should understand further that I will forgive them for offences which can be forgiven; that they should be induced by my example to practise Dharma; and that they should attain happiness in this world and the next.

I transmit these instructions to you in order to discharge my debt [to them] by instructing you and making known to you my will and my unshakable resolution and commitment. You must perform your duties in this way and establish their confidence in the King, assuring them that he is like a father to them, that he loves them as he loves himself, and that they are like his own children.

Having instructed you and informed you of my will and my unshakable resolution and commitment, I will appoint officials to carry out this programme in all the provinces. You are able to inspire the border peoples with confidence in me and to advance their welfare and happiness in this world and the next. By doing so, you will also attain heaven and help me discharge my debts to the people.

This edict has been inscribed here so that my officials will work at all times to inspire the peoples of neighbouring countries with confidence in me and to induce them to practise Dharma.

This edict must be proclaimed every four months [at the beginning of the three seasons—hot, rainy and cold] on Tisya days [i.e., when the moon is in the constellation containing Tisya, Sirius]; it may also be proclaimed in the intervals between those days; and on appropriate occasions it may be read to individuals.

By doing this, you will be carrying out my commands.

Translation by N. A. Nikam and Richard McKeon,
The Edicts of Asoka, op. cit., pp. 53-4

CONFUCIUS

280. THE GOLDEN AGE: THE CONFUCIAN AGE OF GRAND UNITY

(Li-chi', 9)

Once Confucious was taking part in the winter sacrifice. After the ceremony was over, he went for a stroll along the top of the city gate and sighed mournfully. He sighed for the state of Lu.

His disciple Yet Yen [Tzu lu], who was by his side, asked: 'Why should the gentleman sigh?'

Confucius replied: 'The practice of the Great Way, the illustrious men of the Three Dynasties—these I shall never know in person. And yet they inspire my ambition! When the Great Way was practised, the world was shared by all alike. The worthy and the able were promoted to office and men practised good faith and lived in affection. Therefore they did not regard as parents only their own parents, or as sons only their own sons. The aged found a fitting close to their lives, the robust their proper employment; the young were provided with an upbringing and the widow and widower, the orphaned and the sick, with proper care. Men had their tasks and women their hearths. They hated to see goods lying about in waste, yet they did not hoard them for themselves; they disliked the thought that their energies were not fully used, yet they used them not for private ends. Therefore all evil plotting was prevented and thieves and rebels did not arise, so that people could leave their outer gates unbolted. This was the age of Grand Unity.

'Now the Great Way has become hid and the world is the possession of private families. Each regards as parents only his own parents, as sons only his sons; goods and labour are employed for selfish ends. Hereditary offices and titles are granted by ritual law while walls and moats must provide security. Ritual and righteousness are used to

regulate the relationship between ruler and subject, to insure affection
between father and son, peace between brothers, and harmony between
husband and wife, to set up social institutions, organize the farms and
villages, honour the brave and wise, and bring merit to the individual.
Therefore intrigue and plotting come about and men take up arms.
Emperor Yu, kings T'ang, Wen, Wu, and Ch'eng and the Duke of
Chou achieved eminence for this reason: that all six rulers were
constantly attentive to ritual, made manifest their righteousness and
acted in complete faith. They exposed error, made humanity their
law and humility their practice, showing the people wherein they
should constantly abide. If there were any who did not abide by these
principles, they were dismised from their positions and regarded by
the multitude as dangerous. This is the period of Lesser Prosperity.'

Translation by Wm. Theodore de Bary and others, in
de Bary, *et al.* (eds.), *Sources of Chinese Tradition*
(New York: Columbia University Press, 1960), pp.
191-2

281. THE TEACHINGS OF CONFUCIUS

('Analects,' selections)

*'Confucius,' the Latinized form of K'ung Fu-tzu or 'Master K'ung,' is
the title commonly used in referring to him in Chinese. Confucius
was born in 551 B.C. in what is now Shantung Province. His father
died when he was very young, leaving him to struggle alone with
the problem of securing an education and making his way in the
world. Confucius believed that his place was in the world of politics,
and with almost pathetic persistence he sought throughout the states of
China a ruler who would be willing to employ him and his ideas in
the government. But on the whole his political career was a failure,
and more and more he turned his attention to the teaching of young
men. He was said to have had some three thousand students. He died in
479 B.C.*

Confucius said: 'At fifteen, I set my heart on learning. At thirty, I
was firmly established. At forty, I had no more doubts. At fifty, I
knew the will of Heaven. At sixty, I was ready to listen to it. At
seventy, I could follow my heart's desire without transgressing what
was right.' (II, 4.)

When Confucius was in Ch'i, he heard the Shao music and for three months he forgot the taste of meat, saying: 'I never thought music could be so beautiful.' (VII, 13.)

Confucius said: 'When walking in a party of three, I always have teachers, I can select the good qualities of the one for imitation, and the bad ones of the other and correct them in myself.' (VII, 21.)

Confucius said: 'I am a transmitter and not a creator. I believe in and have a passion for the ancients. I venture to compare myself with our old P'eng (China's Methuselah).' (VII, 1.)

Confucius said: 'Sometimes I have gone a whole day without food and a whole night without sleep, giving myself to thought. It was no use. It is better to learn.' (XV, 30.)

There were four things that Confucius was determined to eradicate: a biased mind, arbitrary judgments, obstinacy, and egotism. (IX, 4.)

Confucius said: 'Those who know the truth are not up to those who love it; those who love the truth are not up to those who delight in it.' (VI, 18.)

Confucius said: 'Having heard the Way (Tao) in the morning, one may die content in the evening.' (IV, 8.)

Humanity (jen)

Fan Ch'ih asked about humanity. Confucius said: 'Love men.' (XII, 22.)

Tzu Chang asked Confucius about humanity. Confucius said: 'To be able to practise five virtues anywhere in the world constitutes humanity.' Tzu Chang begged to know what these were. Confucius said: 'Courtesy, magnaminity, good faith, diligence, and kindness. He who is courteous is not humiliated, he who is magnanimous wins the multitude, he who is of good faith is trusted by the people, he who is diligent attains his objective, and he who is kind can get service from the people.' (XVII, 6.)

Confucius said: 'Without humanity a man cannot long endure adversity, nor can he long enjoy prosperity. The humane rest in humanity; the wise find it beneficial' (IV, 2.)

Confucius said: 'Only the humane man can love men and can hate men.' (IV, 3.)

Filial Piety

Tzu Yu asked about filial piety. Confucius said: 'Nowadays a filial son is just a man who keeps his parents in food. But even dogs or horses are given food. If there is no feeling of reverence, wherein lies the difference?' (II, 7.)

Tzu Hsia asked about filial piety. Confucius said: 'The manner is the really difficult thing. When anything has to be done the young people undertake it; when there is wine and food the elders are served —is this all there is to filial piety?' (II, 8.)

Religious Sentiment

Tzu Lu asked about the worship of ghosts and spirits. Confucius said: 'We don't know yet how to serve men, how can we know about serving the spirits?' 'What about death,' was the next question. Confucius said: 'We don't know yet about life, how can we know about death?' (XI, 11.)

Fan Ch'ih asked about wisdom. Confucius said: 'Devote yourself to the proper demands of the people, respect the ghosts and spirits but keep them at a distance—this may be called wisdom.' (VI, 20.)

Translation by Wm. Theodore de Bary and others, in de Bary, *et al.* (eds.), *Sources of Chinese Tradition* (New York: Columbia University Press, 1960), pp. 24-5, 28-31

C. BUDDHA EXPLAINS THE MIDDLE PATH

282. THE PARABLE OF THE ARROW: GOTAMA BUDDHA REFUSES TO DISCUSS METAPHYSICAL PROBLEMS

('Majjhima-nikāya,' I, 426 ff. [LXII *'Cūla-mālunkyā-sutta'*])

Thus I have heard: The Lord was once dwelling near Sāvatthī, at Jetavana in the park of Anāthapindika. Now the elder Mālunkyāputta had retired from the world, and as he meditated the thought arose: 'These theories have been left unexplained by the Lord, set aside, and rejected, whether the world is eternal or not eternal, whether the world is finite or not, whether the soul (life) is the same as the body, or whether the soul is one thing and the body another, whether a Buddha (Tathāgata) exists after death or does not exist after death, and whether a Buddha both exists and does not exist after death, and whether a Buddha is non-existent and not non-existent after death—these things the Lord does not explain to me, and that he does not explain them to me does not please me, it does not suit me. I will approach the Lord, and ask about this matter. . . . If the Lord does not explain to me, I will give up the training, and return to a worldly life.'

[When Mālunkyāputta had approached and put his questions the Lord replied:] 'Now did I, Mālunkyāputta, ever say to you, 'Come Mālunkyāputta, lead a religious life with me, and I will explain to you whether the world is eternal or not eternal [and so on with the other questions]?'' 'You did not, reverend sir.' 'Anyone, Mālunkyāputta, who should say 'I will not lead a religious life with the Lord, until the Lord explains to me whether the world is eternal or not eternal [etc.] . . .' that person would die, Mālunkyāputta, without its being explained. It is as if a man had been wounded by an arrow thickly smeared with poison, and his friends, companions, relatives, and kinsmen were to get a surgeon to heal him, and he were to say, "I will not have this arrow pulled out, until I know by what man I was wounded, whether he is of the warrior caste, or a brahmin, or the agricultural, or the lowest caste." Or if he were to say, "I will not have

this arrow pulled out until I know of what name or family the man is
. . . or whether he is tall, or short, or of middle height . . . or
whether he is black, or dark, or yellowish . . . or whether he comes
from such and such a village, or town, or city. . . . or until I know
whether the bow with which I was wounded was a chāpa or a kondanda,
or until I know whether the bow-string was of swallow-wort, or
bamboo-fibre, or sinew, or hemp, or of milk-sap tree, or until I know
whether the shaft was from a wild or cultivated plant . . . or whether
it was feathered from a vulture's wing or a heron's or a hawk's, or a pea-
cock's, or a sithilahanu-bird's . . . or whether it was wrapped round
with the sinew of an ox, or of a buffalo, or of a ruru-deer, or of a
monkey . . . or until I know whether it was an ordinary arrow, or
a razor arrow, or a vekanda, or an iron arrow, or a calf-tooth arrow,
or one of a karavīra leaf." That man would die, Mālunkyāputta,
without knowing all this.

'It is not on the view that the world is eternal, Mālunkyāputta,
that a religious life depends; it is not on the view that the world is not
eternal that a religious life depends. Whether the view is held that
the world is eternal, or that the world is not eternal, there is still
re-birth, there is old age, there is death, and grief, lamentation, suffering, sorrow, and despair, the destruction of which even in this life I
announce. It is not on the view that the world is finite. . . . It is not
on the view that a Tathāgata exists after death. . . . Therefore, Mālunkyāputta, consider as unexplained what I have not explained, and consider as explained what I have explained. And what, Mālunkyāputta,
have I not explained? Whether the world is eternal I have not explained, whether the world is not eternal . . . whether a Tathāgata is
both non-existent and not non-existent after death I have not explained. And why Mālunkyāputta, have I not explained this? Because
this, Mālunkyāputta, is not useful, it is not concerned with the principle of a religious life, does not conduce to aversion, absence or passion,
cessation, tranquillity, supernatural faculty, perfect knowledge, Nirvāna, and therefore I have not explained it.

'And what, Mālunkyāputta, have I explained? Suffering have I
explained, the cause of suffering, the destruction of suffering, and the
path that leads to the destruction of suffering have I explained. For
this, Mālunkyāputta, is useful, this is concerned with the principle of
a religious life; this conduces to aversion, absence of passion, cessation,
tranquillity, supernatural faculty, perfect knowledge, Nirvāna and
therefore have I explained it. Therefore, Mālunkyāputta, consider as
unexplained what I have not explained, and consider as explained

what I have explained.' Thus spoke the Lord and with joy the elder
Mālunkyāputta applauded the words of the Lord.

Translation by E. J. Thomas, *Buddhist Scriptures* (London, 1913), pp. 64-7. Cf. Lord Chalmers, *Further Dialogues of the Buddha*, vol. 1 (London, 1926, pp. 304 ff.

283. THE MIDDLE PATH WHICH LEADS TO WISDOM AND CONDUCES TO NIRVĀNA

('Mahāvagga,' 1, 6, 17-30)

17. And the Blessed One thus addressed the five Bhikkhus: There are
two extremes, O Bhikkhus, which he who has given up the world,
ought to avoid. What are these two extremes? A life given to pleasures,
devoted to pleasures and lusts: this is degrading, sensual, vulgar, ignoble, and profitless; and a life given to mortifications: this is painful,
ignoble and profitless. By avoiding these two extremes, O Bhikkhus,
the Tathāgata has gained the knowledge of the Middle Path which leads
to insight, which leads to wisdom, which conduces to calm, to knowledge, to the Sambodhi, to Nirvāna.

18. Which, O Bhikkhus, is this Middle Path the knowledge of
which the Tathāgata has gained, which leads to insight, which leads
to wisdom, which conduces to calm, to knowledge, to the Sambodhi, to
Nirvāna? It is the holy eightfold Path, namely, Right Belief, Right
Aspiration, Right Speech, Right Conduct, Right Means of Livelihood,
Right Endeavour, Right Memory, Right Meditation. This, O Bhikkhus,
is the Middle Path the knowledge of which the Tathāgata has gained,
which leads to insight, which leads to wisdom, which conduces to
calm, to knowledge, to the Sambodhi, to Nirvāna.

19. This, O Bhikkhus, is the Noble Truth of Suffering: Birth is
suffering: decay is suffering; illness is suffering; death is suffering.
Presence of objects we hate, is suffering; Separation from objects we
love, is suffering; not to obtain what we desire, is suffering. Briefly, the
fivefold clinging to existence is suffering.

20. This, O Bhikkhus, is the Noble Truth of the Cause of suffering:
Thirst, that leads to re-birth, accompanied by pleasure and lust, finding
its delight here and there. (This thirst is threefold), namely, thirst for
pleasure, thirst for existence, thirst for prosperity.

21. This, O Bhikkhus, is the Noble Truth of the Cessation of suffering: (it ceases with) the complete cessation of this thirst—a cessation which consists in the absence of every passion—with the abandoning of this thirst, with the doing away with it, with the deliverance from it, with the destruction of desire.

22. This, O Bhikkhus, is the Noble Truth of the Path which leads to the cessation of suffering: that holy eightfold Path, that is to say, Right Belief, Right Aspiration, Right Speech, Right Conduct, Right Means of Livelihood, Right Endeavour, Right Memory, Right Meditation. . . .

29. Thus the Blessed One Spoke. The five Bhikkhus were delighted, and they rejoiced at the words of the Blessed One. And when this exposition was propounded, the venerable Kondanna obtained the pure and spotless Eye of the Truth (that is to say, the following knowledge): 'Whatsover is subject to the condition of origination, is subject also to the condition of cessation.

30. And as the Blessed One had founded the Kingdom of Truth (by propounding the four Noble Truths), the earth-inhabiting *devas* shouted: Truly the Blessed One has founded at Benares, in the deer park Isipatana, the highest kingdom of Truth, which may be opposed neither by a Samana nor by a Brāhmana, neither by a deva, nor by Māra, nor by Brahma, nor by any being in the world.

Translation by T. W. Rhys Davids and Hermann Oldenberg, *Vinaya Texts*, part I, in *Sacred Books of the East*, XIII (Oxford, 1881), pp. 94-7

284. PROFITABLE AND UNPROFITABLE DOCTRINES

('Samyutta-nikāya,' V, 437)

At one time the Lord dwelt at Kosambi in the sisu-grove. Then the Lord took a few sisu leaves in his hand and addressed the monks: 'What do you think, monks, which are the more, the few sisu leaves I have taken in my hand, or those that are in the sisu-grove?' 'Small in number, Lord, and few are the leaves that the Lord has taken in his hand: those are far more that are in the sisu-grove.' 'Even so, monks, that is much more which I have realized and have not declared to you; and but little have I declared.

'And why, monks, have I not declared it? Because it is not profitable, does not belong to the beginning of the religious life, and does not tend to revulsion, absence of passion, cessation, calm, higher knowledge, enlightenment, Nirvāna. Therefore have I not declared it.

'And what, monks, have I declared? This is pain, I have declared; this is the cause of pain, I have declared; this is the cessation of pain, I have declared; this is the Way leading to the cessation of pain, I have declared. And why, monks, have I declared it? Because it is profitable, it belongs to the beginning of the religious life, and tends to revulsion, absence of passion, cessation, calm, higher knowledge, enlightenment, Nirvāna. Therefore have I declared it.

'Therefore, monks, to this you must be devoted: this is pain, this is the cause of pain, this is the cessation of pain, this is the Way, leading to the cessation of pain.'

Translation by Edward J. Thomas, *Early Buddhist Scriptures* (London, 1935), pp. 117-18

285. THE BUDDHA EXPLAINS THE NOBLE EIGHTFOLD WAY

('*Samyutta-nikāya*,' v, 8)

'The Noble Eightfold Way, monks, I will expound and analyse to you. Listen to it, reflect on it well, I will speak.' 'Even so, Lord,' the monks replied to the Lord.

The Lord said, 'What, monks, is the Noble Eightfold Way? It is namely right view, right intention, right speech, right action, right livelihood, right effort, right mindfulness, right concentration.

'And what, monks, is the right view? The knowledge of pain, knowledge of the cause of pain, knowledge of the cessation of pain, and knowledge of the way that leads to the cessation of pain: that monks is called right view.

'And what is right intention? The intention to renounce, the intention not to hurt, the intention not to injure: that, monks, is called right intention.

'And what is right speech? Refraining from falsehood, from malicious speech, from harsh speech, from frivolous speech: that, monks, is called right speech.

'And what is right action? Refraining from taking life, from taking what is not given, from sexual intercourse: that, monks, is called right action.

The Middle Path

'And what is right livelihood? Here a noble disciple abandoning a false mode of livelihood gets his living by right livelihood: that, monks, is called right livelihood.

'And what is right effort? Here a monk with the nonproducing of bad and evil thoughts that have not yet arisen exercises will, puts forth effort, begins to make exertion, applies and exerts his mind; with the dispelling of bad and evil thoughts that had arisen he exercises will, puts forth effort, begins to make exertion, applies and exerts his mind; with the producing of good thoughts that had not arisen he exercises will, puts forth effort, begins to make exertion, applies and exerts his mind; with the fixing, freeing from confusion, increasing, enlarging, developing and filling up of good thoughts that had arisen he exercises will, puts forth effort, begins to make exertion, applies and exerts his mind: that, monks, is called right effort.

'And what is right mindfulness? Here (1) on the body: a monk abides contemplating the body, ardent, thoughtful, and mindful, dispelling his longing and dejection towards the world; (2) on feelings: he abides contemplating the feelings, ardent, thoughtful, and mindful, dispelling his longing and dejection towards the world; (3) on the mind: he abides contemplating the mind, ardent, thoughtful, and mindful, dispelling his longing and dejection towards the world; (4) on thoughts: he abides contemplating thoughts, ardent, thoughtful, and mindful, dispelling his longing and dejection towards the world. That, monks is called right mindfulness.

'And what is right concentration? Here (1) a monk free from passions and evil thoughts attains and abides in the first trance of joy and pleasure, which is accompanied by reasoning and investigation and arises from seclusion. (2) With the ceasing of reasoning and investigation, in a state of internal serenity, with his mind fixed on one point, he attains and abides in the second trance of joy and pleasure arising from concentration, and free from reasoning and investigation. (3) With equanimity and indifference towards joy he abides mindful and self-possessed, and with his body experiences pleasure that the noble ones call "Dwelling with equanimity, mindful and happy," and attains and abides in the third trance. (4) Dispelling pleasure and pain, and even before the disappearance of elation and depression, he attains and abides in the fourth trance, which is without pleasure and pain, and with the purity of mindfulness and equanimity: that, monks, is called right concentration.'

Translation by E. J. Thomas, *Early Buddhist Scriptures* (London, 1935), pp. 94-6

286. THE PARABLE OF THE FIRE:
A TATHĀGATA IS LIKE A BURNED-OUT FIRE

('*Majjhima-nikāya*,' I, 485 *ff*. [LXXII '*Aggi-vacchagotta-sutta*'])

'Vaccha, the view that the world is eternal is a jungle, a wilderness, a theatrical show, a perversion, a fetter, and is coupled with suffering, destruction, despair, and pain, and does not tend to aversion, absence of passion, cessation, tranquillity, supernatural faculty, perfect knowledge, Nirvāna. . . . Considering it disadvantageous, Vaccha, I have accordingly none of these views.' 'But has Gotama any view?' 'The Tathāgata, Vaccha, is free from views, for this is what the Tathāgata holds: form, the cause of form, the destruction of form, sensation, the cause of sensation, perception, the aggregates of qualities, consciousness, how they arise and perish. Therefore with the destruction of, and indifference towards, and the ceasing and abandonment of all imaginings, all agitations, all false views of the self or of anything belonging to a self, the Tathāgata is liberated, thus I say.'

'But where is the monk reborn, sir Gotama, whose mind is thus liberated?' 'It does not fit the case, Vaccha, to say he is reborn.' 'Then, sir Gotama, he is not reborn.' 'It does not fit the case, Vaccha, to say he is not reborn.' 'Then, sir Gotama, he is both reborn and not reborn.' 'It does not fit the case, Vaccha, to say he is neither reborn nor not reborn. . . .' 'In this matter, sir Gotama, I feel in a state of ignorance and confusion, and the small amount of faith that I had in Gotama through a former conversation has now disappeared.' 'Enough of your ignorance and confusion, Vaccha, for deep is this doctrine, difficult to be seen and comprehended, good, excellent, beyond the sphere of reasoning, subtle, intelligible only to the wise. It is difficult to be understood by you, who hold other views, another faith, other inclinations, another discipline, and have another teacher. Therefore, Vaccha, I will ask you this, and do you explain it as you may please. Do you think, Vaccha, that if a fire were burning before you, you would know that a fire was burning before you?' 'If a fire was burning before me, sir Gotama, I should know that a fire was burning before me.' 'And if some one asked you on what the fire burning before you depends, how would you explain it? . . .' 'I should say that this fire which is burning before me depends on its clinging to grass and sticks.' 'If the fire before you were to go out, would you know that the fire before you had gone out?' 'If the fire before me were to go out, I should know that the fire had gone out.' 'And if some one were to ask you, "Vaccha, in what direction has the fire gone which has gone out, to the east, west, north or south," if you were thus asked, how would you explain it?' 'It does not fit the case, sir Gotama, to say so, for the fire burned through depending on its clinging to grass and sticks, and through its consuming this, and not getting any other, it is without food, and comes to be what is called extinct.' 'And just so, Vaccha, that form by which one would assert the existence of a Tathāgata has ceased, it is uprooted, it is pulled up like a taliput-palm, made non-existent, and not liable to arise again in the future. The Tathāgata, who is released from what is called form, is deep, immeasurable, hard to fathom, and like a great ocean. It does not fit the case to say he is born again, to say he is not born again, to say he is both born again and not born again, or to say he is neither born again nor not born again.

Translation by E. J. Thomas, *Buddhist Scriptures* (London, 1913), pp. 71-3. Cf. Lord Chalmers, *Further Dialogues of the Buddha*, vol. I (London, 1926), pp. 342 ff.

287. THE PARABLE OF THE OIL LAMP: THE EXTINCTION OF CRAVING

('Samyutta-nikāya,' II, 86)

He dwelt at Sāvatthi. 'In one, monks, who abides reflecting on the enjoyment of things that fetter, craving increases. With craving as a cause there is grasping. With grasping as a cause there is becoming (the desire to be). With the desire to be as a cause there is rebirth. With rebirth as a cause old age and death, grief, lamentation, pain, dejection, and despair arise. Even so is the cause of this whole mass of pain.

'Just as, monks, on account of oil and on account of a wick an oil lamp would burn, and a man from time to time were to pour oil thereon and trim the wick, even so, monks, an oil lamp with that nutriment, that fuel, would burn for a long time.

'Even so, monks, in one who abides reflecting on the enjoyment of things that fetter, craving increases. . . . 'Even so is the cause of this whole mass of pain.

'In one, monks, who reflects on the wretchedness of things that fetter, craving ceases. With the cessation of craving grasping ceases. . . . Even so is the cessation of this whole mass of pain.

'Just as monks, on account of oil and on account of a wick an oil lamp would burn, and a man from time to time were not to pour oil thereon and not to trim the wick, even so, monks, an oil lamp with the exhaustion of the original fuel and being without nutriment through being unfed with any more would become extinct.

'Even so, monks, in one who abides reflecting on the wretchedness of things that fetter, craving ceases. With the ceasing of craving grasping ceases. With the ceasing of grasping the desire to be ceases. With the ceasing of the desire to be rebirth ceases. With the ceasing of rebirth old age and death, grief, lamentation, pain, dejection, and despair cease. Even so is the cessation of this whole mass of pain.'

Translation by E. J. Thomas, *Early Buddhist Scriptures* (London, 1935), pp. 122-3

288. THE BUDDHA'S ADVICE TO SARIPUTRA

('Sutta Nipāta,' 964-975)

The monk alert, rapt farer on the edge,
Should have no fear of these five fears:
Gadflies and stinging bees and things that creep,
Attacks of men and of four-footed beasts.

Nor should he be afraid of others' views,
When the great perils of them he hath seen;
So should the expert seeker overcome
All other troubles that may here befall.

When stricken by disease or hunger's pangs,
Cold and excessive heat should he endure;
When stricken sore by them, that homeless man
Must stir up energy and strive with strength.

Let him not steal nor let him tell a lie,
Let him show amity to weak and strong;
And when he knows disquiet of the mind,
Let him expel that as dark as Mara's gloom.

Nor must he fall a prey to wrath and pride,
But digging up their roots, let him stay poised;
And, as he wrestles, let him overcome
All that is dear to him, all that repels.

With joy in what is lovely, wisdom-led,
Let him then put to flight these troubles here,

The Middle Path

Conquer dislike for his lone lodging place,
Conquer the four that cause him discontent:

With food and clothing timely gotten, he
Must therein measure know for his content;
He, faring thus, restrained and curbed, would speak
In village no harsh words, tho' vexed indeed.

Then let him loiter not, but eyes downcast,
Be ever bent on musing, much awake;
Then let him strive for poise, intent-of-self
Cut doubt and hankering and fretful ways.

Alert, let him rejoice, when urged by words,
Break fallowness in fellow-wayfarers,
Utter in season due the expert word,
Not ponder on the views and talk of folk.

Alert, then let him train to discipline
Those things which are the five dusts in the world;
To conquer lust for forms and sounds and tastes,
To conquer lust for scents and things of touch.

When he hath disciplined desire for these,
Alert, with mind released in full, that monk
As studies he the thing aright, in time
Alone, uplifted, may the darkness rend.

Thus spake the master.

Translation by Edward Conze in Conze (ed.) *Buddhist Scriptures* (Baltimore, 1959), pp. 77-9

289. THE BUDDHA'S 'WAY OF VIRTUE'

('Dhammapada,' selections)

The Dhammapada although accepted at the Council of Ashoka in 240
B.C. as a collection of the sayings of Gotama, was not put into writing
until some generations had passed. It probably contains accretions of
later date.

47. He who is busy culling pleasure, as one plucks flowers, Death
seizes and hurries off, as a great flood bears away a sleeping village.

48. The Destroyer treads him underfoot as he is culling worldly
pleasures, still unsated with lusts of the flesh.

50. Be not concerned with other men's evil words or deeds or neglect of good: look rather to thine own sins and negligence [lit. 'sins of commission and omission': things done and undone.]

51. As some bright flower—fair to look at, but lacking fragrance— so are fair words which bear no fruit in action.

52. As some bright flower, fragrant as it is fair, so are fair words whose fruit is seen in action.

63. The fool who knows his folly is so far wise; but the fool who reckons himself wise is called a fool indeed.

76. Look upon him who shows you your faults as a revealer of treasure: seek his company who checks and chides you, the sage who is wise in reproof: it fares well and not ill with him who seeks such company.

78. Avoid bad friends, avoid the company of the evil: seek after noble friends and men of lofty character.

83. Freely go the righteous; the holy ones do not whine and pine for lusts: unmoved by success or failure, the wise show no change of mood.

85. Few amongst men are they who reach the farther shore: the rest, a great multitude, stand only on the bank.

92. Some there are who have no treasure here, temperate ones whose goal is the freedom which comes of realizing that life is empty and impermanent: their steps are hard to track as the flight of birds through the sky.

93. He whose taints are purged away, who is indifferent to food, whose goal is the freedom which comes of realizing life's emptiness and transiency, is hard to track as the flight of birds in the sky.

94. Even the gods emulate him whose senses are quiet as horses well-tamed by the charioteer, who has renounced self-will, and put away all taints.

100. Better than a thousand empty words is one pregnant word, which brings the hearer peace.

101. Better than a thousand idle songs is a single song, which brings the hearer peace.

102. Better it is to chant one verse of the law, that brings the hearer peace, than to chant a hundred empty songs.

103. If one were to conquer a thousand thousand in the battle—he who conquers self is the greatest warrior.

104, 105. Self-conquest is better than other victories; neither god nor demi-god, neither Māra nor Brahmā, can undo the victory of such a one, who is self-controlled and always calm.

106. If month by month throughout a hundred years, one were to offer sacrifices costing thousands, and if for a moment another were to reverence the self-controlled—this is the better worship.

107. If one for a hundred years tended the sacred fire in the glade, and another for a moment reverenced the self-controlled, this is the better worship.

110. Better than a hundred years of impure and intemperate existence is a single day of moral, contemplative life.

111. Better is one day of wise and contemplative life than a thousand years of folly and intemperance.

141. Not nakedness, nor matted hair, not dirt, nor fastings, not sleeping in sanctuaries, nor ashes, nor ascetic posture—none of these things purifies a man who is not free from doubt.

145. Engineers control the water, fletchers fashion their shafts, carpenters shape the wood: it is themselves that the pious fashion and control.

146. Where is the joy, what the pleasure, whilst all is in flames? Benighted, would ye not seek a torch?

147. Look at this painted image, wounded and swollen, sickly and full of lust, in which there is no permanence;

148. This wasted form is a nest of disease and very frail: it is full of putrid matter and perishes. Death is the end of life.

149. What delight is there for him who sees these grey bones scattered like gourds in autumn?

150. Here is a citadel of bones plastered with flesh and blood, and manned by old age and death, self-will and enmity.

151. Even as the king's bright chariot grows old, so the body of man also comes to old age. But the law of the holy never ages; the holy teach it to the holy.

165. Thou art brought low by the evil thou hast done thyself: by the evil thou hast left undone art thou purified. Purity and impurity are things of man's inmost self; no man can purify another.

169. Follow after virtue, not after vice. The virtuous live happy in this world and the next.

170. The King of Death sees not him who regards the world as a bubble, a mirage. . . .

174. Blinded are the men of this world; few there are who have eyes to see; few are the birds which escape the fowler's net; few are they who go to heaven. . . .

178. Good is kingship of the earth; good is birth in heaven; good is universal empire; better still is the fruit of conversion. . . .

197. O Joy! We live in bliss; amongst men of hate, hating none. Let us indeed dwell among them without hatred.

198. O Joy! In bliss we dwell; healthy amidst the ailing. Let us indeed dwell amongst them in perfect health.

199. Yea in very bliss we dwell: free from care amidst the careworn. Let us indeed dwell amongst them without care.

200. In bliss we dwell possessing nothing: let us dwell feeding upon joy like the shining ones in their splendour.

201. The victor breeds enmity; the conquered sleeps in sorrow. Regardless of either victory or defeat the calm man dwells in peace.

202. There is no fire like lust; no luck so bad as hate. There is no sorrow like existence: no bliss greater than Nirvāna [rest].

211. Take a liking for nothing; loss of the prize is evil. There are no bonds for him who has neither likes nor dislikes.

212. From attachment comes grief, from attachment comes fear. He who is pure from attachment knows neither grief nor fear.

213. From affection comes grief and fear. He who is without affection knows neither grief nor fear.

214. From pleasure comes grief and fear. He who is freed from pleasure knows neither grief nor fear.

215. From lust come grief and fear. He who is freed from lust knows neither grief nor fear.

216. From desire comes grief and fear. He who is free of desire knows neither grief nor fear. . . .

223. By calmness let a man overcome wrath; let him overcome evil by good; the miser let him subdue by liberality, and the liar by truth.

224. Speak the truth, be not angry, give of thy poverty to the suppliant: by these three virtues a man attains to the company of the gods.

237. Thy life is ended; thou art come into the Presence of Death: there is no resting-place by the way, and thou hast no provision for the journey.

238. Make for thyself a refuge; come, strive and play the sage! Burn off thy taints, and thou shalt know birth and old age no more.

252. To see another's fault is easy: to see one's own is hard. Men winnow the faults of others like chaff: their own they hide as a crafty gambler hides a losing throw.

264. Not by his shaven crown is one made a 'religious' who is intemperate and dishonourable. How can he be a 'religious' who is full of lust and greed?

286. 'Here I will pass the wet season; here the winter and summer,' thinks the fool, unmindful of what may befall.

287. Then comes Death and sweeps him away infatuated with children and cattle, and entangled with this world's goods, as a flood carries off a sleeping village.

288. There is no safety in sons, or in father, or in kinsfolk when Death overshadows thee: amongst thine own kith and kin is no refuge;

289. Knowing this clearly, the wise and righteous man straightway clears the road that leads to Nirvāna.

385. Him I call the Brahmin whom desire assails not from within nor from without, in whom is no fear, he is indeed free.

386. Him I call Brahmin who is meditative, clean of heart, solitary, who has done his duty and got rid of taints, who has reached the goal of effort. . . .

393. Not by matted locks, nor by lineage, nor by caste is one a Brahmin; he is the Brahmin in whom are truth and righteousness and purity. . . .

396. Not him do I call Brahmin who is merely born of a Brahmin mother; men may give him salutation as a Brahmin, though he be not detached from the world: but him I call a Brahmin who has attachment to nothing.

397. Him I call a Brahmin who has cut the bonds, who does not thirst for pleasures, who has left behind the hindrances.

398. Whoso has cut the cable, and the rope and the chain with all its links, and has pushed aside the bolt, this wise one I call a Brahmin. . . .

400. He is the Brahmin who does not give way to anger, who is careful of religious duties, who is upright, pure, and controlled, who has reached his last birth.

406. Not opposing those who oppose, calm amidst the fighters, not grasping amidst men who grasp, he is the Brahmin.

Translation by W. D. C. Wagiswara and K. J. Saunders, *The Buddha's 'Way of Virtue'* (London: John Murray, 1912)

See also nos. 220, 225-30

D. THE ULTIMATE REALITY:
QUESTIONS AND ANSWERS

290. ZARATHUSTRA ASKS THE LORD . . .

('Gāthā-Yasna' 44)

This *Gāthā-Yasna* 44 might be called the *Questions to the Lord*, for each of its stanzas, except the last, is introduced by this formula: 'This I ask thee, O Lord, answer me truly . . .'

Stanzas 3 to 7 are concerned with the origin of the world and its organization, and stanzas 8 to 19 with its future. The last four of these in particular are devoted to the mission of Zarathustra and to the expectation of the Saviour. Such is the body of the hymn, preceded by two introductory stanzas and ended by a final stanza.

1. *This I ask thee, O Lord, answer me truly:*
   May a wise one like thee reveal it to a friend such as I am,
   In virtue of my veneration,—such as is due to a being like you—
   And as Righteousness may he lend us his friendly support,
   Coming unto us through the Good Mind!

2. *This I ask thee, O Lord, answer me truly:*
   When the best existence begins,
   Shall they have their fill of the rewards who have desired them?
   For this man, the holy one through Righteousness,
   Holds in his spirit the force which heals existence,
   Beneficent unto all, as a sworn friend, O Wise One.

3. *This I ask thee, O Lord, answer me truly:*
   Who was the first father of Righteousness at the birth?
   Who appointed their path to sun and stars?
   Who but thou is it through whom the moon waxes and wanes?
   This I would know, O Wise One, and other things too!

4. *This I ask thee, O Lord, answer me truly:*
   Who set the Earth in its place below, and the sky of the clouds,
   *   that it shall not fall?*

164

Who the waters and the plants?
Who yoked the two steeds to wind and clouds?
Who, O Wise One, is the creator of the Good Mind?

5. This I ask thee, O Lord, answer me truly:
What artificer made light and darkness?
What artificer sleep and waking?
Who made morning, noon, and night,
To remind the wise man of his task?

11. This I ask thee, O Lord, answer me truly:
Shall Devotion extend to those to whom thy religion shall be
    proclaimed?
From the beginning was I chosen for this by thee:
All others I shall look upon with hostile spirit.

12. This I ask thee, O Lord, answer me truly:
Who among those to whom I speak is righteous and who is
    wicked?
Which of the two? Am I evil myself,
Or is he the evil one who would wickedly keep me far from thy
    salvation?
How should I not think him the wicked one?

13. This I ask thee, O Lord, answer me truly:
(How?) shall we rid ourselves of evil
By throwing it back on these who, full of disobedience,
Care naught for following Righteousness
And do not trouble to take counsel with the Good Mind?

14. This I ask thee, O Lord, answer me truly:
(How?) shall I deliver evil into the hands of Righteousness,
That it may put it down according to the rules of thy doctrine,
That it may cause a mighty schism among the wicked
And bring them blindness and hostilities, O Wise One.

16. This I ask thee, O Lord, answer me truly:
Who will be victorious and protect the living by thy doctrine?
May visible signs be given to me:
Make known the judge that shall heal existence!
And may it be given to obey him, through the Good Mind,
To all those in whom thou seekest it, O Wise One!

17. This I ask thee, O Lord, answer me truly:
    Shall I attain my goal with you, O Wise One?
    May I become one with you and may my word have power,
    That Integrity and Immortality according to thy order
    May join themselves with the follower of Righteousness.

18. This I ask thee, O Lord, answer me truly:
    Shall I receive for my wage, through Righteousness,
    Two mares with a stallion and a camel,
    Which were promised to me, O Wise One,
    Together with thy gift of Integrity and Immortality?

19. This I ask thee, O Lord, answer me truly:
    He that does not give his hire to the one who earned it,
    He that does not give it according to his word,
    What shall be his present punishment,
    —knowing that which shall come to him at the end?

20. Have the false gods ever been good masters?
    This I ask of those who see, in their cult,
    How the sacrificer and the usig deliver the ox to fury,
    And how the sorcerer prince makes him to moan in his soul,
    And who do not sprinkle the water of the cattle on the pastures
    To make it prosper through Righteousness.

Translation and commentary by Jacques Duchesne-Guillemin, in his *The Hymns of Zarathustra* (London, 1952), pp. 63-73

See also nos. 37, 60, 303

291. NACIKETAS' THIRD WISH

('Katha Upanishad,' I, 1, selections)

A poor and pious Brāhman, Vājasravasa, performs a sacrifice and gives as presents to the priests a few old and feeble cows. His son, Naciketas, feeling disturbed by the unreality of his father's observance of the sacrifice, proposes that he himself may be offered as offering (daksinā) to a priest. When he persisted in his request, his father in rage said, 'Unto Yama, (death) I give thee.' Naciketas goes to the abode of Yama and

166

finding him absent, waits there for three days and nights unfed. Yama, on his return, offers three gifts in recompense for the delay and discomfort caused to Naciketas. For the first, Naciketas said, 'Let me return alive to my father.' For the second, 'Tell me how my good works may not be exhausted'; and for the third, 'Tell me the way to conquer re-death.'

20. There is this doubt in regard to a man who has departed, some (holding) that he is and some that he is not. I would be instructed by thee in this knowledge. Of the boons this is the third boon.

21. (Yama said): Even the gods of old had doubt on this point. It is not, indeed, easy to understand; (so) subtle is this truth. Choose another boon, O Naciketas. Do not press me. Release me from this. . . .

23. (Yama said): Choose sons and grandsons that shall live a hundred years, cattle in plenty, elephants, gold and horses. Choose vast expanses of land and life for thyself as many years as thou wilt.

24. If thou deemest (any) boon like unto this, choose (that) as also wealth and long life. O Naciketas, prosper then on this vast earth. I will make thee the enjoyer of thy desires. . . .

26. (Naciketas said): Transient (are these) and they wear out, O Yama, the vigour of all the senses of men. All life (a full life), moreover, is brief. Thine be the chariots, thine the dance and song.

27. Man is not to be contented with wealth. Shall we enjoy wealth when we have seen thee? Shall we live as long as thou art in power? That alone is (still) the boon chosen by me.

28. Having approached the undecaying immortality, what decaying mortal on this earth below who (now) knows (and meditates on) the pleasures of beauty and love, will delight in an over-long life?

29. Tell us that about which they doubt, O Death, what there is in the great passing-on. This boon which penetrates the mystery, no other than that does Naciketas choose.

S. Radhakrishnan (editor and translator), *The Principal Upanishads* (New York: Harper & Row, 1953), pp. 603 ff.

292. 'EXPLAIN TO ME THE BRAHMAN . . .'

('Brihad-āranyaka Upanishad,' III, 4, 1-2)

1. Then Ushasta Cākrāyana asked him: 'Yājñavalkya,' said he, 'explain to me the Brahman that is immediately present and directly perceived, who is the self in all things?' 'This is your self. That is within all things.' 'Which is within all things, Yājñavalkya?' 'He who breathes in with your breathing in is the self of yours which is in all things. He who breathes out with your breathing out is the self of yours which is in all things. He who breathes about with your breathing about is the self of yours which is in all things. He who breathes up with your breathing up is the self of yours which is in all things. He is your self which is in all things.'

2. Ushasta Cākrāyana said: 'This has been explained by you as one might say 'This is cow,' 'This is a horse.' Explain to me the *Brahman* that is immediately present and directly perceived, that is the self in all things.' 'This is your self that is within all things.' 'Which is within all things, Yājñavalkya?' 'You cannot see the seer of seeing, you cannot hear the hearer of hearing, you cannot think the thinker of thinking, you cannot understand the understander of understanding. He is your self which is in all things. Everything else is of evil.' Thereupon Ushasta Cākrāyana kept silent.

S. Radhakrishnan (editor and translator), *The Principal Upanishads, op. cit.,* pp. 219-20

293. 'HOW MANY GODS ARE THERE, YĀJÑAVALKYA?' . . . 'ONE'

('Brihad-āranyaka Upanishad,' III, 9, 1)

1. Then Vidagdha Sakalya asked him: 'How many gods are there Yājñavalkya?' He answered, in accord with the following *nivid* (invocation of the gods). 'As many as are mentioned in the *nivid* of the hymn of praise to the Vishve-devas, namely, three hundred and three, and three thousand and three.' 'Yes,' he said, 'but how many gods are there, Yājñavalkya?' 'Thirty-three.' 'Yes,' he said, 'but how many gods are there, Yājñavalkya?' 'Six.' 'Yes,' said he, 'but how many gods are

there, Yājñavalkya?' 'Three.' 'Yes,' said he, 'but how many gods are there, Yājñavalkya?' 'Two.' 'Yes,' said he, 'but how many gods are there, Yājñavalkya?' 'One and a half.' 'Yes,' said he, 'but how many gods are there, Yājñavalkya?' 'One.' . . .

S. Radhakrishnan (editor and translator), *The Principal Upanishads, op. cit.,* pp. 234-5

294. 'THIS IS THE SELF OF MINE . . . THIS IS BRAHMAN'

('Upanishads,' selections)

1. Verily, this whole world is *Brahman,* from which he comes forth, without which he will be dissolved, and in which he breathes. Tranquil, one should meditate on it.

2. He who consists of mind, whose body is life, whose form is light, whose conception is truth, whose soul is space, containing all works, containing all desires, containing all odours, containing all tastes, encompassing this whole world, being without speech and without concern.

3. This is my self within the heart, smaller than a grain of rice, than a barley corn, than a mustard seed, than a grain of millet or than the kernel of a grain of a millet. This is myself within the heart, greater than the earth, greater than the atmosphere, greater than the sky, greater than these worlds.

4. Containing all works, containing all desires, containing all odours, containing all tastes, encompassing this whole world, without speech, without concern, this is the self of mine within the heart; this is *Brahman.* Into him, I shall enter, on departing hence. Verily, he who believes this, will have no more doubts. *(Chāndogya Upanishad,* III, 14, 1-4.)

. . . But the self *(ātman)* is not this, not this. He is incomprehensible for he is never comprehended. He is indestructible for he cannot be destroyed. He is unattached for he does not attach himself. . . . *(Brihad-āranyaka Upanishad,* IV, 2, 4.)

This self *(ātman)* is (like) honey for all beings and all beings are (like) honey for this self. This shining, immortal person who is in this self and the shining, immortal person who is in this (individual) self, he is just this Self, this is immortal, this is *Brahman*, this is all. *(Brihad-āranyaka Upanishad*, II, 5, 14.)

Manifest, well-fixed, moving, verily, in the secret place (of the heart) such is the great support. In it is centred all this which moves, breathes and winks. Know that as being, as non-being, as the supreme object to be desired, as the highest beyond the reach of man's understanding. *(Mundaka Upanishad*, II, 2, 1.)

S. Radhakrishnan (editor and translator), *The Princi-pal Upanishads, op. cit.*

See also nos. 56, 101, 300

295. WHENEVER ORDER (DHARMA) LANGUISHES, KRISHNA MANIFESTS HIMSELF

('Bhagavad Gītā, IV, 1-9, 14)

The Blessed One said:
1. *This discipline to Vivasvant*
   I proclaimed; 'tis eternal;
   Vivasvant told it to Manu,
   Manu spake it to Ikshvāku.

2. *Thus received in line of succession,*
   The royal seers knew it.
   In a long course of time in this world this
   Discipline became lost, scorcher of the foe.

3. *This very same by Me to thee today,*
   This ancient discipline, is proclaimed.
   Thou art My devotee and friend, that is why;
   For this is a supreme secret.

   Arjuna said:
4. *Later Thy birth,*
   Earlier the birth of Vivasvant:
   How may I understand this,
   That Thou didst proclaim it in the beginning, as Thou sayest?

   The Blessed One said:
5. *For Me have passed many*
   Births, and for thee, Arjuna;

These I know all;
Thou knowest not, scorcher of the foe.

6. Tho unborn, tho My self is eternal.
 Tho Lord of Beings,
 Resorting to My own material nature
 I come into being by My own mysterious power.

7. For whenever of the right
 A languishing appears, son of Bharata,
 A rising up of unright,
 Then I send Myself forth.

8. For protection of the good,
 And for destruction of evil-doers,
 To make a firm footing for the right,
 I come into being in age after age.

9. My wondrous birth and actions
 Whoso knows thus as they truly are,
 On leaving the body, to rebirth
 He goes not; to Me he goes, Arjuna! . . .

14. Actions do not stain Me,
 (Because) I have no yearning for the fruit of actions.
 Who comprehends Me thus
 Is not bound by actions.

Translation by Franklin Edgerton. *The Bhagavad Gītā*, vol I Harvard Oriental Series, Vol. 38 (Cambridge: Harvard University Press, 1944)

296. THE TEACHINGS OF THE BHAGAVAD GĪTĀ: 'WHATEVER THOU DOEST, DO AS AN OFFERING TO ME'

(*'Bhagavad Gītā*, IX, VI, VIII, selections)

4. By Me is pervaded all this
 Universe, by Me in the form of the unmanifest.
 All beings rest in Me,
 And I do not rest in them.

5. And (yet) beings do not rest in Me:
 Behold My divine mystery (or magic)!
 Supporter of being, and not resting in beings,
 Is My Self, that causes beings to be.

6. As constantly abides in the ether
   The great wind, that penetrates everywhere,
   So all beings
   Abide in Me; make sure of that.

7. All beings, son of Kuntī,
   Pass into My material nature
   At the end of a world-eon; them again
   I send forth at the beginning of a (new) world-eon.

8. Taking as base My own material nature
   I send forth again and again
   This whole host of beings,
   Which is powerless, by the power of (My) material nature.

9. And Me these actions do not
   Bind Dhanamjaya,—
   Sitting in as one sitting out (participating as one indifferent),
   Unattached to these actions.

10. With Me as overseer, material nature
    Brings forth (the world of) moving and unmoving (beings);
    By this motive force, son of Kuntī,
    The world goes around.

11. Fools despise Me
    That have assumed human form,
    Not knowing the higher state
    Of Me, which is the great lord of beings. . . .

16. I am the ritual act, I am the act of worship,
    I am the offering to the dead, I am the medicinal herb,
    I am the sacred formula, I alone am the sacrificial butter,
    I am the fire of offering, I am the poured oblation.

17. I am the father of this world,
    The mother, the establisher, the grandsire,
    The object of knowledge, the purifier, the sacred syllable om,
    The verse of praise, the chant, and the sacrificial formula.

18. The goal, supporter, lord, witness,
    The dwelling-place, refuge, friend,
    The origin, dissolution, and maintenance,
    The treasure-house, the imperishable seed.

19. I give heat; the rain I
     Hold back and send forth;
   Both immortality and death,
     Both the existent and the non-existent am I, Arjuna. . . .

23. Even those who are devotees of other gods,
     And worship them permeated with faith,
   It is only Me, son of Kuntī, that even they
     Worship, (tho) not in the enjoined fashion.

24. For I of all acts of worship
     Am both the recipient and the lord;
   But they do not recognize Me
     In the true way; therefore they fall (from the 'heaven' they
       win).

25. Votaries of the gods go to the gods,
     Votaries of the (departed) fathers go to the fathers,
   Worshippers of goblins go to the goblins,
     Worshippers of Me also go to Me.

26. A leaf, a flower, a fruit, or water,
     Who presents to Me with devotion,
   That offering of devotion I
     Accept from the devout-souled (giver).

27. Whatever thou doest, whatever thou eatest,
     Whatever thou offerest in oblation or givest,
   Whatever austerity thou performest, son of Kuntī,
     That do as an offering to Me. . . .

30. Even if a very evil doer
     Reveres Me with single devotion,
   He must be regarded as righteous in spite of all;
     For he has the right resolution.

31. Quickly his soul becomes righteous,
     And he goes to eternal peace.
   Son of Kuntī, make sure of this:
     No devotee of Mine is lost.

32. For if they take refuge in Me, son of Prithā,
     Even those who may be of base origin,
   Women, men of the artisan caste, and serfs too,
     Even they go to the highest goal. (IX, 4-11, 16-19, 23-7, 30-2.)

30. Who sees Me in all,
    And sees all in Me,
  For him I am not lost,
    And he is not lost for Me.

31. Me as abiding in all beings whoso
    Reveres, adopting (the belief in) one-ness,
  Tho abiding in any possible condition,
    That disciplined man abides in Me. (VI, 30-1.)

5. And at the hour of death, on Me alone
   Meditating, leaving the body
  Whoso dies, to My estate he
   Goes; there is no doubt of that.

6. Whatsoever state (of being) meditating upon
   He leaves the body at death,
  To just that he goes, son of Kuntī,
   Always, being made to be in the condition of that.

7. Therefore at all times
   Think on Me, and fight;
  With thought-organ and consciousness fixed on Me
   Thou shalt go just to Me without a doubt. (VIII, 5-7.)

Translation by Franklin Edgerton, *The Bhagavad Gītā*
vol. I, Harvard Oriental Series, vol. 38 (Cambridge:
Harvard University Press, 1944)

See also nos. 28, 117, 264

297. TAO, THE ULTIMATE REALITY

('Tao Tê Ching,' selections)

Tao is the way that those must walk who would 'achieve without doing.' But tao is not only a means, a doctrine, a principle. It is the ultimate reality in which all attributes are united, 'it is heavy as a stone, light as a feather'; it is the unity underlying unity. 'It is that by losing of which men die; by getting of which men live. Whatever is done without it, fails; whatever is done by means of it, succeeds. It has neither root nor stalk, leaf nor flower. Yet upon it depends the generation and growth of the ten thousand things, each after its kind' (Kuan Tzu, 49).

The Ultimate Reality

We do not know, and it is unlikely that we shall ever know, who wrote the Tao Tê Ching. But for two thousand years the name of Lao Tan or 'Master Lao' (Lao Tzu) has been connected with this book.

Chapter IV

The Way is like an empty vessel
That yet may be drawn from
Without ever needing to be filled.
It is bottomless; the very progenitor of all things in the world.
In it all sharpness is blunted,
All tangles untied,
All glare tempered,
All dust[1] smoothed.
It is like a deep pool that never dries.
Was it too the child of something else? We cannot tell,
But as a substanceless image[2] it existed before the Ancestor.[3]

Notes

1 Dust is the Taoist symbol for the noise and the fuss of everyday life.
2 A *hsiang*, an image such as the mental images that float before us when we think.
3 The Ancestor in question is almost certainly the Yellow Ancestor who separated Earth from Heaven and so destroyed the Primal Unity, for which he is frequently censured in Chuang Tzu.

Chapter VI

The Valley Spirit never dies.
It is named the Mysterious Female.
And the Doorway of the Mysterious Female
Is the base from which Heaven and Earth sprang.
It is there within us all the while;
Draw upon it as you will, it never runs dry.

Chapter VII

Heaven is eternal, the Earth everlasting.
How come they to be so? It is because they do not foster their
    own lives;
That is why they live so long.
Therefore the Sage

Puts himself in the background; but is always to the fore.
Remains outside; but is always there.
Is it not just because he does not strive for any personal end
That all his personal ends are fulfilled?

Chapter XI

We put thirty spokes together and call it a wheel;
But it is on the space where there is nothing that the
    usefulness of the wheel depends.
We turn clay to make a vessel;
But it is on the space where there is nothing that the
    usefulness of the vessel depends.
We pierce doors and windows to make a house;
And it is on these spaces where there is nothing that the
    usefulness of the house depends.
Therefore just as we take advantage of what is, we should
    recognize the usefulness of what is not.

Chapter XXII

'To remain whole, be twisted!
To become straight, let yourself be bent.
To become full, be hollow.
Be tattered, that you may be renewed.
Those that have little, may get more,
Those that have much, are but perplexed.
Therefore the Sage
Clasps the Primal Unity,
Testing by it everything under heaven.
He does not show himself; therefore he is seen everywhere.
He does not define himself, therefore he is distinct.
He does not boast of what he will do, therefore he succeeds.
He is not proud of his work, and therefore it endures.
He does not contend,
And for that very reason no one under heaven can contend with him.

So then we see that the ancient saying 'To remain whole, be twisted!'
was no idle word; for true wholeness can only be achieved by return.[1]

Note

1 To the way.

The Ultimate Reality

Chapter XXV

There was something formless yet complete,
That existed before heaven and earth;
Without sound, without substance,
Dependent on nothing, unchanging,
All pervading, unfailing.
One may think of it as the mother of all things under heaven.
Its true name[1] we do not know;
'Way' is the by-name that we give it.
Were I forced to say to what class of things it belongs I should call
    it Great (ta).
Now ta also means passing on,
And passing on means going Far Away,
And going far away means returning.[2]
Thus just as Tao[3] has 'this greatness' and as earth has it
and as heaven has it, so may the ruler also have it. Thus
'within the realm there are four portions of greatness,' and
one belongs to the king. The ways of men are conditioned by
those of earth. The ways of earth, by those of heaven. The
ways of heaven by those of Tao, and the ways of Tao by the Self-so.[4]

Notes

1 I.e., we do not know to what class of things it belongs.
2 Returning to 'what was there at the Beginning.'
3 Henceforward I shall use the Chinese word Tao instead of the Way; to do
 so avoids many inconveniences.
4 The 'unconditioned'; the 'what-is-so-of-itself.'

Chapter XXVII

Perfect activity leaves no track behind it;
Perfect speech is like a jade-worker whose tool leaves no mark
The perfect reckoner needs no counting-slips;
The perfect door has neither bolt nor bar,
Yet cannot be opened.
The perfect knot needs neither rope nor twine,
Yet cannot be untied.
Therefore the Sage
Is all the time in the most perfect way helping men,
He certainly does not turn his back on men;
Is all the time in the most perfect way helping creatures,
He certainly does not turn his back on creatures. . . .

Chapter XXXIV

Great Tao is like a boat that drifts;
It can go this way; it can go that.
The ten thousand creatures owe their existence to it and it does
    not disown them;
Yet having produced them, it does not take possession of them.
Tao, though it covers the ten thousand things like a garment,
Makes no claim to be master over them,
And asks for nothing from them.
Therefore it may be called the Lowly.
The ten thousand creatures obey it,
Though they know not that they have a master;
Therefore it is called the Great.
So too the Sage just because he never at any time makes a show
of greatness in fact achieves greatness.

Chapter XLII

Tao gave birth to the One; the One gave birth successively to two things, three things, up to ten thousand.[1] These ten thousand creatures cannot turn their backs to the shade without having the sun on their bellies,[2] and it is on this blending of the breaths[3] that their harmony[4] depends. To be orphaned, needy, ill-provided is what men most hate, yet princes and dukes style themselves so. Truly, 'things are often increased by seeking to diminish them and diminished by seeking to increase them.' The maxims that others use in their teaching I too will use in mine. Show me a man of violence that came to a good end, and I will take him for my teacher.

Commentary

To be a prince is a 'sunny' as opposed to a 'shady' thing. But a prince does not feel properly 'harmonized' unless he also has 'the shade at his back,' which he obtains by humbling himself.

A proverb says: 'The man of violence never yet came to a good end; nor did he that delights in victory fail to meet his match.' Another proverb says: 'The best doctor cannot save one whose life-span has run out; nor can the man of violence strive with Heaven.' It is possible that Ch'iang-liang, 'man of violence,' is in reality the name of a mythological figure, a sort of Titan who warred unsuccessfully against Heaven. Chi'iang means 'violent'; but liang means 'rafter,' and though the two together are said to mean 'man of violence,' no proof is adduced; and I suspect that this Titan was called 'Rafter' because his image was carved on the ends of rafters. This theory is borne out by a passage in *Chuang Tzu* (VI, 9) which speaks of a strong man called Chü-liang, 'holder of the rafters' who like Samson 'lost his strength.' In order to conform to a quotation by Huai-nan Tzu, many modern editors have tampered with the text at the beginning of the chapter.

Notes

1 I.e., everything.
2 Which symbolizes the fact that they are themselves a mixture of light and dark, hard and soft, water and fire, etc.
3 The warm 'breath' of the sun and the cold 'breath' of the shade. Hence 'breath' comes to mean a 'state of the atmosphere' in a wider sense.
4 Or 'balance,' as we should say.

Chapter LII

That which was the beginning of all things under heaven
We may speak of as the 'mother' of all things.
He who apprehends the mother[1]
Thereby knows the sons.[2]
And he who has known the sons
Will hold all the tighter to the mother,
And to the end of his days suffer no harm:
'Block the passages, shut the doors,
And till the end your strength shall not fail.
Open up the passages, increase your doings,
And till your last day no help shall come to you.'
As good sight means seeing what is very small
So strength means holding on to what is weak.[3]
He who having used the outer-light[4] *can return to the*
*   inner-light*
Is thereby preserved from all harm.
This is called resorting to the always-so.

Notes

1 Tao, the One, the Whole.
2 The Many, the universe.
3 I.e., Tao.
4 This corresponds to 'knowing the sons.' Ming ('inner-light') is self-knowledge.

Chapter LVI

Those who know do not speak;
Those who speak do not know.
Block the passages,
Shut the doors,
Let all sharpness be blunted,
All tangles untied,
All glare tempered.
All dust smoothed.
This is called the mysterious levelling.
He who has achieved it cannot either be drawn into friendship
    or repelled,
Cannot be benefited, cannot be harmed,
Cannot either be raised or humbled,
And for that very reason is highest of all creatures under
    heaven.

Chapter LVII

'Kingdoms can only be governed if rules are kept;
Battles can only be won if rules are broken.'[1]
But the adherence of all under heaven can only be won by letting-
    alone.
How do I know that it is so?
By this.[2]
The more prohibitions there are, the more ritual avoidances,
The poorer the people will be.
The more 'sharp weapons'[3] there are,
The more benighted will the whole land grow.
The more cunning craftsmen there are,
The more pernicious contrivances[4] will be invented.
The more laws are promulgated,
The more thieves and bandits there will be.
Therefore a sage has said:
So long as I 'do nothing' the people will of themselves be trans-
    formed.
So long as I love quietude, the people will of themselves go
    straight.

So long as I act only by inactivity the people will of themselves
  become prosperous.
So long as I have no wants the people will of themselves return to
  the 'state of the Uncarved Block.'

Notes

1 A military maxim, to the pattern of which the author proceeds to fit his
Taoist formula. Cf. Lionel Giles, *Sun Tzu*, pp. 34, 35. Ch'i means unexpected
manoeuvres. Cheng 'rules kept' is not here used in its technical military sense
of 'open attack.'
2 Through what I have found inside myself, 'in the belly'; through the light of
my inner vision.
3 I.e., clever people.
4 Cf. the story in *Chuang Tzu* (XII 11) about the man in whom the idea of a
simple labour-saving contrivance inspired feelings similar to those aroused in
Wordsworth by the sight of a railway train.

Chapter LXXXI

True words are not fine-sounding;
Fine-sounding words are not true.
The good man does not prove by argument;
And he who proves by argument is not good.
True wisdom is different from much learning;
Much learning means little wisdom.
The Sage has no need to hoard;
When his own last scrap has been used up on behalf of others,
Lo, he has more than before!
When his own last scrap has been used up in giving to others,
Lo, his stock is even greater than before!
For Heaven's way is to sharpen without cutting,
And the Sage's way is to act without striving.

> Translation, commentary, and notes by Arthur
> Waley, in his *The Way and Its Power: A Study of
> the Tao Tê Ching* (Grove Press, New York)

298. CHUANG TZU DISCOURSES ON TAO

The second great figure of the early Taoist school is the philosopher
Chuang Tzu or Chuang Chou, whose dates are tentatively given as
369 to 286 B.C., making him a contemporary of Mencius. Although he

was a minor official at one time, he seems to have lived most of his life as a recluse and almost nothing is known about him. The book which bears his name, actually probably a combination of his own essays and those of his disciples and imitators, is one of the most witty and imaginative works of all Chinese literature. Like the *Lao Tzu* it does not depend for its effect upon methodical argumentation, but upon the use of parable and allegory, paradox and fanciful imagery. A favourite device of the work is to make an actual historical figure like Confucius serve as an illustration of Taoist ideas, thus involving the great men of Chinese history in all sorts of whimsical and purely imaginative anecdotes.

Chuang Tzu shares with the *Lao Tzu* its central conception of the Tao as the principle underlying and governing all existence. He is, however, less concerned with the Tao as a guide in life than as that which possesses a supreme value in itself, transcending all mundane uses. . . . Chuang Tzu is almost indifferent to human society. He seeks neither to reform things nor to keep them as they are, but only to rise above them. The philosophy of Chuang Tzu is essentially a plea for the freedom of the individual. But it is a kind of spiritual freedom, liberating the individual more from the confines of his own mind than from external restraints. What he must be freed from are his own prejudices, his own partial view of things, his tendency to judge all else in terms of himself.

The Identity of the Opposites

Whereby is the Tao vitiated that there should be a distinction of true and false? Whereby is speech vitiated that there should be a distinction of right and wrong? How could the Tao depart and be not there? And could there be speech and yet it be not appropriate? The Tao is vitiated by petty virtues. Speech is vitiated by flowery eloquence. So it is that we have the contentions between the Confucianists and the Mo-ists, each affirming what the other denies and denying what the other affirms. But if we are to decide on their several affirmations and denials, there is nothing better than to employ the light of reason.

Everything is its own self; everything is something else's other. Things do not know that they are other things' other; they only know that they are themselves. Thus it is said, the other arises out of the self, just as the self arises out of the other. This is the theory that self and others give rise to each other. Besides, where there is life, there is death; and where there is death, there is life. Where there is impossibility, there is possibility; and where there is possibility, there is impossibility. It is because there is right, that there is wrong; it is because there is wrong, that there is right. This being the situation, the sages do not approach things at this level, but reflect the light of nature. Thereupon the self is also the other; the other is also the self. According to the other, there is one kind of right and wrong. According to the self there is another kind of right and wrong. But really are there such distinctions as the self and the other, or are there no such distinctions? When the self and the other [or the this and the that] lose their contrariety, there we have the very essence of the Tao. Only the essence of the Tao may occupy the centre of the circle, and respond therefrom to the endless opinions from all directions. Affirmation [of the self] is one of the endless opinions; denials [of the other] is another. Therefore it is said that there is nothing better than to employ the light of reason. . . .

The possible is possible; the impossible is impossible. The Tao operates and things follow. Things are what they are called. What are they? They are what they are. What are they not? They are not what they are not. Everything is what it is, and can be what it can be. There is nothing that is not something, and there is nothing that cannot be something. Therefore, for instance, a stalk and a pillar, the ugly and the beautiful, the common and the peculiar, the deceitful and the strange—by the Tao this great variety is all brought into a single unity. Division to one is construction to another; construction to one is destruction to another. Whether in construction or in destruction, all things are in the end brought into unity. . . .

The Decline of Tao

The knowledge of the ancients was perfect. In what way was it perfect? They were not yet aware that there were things. This is the most perfect knowledge; nothing can be added. Then, some were aware that there were things, but not aware that there were distinctions among them. Then, some were aware that there were distinctions, but not yet aware that there was right and wrong among them. When right and wrong became manifest, the Tao thereby declined. With the decline of the Tao came the growth of love. But was there really a growth and a decline? Or was there no growth or decline?

Now I have something to say [namely, that there is no such thing as right and wrong]. I do not know whether or not what I say agrees with what others say [namely, that there is right and wrong].

Whether or not what I say and what others say agree [in maintaining right and wrong], they at least agree [in assuming that there is right and wrong]. Then there is hardly any difference between what I say and what others say. But though this may be the case, let me try to explain myself. There was a beginning. There was a no-beginning [before the beginning]. There was a no-no-beginning [previous to the no-beginning before the beginning]. There was being. There was nonbeing [before there was being]. There was no-nonbeing [before there was nonbeing]. There was no-no-nonbeing [before there was no-nonbeing]. Suddenly being and nonbeing appeared. And yet, between being and nonbeing, I do not know which is really being and which is really nonbeing. Just now I have said something, and yet I do not know whether what I have said really means something, or does not mean anything at all.

The Great Awakening

Leaning against the sun and the moon and carrying the universe under his arm, the sage blends everything into a harmonious whole. He is unmindful of the confusion and the gloom, and equalizes the humble and the honourable. The multitude strive and toil; the sage is primitive and without knowledge. He comprehends ten thousand years as one unity, whole and simple. All things are what they are, and are thus brought together.

How do I know that the love of life is not a delusion? How do I know that he who is afraid of death is not like a man who left his home as a youth and forgot to return? Lady Li was the daughter of the border warden of Ai. When she was first brought to the state of Chin, she wept until the bosom of her robe was drenched with tears. But when she came to the royal residence, shared with the king his luxurious couch and ate sumptuous food, she regretted that she had wept. How do I know that the dead do not repent of their former craving for life? Those who dream of a merry drinking party may the next morning wail and weep. Those who dream of wailing and weeping may in the morning go off gaily to hunt. While they dream they do not know that they are dreaming. In their dream, they may even try to interpret their dream. Only when they have awakened do they begin to know that they have dreamed. By and by comes the great awakening, and then we shall know that it has all been a great dream. Yet all the while the fools think that they are awake; this they are sure of. With minute nicety, they discriminate between

princes and grooms. How stupid! Confucius and you are both in a
dream. And when I say that you are in a dream, this is also a dream.
This way of talking may be called paradoxical. If after ten thousand
generations we could once meet a great sage who knew how to explain
the paradox, it would be as though we met him after only one morning
or one evening.

Chuang Tzu and the Butterfly

Once upon a time, Chuang Chou [i.e., Chuang Tzu] dreamed that he
was a butterfly, a butterfly fluttering about, enjoying itself. It did not
know that it was Chuang Chou. Suddenly he awoke with a start and
he was Chuang Chou again. But he did not know whether he was
Chuang Chou who had dreamed that he was a butterfly, or whether
he was a butterfly dreaming that he was Chuang Chou. Between
Chuang Chou and the butterfly there must be some distinction. This
is what is called the transformation of things.

The Natural and the Artificial

'The Tao is without beginning and without end. Things are born and
die, without holding to any permanence. They are now empty, now
full, without maintaining a constant form. The years cannot be made
to abide; time cannot be arrested. Processes of increase and decrease
are in operation and every end is followed by a new beginning. Thus
may we speak of the great norm [of the Tao] and the principle pervading all things.

'The life of things passes by like a galloping horse. Every movement
brings a change, and every hour makes a difference. What is one to
do or what is one not to do? Indeed everything will take its own
course. . . .

'Therefore it has been said that the natural abides within, the artificial without, and virtue (te) resides in the natural. If one knows
the course of nature and man, taking nature as the fundamental and
abiding by virtue, one may feel free either to proceed or retreat, either
to contract or extend, for there is always a return to the essential and
to the ultimate.'

'What do you mean,' enquired the Earl of the River, 'by the natural
and the artificial?'

'Horses and oxen,' answered the spirit of the Ocean, 'have four feet.
That is the natural. Putting a halter on a horse's head, a string through
a bullock's nose—that is the artificial.'

'Therefore it has been said, do not let the artificial obliterate the natural; do not let effort obliterate destiny; do not let enjoyment be sacrificed to fame. Diligently observe these precepts without fail, and thus you will revert to the original innocence.'

'The hard will be crushed . . .'

Lao Tzu said: 'Know the masculine but maintain the feminine; become thereby a ravine for the world. Know purity but endure disgrace; become thereby a valley for the world.' Men all reach for the first; he alone took the last. He said, 'Receive unto yourself the refuse of the world.' Men all seek the substantial; he alone took the empty. Because he did not hoard, he had abundance; indeed great was his abundance. His actions were effortless and without waste. He believed in doing nothing, and laughed at the ingenious. Men all seek for happiness; he alone sought self-preservation through adaptation. He said: 'Let us be free from reproach.' He believed in depth for one's foundation, and simplicity as the rule of outward conduct. He said: 'The hard will be crushed; the sharp will be blunted.' He was always generous and tolerant toward things. He would not exploit others. This may be considered the height of perfection. Kuan Yin and Lao Tan—they belonged with the great and true men of old!

Translation and commentary by Y. P. Mei, in Wm. Theodore de Bary, *et al.* (ed.), *Sources of Chinese Tradition* (Columbia University Press, 1960), pp. 64-5, 70-5, 78-9, 85

E. REFLECTING ON GODS, THE SELF,
AND THE GOD

299. NUER CONCEPTION OF GOD

The Nuer word we translate 'God' is *kwoth*, Spirit. Nuer also speak of him more definitely as *kwoth nhial* or *kwoth a nhial*, Spirit of the sky or Spirit who is in the sky. There are other and lesser spirits which they class as *kuth nhial*, spirits of the sky or of the above, and *kuth piny*, spirits of the earth or of the below. I discuss the conception of God first because the other spiritual conceptions are dependent on it and can only be understood in relation to it. . . .

We may certainly say that the Nuer do not regard the sky or any celestial phenomenon as God, and this is clearly shown in the distinction made between God and the sky in the expressions 'Spirit of the sky' and 'Spirit who is in the sky.' Moreover, it would even be a mistake to interpret 'of the sky' and 'in the sky' too literally.

It would equally be a mistake to regard the association of God with the sky as pure metaphor, for though the sky is not God, and though God is everywhere, he is thought of as being particularly in the sky, and Nuer generally think of him in a spatial sense as being on high. Hence anything connected with the firmament has associations with him. Nuer sometimes speak of him as falling in the rain and of being in lightning and thunder. . . .

It would be quite contrary to Nuer thought, as I have remarked, and it would even seem absurd to them, to say that sky, moon, rain, and so forth are in themselves, singly or collectively, God. God is Spirit, which, like wind and air, is invisible and ubiquitous. But though God is not these things he is in them in the sense that he reveals himself through them. In this sense, he is in the sky, falls in the rain, shines in the sun and moon, and blows in the wind. These divine manifestations are to be understood as modes of God and not as his essence, which is Spirit.

God being above, everything above is associated with him. This is why the heavenly bodies and the movements and actions connected with them are associated with him. This is why also the spirits of the air are regarded as *gaat kwoth*, children of God, in a way other spirits are not, for they, unlike other spirits, dwell in the air and are also thought of as being in the clouds, which are nearest to the sky. This is why also the *colwic* spirits are so closely associated with God, for he touched them with his fire from heaven and took them to himself. . . .

Nuer say that God is everywhere, that he is 'like wind' and 'like air.' According to Father Crazzolara, he may be spoken of by the epithets *jiom*, wind, and *ghau*, universe, but these words only stand for God in poems or in an allegorical sense and are illustrations of the liking the Nilotic people show in their poetry for metonymy and synecdoche. God is not wind, but *cere jiom*, like wind; and he is not *ghau*, the universe, but *cak ghaua*, the creator of the universe. Another poetic epithet by which he may be referred to is *tutgar*. This is an ox-name, taken from an ox of the kind Nuer call *wer*, which has wide spreading horns and is the most majestic of their beasts. The name is a combination of two words; *tut*, which has the sense of 'strength' or 'greatness,' and *gar*, which has the sense of 'omnipresent,' as in another of God's titles, *kwoth me gargar*, the omnipresent God (*gargar* can also be translated 'limitless'). But the commonest Nuer way of trying to express their idea of the nature of God is to say that he is like wind or air, a metaphor which seems appropriate to us because it is found throughout the hierological literature of the world and we are particularly familiar with it in the Old Testament. Among the Nuer the metaphor is consistent not only with the absence of any fixed abode of God but also of any places where he is thought particularly to dwell, for air and wind are everywhere. Unlike the other spirits God has no prophets or sanctuaries or earthly forms.

God, Spirit in the heavens who is like wind and air, is the creator and mover of all things. Since he made the world he is addressed in prayers as *kwoth ghaua*, Spirit of the universe, with the sense of creator of the universe. The word *cak*, used as a noun, can mean the creation, that is, all created things, and hence the nature or character proper to a person or thing; it can be used in a very special sense to refer to an abnormality, *cak kwoth*, a freak; and, though I think rarely, it is used as a title of God, the creator, as in the expression *cak nath*, creator of men. As a verb 'to create' it signifies creation *ex nihilo*, and when speaking of things can therefore only be used of God. However, the word can be used of men for imaginative constructions, such as the thinking of a name to give a child, inventing a tale, or composing a poem, in the same figurative sense as when we say that an actor creates a part. The word therefore means not only creation from nothing but also creation by thought or imagination, so that 'God created the universe' has the sense of 'God thought of the universe' or 'God imagined the universe.'. . .

Whether they are speaking about events which happened *ne walka*, in the beginning or long ago, or about happenings of yesterday or today, God, creative Spirit, is the final Nuer explanation of everything. When asked how things began or how they have come to be what they are they answer that God made them or that it was his will that they have come to be what they are. The heavens and the earth and the waters on the earth, and the beasts and birds and reptiles and fish were made by him, and he is the author of custom and tradition. The Nuer herd cattle and cultivate millet and spear fish because God gave them these things for their sustenance. He instituted their marriage prohibitions. He gave ritual powers to some men and not to others. He decreed that the Nuer should raid the Dinka and that Europeans should conquer the Nuer. He made one man black and another white (according to one account our white skins are a punishment by God for incest committed by our ancestor with his mother), one man fleet and another slow, one strong and another weak. Everything in nature, in culture, in society, and in men is as it is because God made or willed it so. . . .

In the Nuer conception of God he is thus creative Spirit. He is also a *ran*, a living person, whose *yiegh*, breath or life, sustains man. I have never heard Nuer suggest that he has human form, but though he is himself ubiquitous and invisible, he sees and hears all that happens and he can be angry and can love. . . . Man's relation to him is, as it is among other peoples, on the model of a human social relationship. He is the father of men. . . .

A very common mode of address to the Deity is *'gwandong,'* a word which means 'grandfather' or 'ancestor,' and literally 'old father,' but in a religious context 'father' or 'our father' would convey the Nuer sense better; and *'gwara'* and *'gwandan,'* 'our father,' and the respectful form of address *'gwadin,'* 'father,' are also often used in speaking to or about God. God is the father of men in two respects. He is their creator and he is their protector. . . .

But though God is sometimes felt to be present here and now, he is also felt to be far away in the sky. If he hears a whispered prayer, it is spoken with eyes and hands raised to the distant heavens. However, heaven and earth, that is, God and man, for we are justified here in treating the dichotomy anagogically, are not entirely separated. There are comings and goings. God takes the souls of those he destroys by lightning to dwell with him and in him they protect their kinsmen;

he participates in the affairs of men through divers spirits which haunt the atmosphere between heaven and earth and may be regarded as hypostasizations of his modes and attributes; and he is also everywhere present in a way which can only be symbolized, as his ubiquitous presence is symbolized by the Nuer, by the metaphor of wind and air. Also he can be communicated with through prayer and sacrifice, and a certain kind of contact with him is maintained through the social order he is said to have instituted and of which he is the guardian. . . .

E. E. Evans-Pritchard, *Nuer Religion* (London: Oxford University Press, 1957), pp. 1-10

See also nos. 2-7, 51, 67, 91, 126, 127

300. WISDOM, LIBERATION, IMMORTALITY

('Shvetāshvatara Upanishad,' III, V, VI, *selections*)

III, 7. Higher than this is *Brahman*, the supreme, the great hidden in all creatures according to their bodies, the one who envelopes the universe, knowing Him, the Lord, (men) become immortal.

8. I know the Supreme Person of sunlike colour (lustre) beyond the darkness. Only by knowing Him does one pass over death. There is no other path for going there.

9. Than whom there is naught else higher, than whom there is naught smaller, naught greater, (the) one stands like a tree established in heaven, by Him, the Person, is the whole universe filled.

10. That which is beyond this world is without form and without suffering. Those who know that become immortal, but others go only to sorrow.

11. He who is in the faces, heads and necks of all, who dwells in the cave (of the heart) of all beings, who is all-pervading, He is the Lord and therefore the omnipresent *Shiva*.

12. That person indeed is the great lord, the impeller of the highest being. (He has the power of) reaching the purest attainment, the imperishable light.

13. A person of the measure of a thumb is the inner self, ever dwelling in the heart of men. He is the lord of the knowledge framed by the heart and the mind. They who know that become immortal.

14. The person has a thousand heads, a thousand eyes, a thousand feet. He surrounds the earth on all sides and stands ten fingers' breadth beyond.

15. The person is truly this whole world, whatever has been and whatever will be. He is also the lord of immortality, and whatever grows up by food. . . .

19. Without foot or hand, (yet) swift and grasping, he sees without eye, he hears without ear. He knows whatever is to be known; of him there is none who knows. They call him the Primeval, the Supreme Person.

20. Subtler than the subtle, greater than the great is the Self that is set in the cave of the (heart) of the creature. One beholds Him as being actionless and becomes freed from sorrow, when through the grace of the Creator he sees the Lord and His majesty.

21. I know this undecaying, ancient (primeval) Self of all, present in everything on account of infinity. Of whom they declare, there is stoppage of birth. The expounders of *Brahman* proclaim Him to be eternal.

v, 9. This living self is to be known as a part of the hundredth part of the point of a hair divided a hundredfold, yet it is capable of infinity. . . .

11. By means of thought, touch, sight and passions and by the abundance of food and drink there are the birth and development of the (embodied) self. According to his deeds, the embodied self assumes successively various forms in various conditions.

12. The embodied self, according to his own qualities, chooses (assumes) many shapes, gross and subtle. Having himself caused his union with them, through the qualities of his acts and through the qualities of his body, he is seen as another.

13. Him who is without beginning and without end, in the midst of chaos, the creator of all, of manifold form, who alone embraces the universe, he who knows God is freed from all fetters.

14. Him who is to be grasped by the mind, who is called incorporeal, who makes existence and non-existence, the kindly (the auspicious), the maker of creation and its parts, the Divine, they who know Him have left the body behind.

vi, 1. Some wise men speak of inherent nature, others likewise of time (as the first cause), being deluded. But it is the greatness of God in the world, by which this Brahma-wheel is made to turn.

2. He by whom this whole world is always enveloped, the knower, the author of time, the possessor of qualities and all knowledge. Controlled by Him (this) work (of creation) unfolds itself, that which is regarded as earth, water, fire, air and ether. . . .

6. Higher and other than the forms of the world-tree and time is he from whom this world revolves, who brings good and removes evil, the lord of prosperity, having known Him as in one's own self, the immortal, the support of all (he attains *Brahman*).

7. He in whom is the Supreme Lord of lords, who is the highest deity of deities, the supreme master of masters, transcendent, him let us know as God, the lord of the world, the adorable.

8. There is no action and no organ of his to be found. There is not seen his equal or his better. His high power is revealed to be various indeed. The working of his intelligence and strength is inherent (in him). . . .

10. The one God who, according to his own nature, covers himself like a spider with threads produced from *pradhāna* (unmanifested matter), may He grant us entrance into *Brahman*.

11. The one God hidden in all beings, all-pervading, the inner self of all beings, the ordainer of all deeds, who dwells in all beings, the witness, the knower, the only one, devoid of qualities.

12. The one controller of the many, inactive, who makes the one seed manifold, the wise who perceive Him as abiding in their self, to them belongs eternal happiness, not to others.

13. He is the eternal among the eternals, the intelligent among the intelligences, the one among many, who grants desires. That cause which is to be apprehended by discrimination (of *sāmkhya*) and discipline (*yoga*)—by knowing God, one is freed from all fetters. . . .

16. He is the maker of all, the knower of all, the self-caused, the knower, the author of time, the possessor of qualities, the knower of everything, the ruler of nature and of the spirit, the lord of qualities, the cause of worldly existence, and of liberation, of continuance and of bondage.

17. Becoming that, immortal, existing as the lord, the knower, the omnipresent, the guardian of this world is He who rules this world for ever, for no other cause is found for the ruling.

18. To Him who, of old, creates Brahmā and who, verily, delivers to him the Vedas, to that God who is lighted by His own intelligence, do I, eager for liberation, resort for refuge.

19. To Him who is without parts, without activity, tranquil, irreproachable, without blemish, the highest bridge to immortality like a fire with its fuel burnt.

S. Radhakrishman (editor and translator), *The Principal Upanishads* (New York: Harper & Row, 1953), pp. 727 ff.

Gods, the Self, and the God

301. SHANKARA ON THE NATURE OF BRAHMAN

Shankara (ca. 788-820), founder of the standard system of philosophical Hinduism, was an orthodox Shaivite Brāhmán who left his native South India to establish monasteries and to teach throughout India his philosophy of Advaita (Nonduality). Shankara derived his nonsectarian doctrines from the Upanishads, emphasizing salvation (moksha) as the realization through meditation of the identity of the individual soul (ātman) with the Absolute (Brahman). As Brahman is impersonal the phenomenal world is understood by Advaita Vedānta to be appearance or illusion (māyā), altogether outside the ultimate reality of absolute Being-Consciousness-Bliss.

But, it may be asked, is Brahman known or not known (previously to the enquiry into its nature)? If it is known we need not enter on an enquiry concerning it; if it is not known we can not enter on such an enquiry.

We reply that Brahman is known. Brahman, which is all-knowing and endowed with all powers, whose essential nature is eternal purity, intelligence, and freedom, exists. For if we consider the derivation of the word 'Brahman,' from the root *brih*, 'to be great,' we at once understand that eternal purity, and so on, belong to Brahman. Moreover the existence of Brahman is known on the ground of its being the Self of every one. For every one is conscious of the existence of (his) Self, never thinks 'I am not.' If the existence of the Self were not known, everyone would think 'I am not.' And this Self (of whose existence all are conscious) is Brahman. But if Brahman is generally known as the Self, there is no room for an enquiry into it! Not so, we reply; for there is a conflict of opinions as to its special nature. Unlearned people and the Lokāyatikas are of opinion that the mere body endowed with the quality of intelligence is the Self; others that the organs endowed with intelligence are the Self; others maintain that the internal organ is the Self; others, again, that the Self is a mere momentary idea; others, again, that it is the Void. Others, again (to proceed to the opinion of such as acknowledge the authority of the Veda), maintain that there is a transmigrating being different from the body, and so on, which is both agent and enjoyer (of the fruits of action); others teach that being is enjoying only, not acting; others believe that in addition to the individual souls, there is an all-knowing, all-powerful Lord. Others, finally (i.e., the Vedāntins), maintain that

193

the Lord is the Self of the enjoyer (i.e., of the individual soul whose individual existence is apparent only, the produce of Nescience).

Thus there are many various opinions, basing part of them on sound arguments and scriptural texts, part of them on fallacious arguments and scriptural texts misunderstood. If therefore a man would embrace some one of these opinions without previous consideration, he would bar himself from the highest beatitude and incur grievous loss [I, 1, 1.]

'He knows the highest Brahman becomes even Brahman'

That same highest Brahman constitutes—as we know from passages such as 'that art thou'—the real nature of the individual soul [i.e., *ātman*], while its second nature, i.e., that aspect of it which depends on fictitious limiting conditions, is not its real nature. For as long as the individual soul does not free itself from Nescience in the form of duality—which Nescience may be compared to the mistake of him who in the twilight mistakes a post for a man—and who does not rise to the knowledge of the Self, whose nature is unchangeable, eternal Cognition—which expresses itself in the form 'I am Brahman'—so long it remains the individual soul. But when, discarding the aggregate of body, sense-organs and mind, it arrives, by means of Scripture, at the knowledge that it is not itself that aggregate, that it does not form part of transmigratory existence, but is the True, the Real, the Self, whose nature is pure intelligence; then knowing itself to be of the nature of unchangeable, eternal Cognition, it lifts itself above the vain conceit of being one with this body, and itself becomes the Self, whose nature is unchanging, eternal Cognition. As is declared in such scriptural passages as 'He who knows the highest Brahman becomes even Brahman' (*Mundaka Upanishad*, III, 2, 9). And this is the real nature of the individual soul by means of which it arises from the body and appears in its own form. [I, 3, 19.]

There is only one highest Lord ever unchanging, whose substance is cognition [i.e., of whom cognition is not a mere attribute], and who, by means of Nescience, manifests himself in various ways, just as a thaumaturg appears in different shapes by means of his magical power. . . . To the highest Self which is eternally pure, intelligent and free, which is never changing, one only, not in contact with anything, devoid of form, the opposite characteristics of the individual soul are erroneously ascribed; just as ignorant men ascribe blue colour to the colourless ether. [I, 3, 19.]

Gods, the Self, and the God

The Serpent and the Rope

A man may, in the dark, mistake a piece of rope lying on the ground for a snake and run away from it, frightened and trembling; thereon another man may tell him, 'Do not be afraid, it is only a rope, not a snake'; and he may then dismiss the fear caused by the imagined snake, and stop running. But all the while the presence and subsequent absence of his erroneous notion, as to the rope being a snake, make no difference whatever in the rope itself. Exactly analogous is the case of the individual soul which is in reality one with the highest soul, although Nescience makes it appear different. [1, 4, 6.]

As therefore the individual soul and the highest Self differ in name only, it being a settled matter that perfect knowledge has for its object the absolute oneness of the two; it is senseless to insist (as some do) on a plurality of Selfs, and to maintain that the individual soul is different from the highest Self, and the highest Self from the individual soul. For the Self is indeed called by many different names, but it is one only. Nor does the passage, 'He knows Brahman which is real, knowledge, infinite, as hidden in the cave' (*Taittirīya Upanishad*, II, 1), refer to some one cave (different from the abode of the individual soul). And that nobody else but Brahman is hidden in the cave we know from a subsequent passage, viz. 'Having sent forth he entered into it' (*Taittirīya Upanishad*, II, 6) according to which the creator only entered into the created beings.—Those who insist on the distinction of the individual and the highest Self oppose themselves to the true sense of the Vedānta-texts, stand thereby in the way of perfect knowledge, which is the door to perfect beatitude, and groundlessly assume release to be something effected, and therefore non-eternal. (And if they attempt to show that *moksha*, although effected, is eternal) they involve themselves in a conflict with sound logic. [1, 4, 22.]

Brahman and the World

That Brahman is at the same time the operative cause of the world, we have to conclude from the circumstance that there is no other guiding being. Ordinarily material causes, indeed, such as lumps of clay and pieces of gold, are dependent, in order to shape themselves into vessels and ornaments, on extraneous operative causes such as potters and goldsmiths; but outside Brahman as material cause there is no other operative cause to which the material cause could look; for Scripture says that previously to creation Brahman was one without a second.—

The absence of a guiding principle other than the material cause can moreover be established by means of the argument made use of in the Sūtra, viz. accordance with the promissory statements and the illustrative examples. If there were admitted a guiding principle different from the material cause, it would follow that everything cannot be known through one thing, and thereby the promissory statements as well as the illustrative instances would be stultified.—The Self is thus the operative cause, because there is no other ruling principle, and the material cause because there is no other substance from which the world could originate. [I, 4, 23.]

'When the sleeper wakes . . .'

The entire complex of phenomenal existence is considered as true as long as the knowledge of Brahman being the Self of all has not arisen; just as the phantoms of a dream are considered to be true until the sleeper wakes. For as long as a person has not reached the true knowledge of the unity of the Self, so long as it does not enter his mind that the world of effects with its means and objects of right knowledge and its results of actions is untrue; he rather, in consequence of his ignorance, looks on mere effects (such as body, offspring, wealth, etc.) as forming part of and belonging to his Self, forgetful of Brahman being in reality the Self of all. Hence, as long as true knowledge does not present itself, there is no reason why the ordinary course of secular and religious activity should not hold on undisturbed. The case is analogous to that of a dreaming man who in his dream sees manifold things, and, up to the moment of waking, is convinced that his ideas are produced by real perception without suspecting the perception to be a merely apparent one. [II, 7, 14.]

Shankara's *Commentary on Vedānta Sūtra*, as translated by George Thibaut, vol. I, in *Sacred Books of the East*, XXXIV (Oxford, 1890), pp. 14-15, 185-6, 190. 251, 282-3, 285-6, 324

302. RĀMĀNUJA ON BRAHMAN: 'BRAHMAN IS TO BE MEDITATED UPON AS CONSTITUTING THE SELF OF THE MEDITATING DEVOTEE'

Rāmānuja (ca. 1017-1137), a South-Indian Vaishnavite teacher who provided the initial philosophical framework for the new forms of devotional Hinduism (bhakti) which had emerged and spread north from Tamilnad since the ninth century, taught, as did Shankara, in various parts of India and wrote numerous commentaries. His system, Vishishtādvaita (Qualified Nonduality), deriving some of its doctrines from the Pāncarātras, differed from Advaita by emphasizing the reality of the phenomenal world and the essential distinction between the individual soul and a personal God (Vishnu). Salvation, by intense devotion or by abandonment of self (prapatti) to God's grace, returns the ātman to a state neither of annihilation nor of absorption but of love in the eternal presence of God.

But how can the Devotees claim that Brahman which is a different being is their 'Ego'?—Because the texts enable them to apprehend this relation as one free from contradiction. 'He who dwelling within the Self is different from the Self, whom the Self does not know, of whom the Self is the body, who rules the Self from within; he is thy Self, the inner ruler, the immortal one' (Brihad-āranyaka Upanishad, III, 7, 3); 'In the True all these beings have their root, they dwell in the True, they rest in the True; in that all that exists has its Self' (Khata Upanishad, VI, 8); 'All this indeed is Brahman' (Khata Upanishad, III, 14, 1)—all these texts teach that all sentient and nonsentient beings spring from Brahman, are merged in him, breathe through him, are ruled by him, constitute his body; so that he is the Self of all of them. In the same way therefore as, on the basis of the fact that the individual soul occupies with regard to the body the position of a Self, we form such judgments of co-ordination as 'I am a god—I am a man'; the fact of the individual Self being of the nature of Self justifies us in viewing our own Ego as belonging to the highest Self. On the presupposition of all ideas being finally based on Brahman and hence all words also finally denoting Brahman, the texts therefore make such statements of mutual implication as 'I am thou, O holy divinity, and thou art me.' On this view of the relation of individual soul and highest Self there is no real contradiction between two, apparently contradictory, sets of texts, viz., those on the one hand which negative the view of the soul being different from the highest Self, 'Now if a man meditates upon another divinity, thinking "the divinity is one and I another," he does not know'; 'He is incomplete, let him meditate upon Him as the Self; 'Everything abandons him who views anything apart from the Self' (Brihad-āranyaka Upanishad, I, 4, 10; II, 4, 6); and on the other hand those texts which set forth the view of the soul and the highest Self being different entities. 'Thinking of the (individual) Self and the Mover as different' (Shvetāshvatara Upani-

shad, 1, 6). For our view implies a denial of difference in so far as the individual 'I' is of the nature of the Self; and it implies an acknowledgment of difference in so far as it allows the highest Self to differ from the individual soul in the same way as the latter differs from its body. The clause 'he is incomplete' (in one of the texts quoted above) refers to the fact that Brahman which is different from the soul constitutes the Self of the soul, while the soul constitutes the body of Brahman. It thus remains a settled conclusion that Brahman is to be meditated upon as constituting the Self of the meditating Devotee.

Rāmānuja, *Commentary on Vedānta-Sūtras*, IV, 1, 3, as translated by George Thibaut, in *Sacred Books of the East*, XLVIII (Oxford, 1904), pp. 717-18

303. ZOROASTRIAN DUALISM: A SYSTEMATIC PRESENTATION

(*'Shikand Gumānī Vazār,'* chapter VIII)

Mardān-Farrukh, the author of Shikand Gumānī Vazār, *an 'Analytical Treatise for the Dispelling of Doubts,' lived in the ninth century* A.D. *According to R. C. Zaehner, his work is 'in some ways the most interesting of all the Zoroastrian books since it presents a philosophical justification of Zoroastrian dualism in a more or less coherent form; and it further contains a detailed critique of the monotheistic creeds, Islam, Judaism and Christianity as well as an attack on Zoroastrianism's dualistic rival, Manichaeanism.' The great merit of Zoroastrian dualism is that it absolves God from any breath of evil and explains why creation was actually necessary.*

(1) Another proof that a contrary principle exists is (2) that good and evil are observable in the world, (3) and more particularly in so far as both good [and bad] conduct are defineable as such, (4) as are darkness and light, (5) right knowledge and wrong knowledge, (6) fragrance and stench, (7) life and death, (8) sickness and health, (9) justice and injustice, (10) slavery and freedom, (11) and all the other contrary activities which indisputably exist and are visible in every country and land at all times; (12) for no country or land exists, has existed, or ever will exist (13) in which the name of good and evil and what that name signifies has not existed or does not exist. (14) Nor can any time or

place be mentioned in which good and evil change their nature essentially.

(15) There are also other contraries whose antagonism is not [one of essence but] one of function, species, or nature. (16) Such is the mutual antagonism of things of like nature as (for example) male and female, (17) (the different) scents, tastes and colours; the Sun, Moon and stars whose dissimilarity is not one of substance but one of function, nature, and constitution, each being adapted to its own particular work. (18) But the dissimilarity of good and evil, light, darkness, and other contrary substances is not one of function but one of substance. (19) This can be seen from the fact that their natures cannot combine and are mutually destructive. (20) For where there is good, there cannot possibly be evil. (21) Where light is admitted, darkness is driven away. (22) Similarly with other contraries, the fact that they cannot combine and are mutually destructive is caused by their dissimilarity in substance. (23) This substantial dissimilarity and mutual destructiveness is observable in phenomena in the material world.

(24) That material world is the effect of the spiritual, and the spiritual is its cause, (25) for the effect is understood through the cause. (26) That the former gives testimony of the latter is obvious to any expert in these matters. (27) That the material is an effect and the spiritual the cause can be proved by the fact that (28) every visible and tangible thing emerges from an unmanifest to a manifest state. . . .

(35) Since we have seen that in the material world contrary substances exist and that they are sometimes mutually co-operative and sometimes mutually destructive, so (must it also be) in the spiritual world (36) which is the cause of the material, (37) and material things are its effects. That this is so is not open to doubt (38) and follows from the very nature of contrary substances. (39-40) I have shown above that the reason and occasion for the wise activity of the Creator which is exemplified in the creative act is the existence of an Adversary. . . .

(57) Now the goodness of the wise Creator can be inferred from the act of creation and from the fact that he cherishes and protects (his creatures), that he ordains and teaches a way and method by which evil can be repelled and sin averted, (58-60) and that he repels and wards off the Adversary who attacks the body; (it can be inferred too) from the organs and faculties of the body (afflicted as they are) by pain and sickness (which come to them) from outside and (which also are) inside the body. . . .

(64) It is suffering and death that destroy the body, not the Creator whose will is good and who preserves and maintains the body. (65) This is clearly so because a wise Creator does not regret or repent of what he has done, (66) nor does he destroy his creatures or make them of no effect, (67) for he is wise and omniscient. (68) It is only possible to attribute regret and repentance for what one has done to one whose knowledge is defective, whose reason is imperfect, and who is ignorant of the final outcome, (69) for knowing and wise persons do not commit actions without cause or occasion. (70) Similarily the actions of ignorant men of perverted intelligence who are ignorant of the final outcome will be haphazard, without cause or occasion.

(71) But the wise (Creator) will dispose wisely and act in accordance with discrimination in warding off from his creatures (the Adversary) whose actions are haphazard and who does not know the final outcome. (72) He, the (demon) whose actions are haphazard, is walled up and circumscribed within a trap and a snare; (73) for it is plain that a moving and living substance cannot be warded off or destroyed in an infinite void, nor is there any security against his harmfulness (74) unless he is circumscribed, uprooted, and made captive. (75) When he is circumscribed and made captive, he is susceptible to suffering and heavy chastisement. (76) But until he is completely conscious of his suffering and fully aware that his actions are based on a wrong knowledge, he continues to have utterly false views of what has befallen him. (77) His experience of suffering (is due to) the complete power of the omnipotent Creator.

(78) When once he has reached full realization of what he suffers at the hands of omnipotence, the wise Creator puts him out of action and hurls him into the infinite Void. (79) Then the good creation will have no fear of him; it will be immortal and free from adversity. (80) Perfect is the wisdom and discrimination of the omniscient Creator of the good and (perfect is) his foreknowledge of what needs to be done. . . .

(103) From this we must infer (104) that what is perfect and complete in its goodness cannot produce evil. (105) If it could, then it would not be perfect, (106) for when a thing is described as perfect, there is no room for anything else (in it); (107) and if there is no room for anything else, nothing else can proceed from it. (108) If God is perfect in goodness and knowledge, plainly ignorance and evil cannot proceed from Him; (109) or if it can, then he is not perfect; (110) and if he is not perfect, then he should not be worshipped as God or as perfectly good.

(111) If (on the other hand) both good and evil originate in God, then he is imperfect so far as goodness is concerned. (112) If he is imperfect in respect of goodness, then he is imperfect in respect of right knowledge. (113) And if he is imperfect in respect of right knowledge, then he is imperfect in respect of reason, consciousness, knowledge, wit, and in all the faculties of knowing. (114) And if he is imperfect in reason, consciousness, wit, and knowledge, he must be imperfect in respect of health; (115) and if he is imperfect in respect of health, he must be sick; (116) and if he must be sick, then he is imperfect in respect of life.

> Translation by R. C. Zaehner, in *The Teachings of the Magi* (London, 1956), pp. 59-66

See also nos. 60, 37-9, 290

304. EPICURUS ON THE GODS

('Letter to Menoeceus,' 123-6)

Epicurus (342?-270 B.C.) was the founder and head of the philosophical school which bears his name. He was born on the island of Samos and taught at Athens from 306 B.C. onward.

First of all believe that God is a being incorruptible [i.e., immortal and unchangeable] and blessed, just as in the common idea of God which is engraved on the mind, and do not assign to him anything contrary to his incorruption or unsuited to his blessedness, and believe about him whatever safeguards his blessedness and incorruption. For gods there certainly are, since the knowledge of them is a matter of immediate perception. But they are not what the majority of men believe them to be, in fact, they do not take care to represent them as they really believe them to be. And the irreligious man is not the one who denies the gods of the majority, but the one who applies to the gods the opinions of the majority. For what the majority say about the gods are not conceptions derived from sensation [*prolepseis*], but false suppositions [*hypolepseis*], according to which the greatest injuries overtake the wicked and the greatest blessings come to [the good] from the gods. For since men are always accustomed to their own virtues, they welcome those who are like themselves, but whatever is not of this sort they regard as alien.

Get accustomed to the idea that death means nothing to us. For all good and evil consist in sensation, and death is only the deprivation of sensation. Hence a real understanding that death means nothing to us makes the mortality of [our] life enjoyable, not by adding to it an unlimited length of time, but by taking away the desire for immortality. For there is nothing dreadful in life for the man who has really grasped the idea that there is nothing dreadful in not living. So that anyone is foolish who says that he is afraid of death, not because it will be painful when it comes, but because it is painful in prospect. For what gives [us] no trouble when it comes is only an empty pain as we look forward to it. So death, the most terrifying of evils, is nothing to us, for as long as we exist death is not present with us, and when death comes then we no longer exist. It is no concern, therefore, either of the living or the dead; for the former it does not exist, while the latter themselves no longer exist.

But the majority at one time flee from death as the greatest of all evils, but at another time [they yearn for it] as a rest from the [evils] in life. [But the wise man neither seeks to escape from life] nor fears to cease living, for neither does life annoy him nor does nonliving seem to be anything evil. Just as in the case of food he does not by any means choose the larger share, but rather the most delicious, so he seeks to enjoy [literally, plucks as fruit], not the longest period of time, but the most pleasant.

> Translation by Frederick C. Grant, in his *Hellenistic Religions*, (New York, 1953), pp. 157-8

See also no. 139

305. THE MUSLIM DOCTRINE OF GOD

(Jamāl ad-Dīn al-Qāsimī)

What Muslims believe about the essential nature of the High and Holy One is that He is One God who has no partner. He is from everlasting, having none prior to Him, and He will continue endlessly to exist, having none come after Him. He is eternal, having no ending, continuing without ever being cut off, One who has not ceased and will not cease to be. He is to be described by the attributes of Majesty. For him there is prescribed no consummation or disjunction by the ceasing of perpetuity or the expiration of fixed terms. Nay, rather (LVII, 3): 'He is the First and the Last, the Outward and the Inward, and He knows all things.' Yet He is not a body that has been formed, nor does He resemble any created thing, nor any created thing resemble Him. Space does not encompass Him, nor do the earths[1] and the heavens contain Him, although He is seated on the Throne in that manner of which He speaks and in that sense which He means.[2] He is above the Throne and the heavens, above everything, and yet also beneath the lowest reaches of the watery abyss.[3] His being above does not make Him nearer the Throne and the heaven nor further from the earth and the watery abyss. Nay, rather He is many stages higher than the Throne or the heavens, as He is many stages beyond the earth and the watery abyss, yet in spite of this He is near to every existing thing. He is nearer to man than his jugular vein (I, 16/15), though His being near does not resemble bodily nearness, just as His essential being does not resemble the the essential being of bodily things. He does not come to rest in anything, just as nothing comes to rest in Him. High exalted is He from being included in any space, just as He is far removed from being limited by any time. Nay, indeed, He was before. He created time and space, and He is now as He was.

He is known by the intelligence to be existing in His essential being. As such essential being He will be perceived by the sight in the Lasting Abode,[4] as an act of grace on His part and a kindness to the righteous, in some sort a perfecting of His bounties by letting them look upon His noble face. And He—exalted be He—is living, powerful, mighty, overcoming, free from all shortcomings and any inability. 'Slumber takes Him not nor sleep' (II, 255/256), and no passing away, no death ever comes upon Him. None but He can create and invent, for He stands uniquely alone in producing and innovating. He knows everything that is knowable, is aware of all that is taking place from the lowest depths of the earths to the highest reaches of the heavens, so that not an atom's weight of anything either on earth or in heaven exists apart from His knowledge. He is aware of the crawling of a black ant upon a hard stone in the darkness of the night, and He perceives the movement of each mote in the atmosphere. 'He knows the secret and the most hidden thing' (XX, 7/6). He is acquainted with the promptings of men's consciences, with the movements of their fancies, with their most deeply concealed secrets, [knowing all this] with a knowledge that is from of old and is to eternity, for He will not cease having this attribute for ever and ever.

He—exalted be He—is the One who wills that existing things be, who manages the things that come to pass, so that no affair happens in the world visible or the world invisible[5] except by His determining, His decree, His decision, His will, so that what He wills is, and what He did not will is not, and there is no one who may resist His command or make a change in His decision. He—exalted be He—both hears and sees (XXII, 61/60). There is nothing that may be heard, however faint, that escapes His hearing, and nothing that may be seen, however minute, that is hidden from His vision. Distance does not dim His hearing, nor does darkness hinder His vision, yet His hearing and His seeing have no resemblance to the hearing and seeing of creatures, just as His essential being has no resemblance to that of creatures. He also —exalted be He—speaks, both to bid and to forbid, to promise and to threaten. The Qur'an, the Torah, the Evangel, and the Psalter are Scriptures of His which He sent down to His messengers—on whom be peace. He also—exalted be He—spoke to Moses with the speech which is an attribute of His essence and not a created thing that may perish, nor an attribute of any created thing so that it should be exhausted.

Now He—exalted be He—[is unique in the sense] that there is beside Him no existing thing save that which came into being by His act, proceeding from His equity in the finest and most perfect, in the most complete and equitable way. He is wise in all His actions, just in all His decrees. Everything apart from Him, whether men or jinn or angels, whether heaven or earth, whether animal or plant or mineral, whether perceived of the mind or by the senses, is a new creation which He produced by His power, being brought out from non-existence and produced as a created thing when it had been no thing. Since He was existing in eternity He was alone, and there was no other with Him. Then He brought forth the creation after that, as a demonstration of His power, a fulfillment of that which He had previously willed, and a verification of the word that He had spoken in eternity. It was not that He had any need for it or was in want of it, for it is as a favour that He creates and produces and undertakes things, not out of necessity, and it is as a service that He grants favours and not because He must. So it is He who is the One who grants favours and benefactions, blessings and grace.

Notes

1 Plural because there are seven earths as there are seven heavens.
2 This is the famous problem of the *istiwā'* which so exercised Muslims theologians. Some seven times in the Qu'an it is stated that Allah *istawā* on the Throne, which, if used of some earthly monarch, would mean that he 'sat upon the throne.'
3 *Ath-tharā* in the old cosmology is what is below the lowest depths. Sura xx, 6/5 says 'To Him belongs what is in the heavens, what is on earth, what is between them both, and what is below the *tharā*.'
4 *Dār al-Qarār* is one of the names of Paradise, so this is a reference to the Muslim doctrine of the beatific vision.
5 *Mulk wa malakūt*, words which both mean 'kingdom,' but refer more particularly to the kingdom of things seen and the kingdom of things unseen.

Translation and notes by Arthur Jeffery, *Islam: Muhammad and His Religion* (New York: Liberal Arts Press, 1958), pp. 90-2

See also nos. 70-3, 231-7, 252, 268, 269

306. THE ESSENCE OF ISLAM

(Al-Malatī, 'Kitāb at-Tanbīh')

Ibn 'Umar has said: Islam is built upon five things: on confessing that that there is no deity save Allah, performing prayers (*salat*), giving the legal alms (*zakat*), going on pilgrimage to the House (i.e., the Ka'ba at Mecca), and fasting during [the month of] Ramadan. Thus did the Apostle of Allah hand it on to us, but beyond that there is holy war (*jihad*), which is an excellent thing. Said Hudaifa: Verily, I know people of two religions among the people of your religion, two religions which are due for hell fire, namely, folk who say that faith is a matter of words [and a man may be a true believer] even though he fornicates and murders, and those who say [that men can be true believers] even if they are patrons of error, claiming that there are not five daily prayers but only two, morning prayer and evening prayer.

'Abdallah al-Yashkuri said: I went to Kufa to procure some mules, and I entered the mosque where there was a man of Qais named Ibn al-Muntafiq who was saying: Someone described to me the Apostle of Allah, and it was pleasing to me, so I went to Mecca to find him, but they said that he was at Muna. So I went to Muna to find him, but they said that he was at 'Arafat. Finally I found him and approached him, getting so close that I could catch the bridle of his mount—or perhaps he said: till I could catch hold of the neck-rein of his mount—so that the necks of our two steeds crossed. I said: 'There are two things about which I want to ask you. What will save me from Hell, and what will assure me entrance to Paradise?' He looked up at the sky, then he turned to face me, and said: 'Even though you have put the matter in short, you are on to something that is immense and really needs a long answer. Nevertheless take this from me: You should worship Allah, associating nothing with Him, perform the prayers that have been prescribed, fast the month of Ramadan, act with people the way you would like them to act with you, do not be averse to folk coming to you but let the people do it, and let go the neck-rein of my riding beast.'

It is related from al-Hasan that the Apostle of Allah said: 'O sons of Adam, prayer prohibits immorality, yet you do not pray.' Ibn 'Abbas quoted the verse (XXXV, 10/11): 'To Him rises up the good word, and the righteous deed He will exalt,' and said: The good word is the making mention of Allah, and the righteous deed is performing the prescribed religious duties (*fara'id*). So whoever makes mention of Allah while performing the prescribed duties is carried on the remembrance of Allah and taken up to the heavens, but he who makes mention of Allah yet does not perform the prescribed duties has his words set in charge of his deeds, which is what he was well entitled to. Said the Apostle of Allah: 'The first thing about which a man will have to give reckoning [at Judgment] will be the fara'id. Should any deficiency be found in them [Allah will say]: "Has my servant any voluntary deeds (*tatawwu'*)?"[1] If such are found He will say: "Fill up [the deficiency in the] *fara'id* from the *tatawwu'*."'

According to Ka'ab the Apostle of Allah said: 'Whoever performs the prayers, and gives the legal alms, and hears and obeys, has a middling sort of faith, but he who loves and hates only for Allah's sake, who gives and withholds only for Allah's sake, has attained a perfect faith.' To the delegation that came from the 'Abd al-Qais, the Apostle of Allah said: 'I command you four things, the first of which is faith in Allah. Do you know what faith in Allah is?' They replied: 'Allah and His Apostle know better.' He said: 'It consists in testifying that there is no deity save Allah, performing the prayers, giving the legal alms, and giving the fifth of the booty.'[2]

Said Ibn 'Umar: 'There are three [necessary things] of which should a man have two but not have the third [his religion] will not be acceptable. [These three are] prayer, fasting, and the washing oneself pure from that which makes legally impure (*janaba*).'

Notes

1 I.e., deeds which religiously are good deeds but which are not among the prescribed duties of religion covered by the fara'id. An example would be extra prayers beyond the prescribed five daily prayers.
2 The reference is to the prescription in Sura VIII, 41/42.

Translation and notes by Arthur Jeffery, *Islam: Muhammad and His Religion* (New York: Liberal Arts Press, 1958), pp. 81-3, from Al-Malati's *Kitāb at-Tanbīh*, in Sven Dedering (ed.), 'Die Widerlegung der Irrgläubigen und Neuerer, von Abū'l-Husain al-Malāti', *Bibliotheca Islamica* (Leipzig, 1936), IX, 110-11

Acknowledgments

Bibliography

Index

ACKNOWLEDGMENTS

Acknowledgment is made to the following for permission to reprint copyrighted material:

GEORGE ALLEN AND UNWIN, LTD for extracts from *The Koran*, translated by A. J. Arberry; *Sufism* by A. J. Arberry; *The Way and its Power* by Arthur Waley; and *The Teachings of the Magi* by R. C. Zaehner.

GEORGE BRAZILLER, INC for extract from *Islam* by John Alden Williams, copyright © 1961 by John Alden Williams, reprinted by permission of George Braziller, Inc.

CAMBRIDGE UNIVERSITY PRESS for extracts from *The Presocratic Philosophers*, translated by G. S. Kirk and J. E. Raven.

CATHOLIC UNIVERSITY OF AMERICA PRESS for extracts from *The Apinaye* by Curt Nimuendaju.

THE CLARENDON PRESS, OXFORD for extracts from *Nuer Religion* by E. E. Evans-Pritchard; *Jaina Sutras*, parts I and II, translated by H. Jacobi; reprinted by permission of the Clarendon Press, Oxford.

COLUMBIA UNIVERSITY PRESS for extracts from *The Religion of the Kwakiutl Indians* by Franz Boas, copyright 1930 by Columbia University Press, New York; *Sources of Chinese Tradition*, edited by William Theodore de Bary, copyright © 1960 by Columbia University Press, New York; *Sources of Indian Tradition*, edited by William Theodore de Bary, copyright © 1958 by Columbia University Press, New York; *Sources of Japanese Tradition*, edited by William Theodore de Bary, copyright © 1958 by Columbia University Press, New York.

DOVER PUBLICATIONS, INC for extracts from *Jaina Sutras*, parts I and II, translated by Herman Jacobi.

THE ESTATE OF WALTER Y. EVANS-WENTZ, DECEASED for extracts from his *Tibet's Great Yogi Milarepa*.

HARVARD UNIVERSITY PRESS for extracts from *Nichiren: the Buddhist Prophet*, reprinted by permission of the publishers.

LIBERAL ARTS DIVISION OF THE BOBBS-MERRILL COMPANY INC for extracts from *Ancient Roman Religion*, Frederick C. Grant, editor, copyright © 1957 by the Liberal Arts Press; *Hellenistic Religions*, edited by Frederick C. Grant, copyright © 1953 by the Liberal Arts Press; *Islam: Muhammad and his Religion*, edited by Arthur Jeffery, copyright © 1958 by the Liberal Arts Press.

THE MACMILLAN COMPANY for extracts from *The Koran*, translated by A. J. Arberry; *The Teachings of the Magi* by R. C. Zaehner.

METHUEN AND COMPANY LTD for extracts from *The Greeks and Their Gods* by W. C. K. Guthrie; *Orpheus and the Greek Religion* by W. C. K. Guthrie.

JOHN MURRAY for extracts from *The Hymns of Zarathustra*, translated by J. Duchesne-Guillemin; *Buddhist Scriptures* by E. J. Thomas; *The Buddha's Way of Virtue* by W. D. C. Wagiswara and K. S. Saunders.

Acknowledgments

THOMAS NELSON & SONS LTD for extracts from *Documents from Old Testament Times* edited by D. Winton Thomas (1958).

THE PALI TEXT SOCIETY for extracts from *Further Dialogues of the Buddha,* vol. I, translated by Lord Robert Chalmers.

PENGUIN BOOKS LTD, BALTIMORE, MARYLAND for extracts from *Buddhist Scriptures,* translated by Edward Conze.

ROUTLEDGE AND KEGAN PAUL LTD for extracts from *Life of Gotama the Buddha* by Earl Brewster; *Early Buddhist Scriptures;* translated by E. J. Thomas.

THAMES AND HUDSON LTD for extracts from *Myth and Symbol in Ancient Egypt* by R. T. Rundle Clark; *Burning Water* by Laurette Séjourné.

THE UNIVERSITY OF CHICAGO PRESS for extracts from Aeschylus' 'Agamemnon', translated by Richard Lattimore in *The Complete Greek Tragedies,* edited by David Grene and Richard Lattimore; and *The Edicts of Asoka,* translated and edited by N. A. Nikam and Richard McKeon.

VANGUARD PRESS, INC for extracts reprinted by permission of the publishers, The Vanguard Press, from *Burning Water* by Laurette Séjourné.

MONICA WILSON for extracts from her *Communal Rituals of the Nyakusa,* published by Oxford University Press under the auspices of the International African Institute.

BIBLIOGRAPHY

Chapter 1 : *Specialists of the Sacred: From Medicine Men to Mystics and Founders of Religions*

Nos. 198 ff. On the initiation of the Australian medicine men, see A. P. Elkin, *Aboriginal Men of High Degree* (Sydney, 1945).

No. 202. On North American shamanism, see Willard Z. Park, *Shamanism in Western North America: A Study in Cultural Relationships* (Evanston-Chicago, 1938); Marcelle Bouteiller, *Chamanisme et guérison magique* (Paris, 1950); M. Eliade, *Shamanism: Archaic Techniques of Ecstasy* (New York and London, 1964), pp. 297 ff.

Nos. 203 ff. On the different types of shamanistic initiations and seances, see M. Eliade, *Shamanism, op. cit.,* pp. 33 ff., 181 ff., and *passim.*

No. 210. On black magic, see E. E. Evans-Pritchard, *Witchcraft, Oracles and Magic among the Azande* (Oxford, 1937); see also the bibliography listed in M. Eliade, *Patterns in Comparative Religion,* (London and New York: Sheed and Ward, 1958; Meridian paperback, 1963)), pp. 36-7.

No. 211. On the African divine kingship, see the bibliography of Charles H. Long, 'Primitive Religion,' in Adams (ed.), *A Reader's Guide to the Great Religions,* p. 19.

No. 214. On *Flamen dialis,* see the numerous works of Georges Dumézil, summarized in his *L'Idéologie tripartie des Indo-Européens* (Bruxelles, 1955).

Nos. 218 ff. On different forms of asceticism, cf. O. Hardmann, *The Ideals of Ascetism. An Essay in the Comparative Study of Religion* (London, 1924); P. V. Kane, *History of Dharmashāstra,* vol. II, part 2 (Poona, 1941), pp. 917-75; and the bibliographies listed in M. Eliade, *Yoga: Immortality and Freedom* (New York and London, 1958), pp. 381-5, 391-2, 404-5, 409-10, 419-20, 423-5.

No. 224. On Zarathustra, cf. the bibliography for nos. 37-9.

Nos. 225 ff. On Buddha and Buddhism, cf. the bibliography for nos. 21 ff., 29, 30.

Nos. 231 ff. On Muhammad and Islam, cf. the bibliographies listed for nos. 40 ff.

No. 238. On the arts and effects of ecstasy in Hellenistic times, see the bibliographies in Frederick C. Grant, *Hellenistic Religions: The Age of Syncretism* (New York, 1953), pp. 151, 169.

Nos. 239-42. On the techniques of Yoga, cf. M. Eliade, *Yoga: Immortality and Freedom, op. cit., passim,* and the bibliography listed p. 372.

Nos. 243 ff. On the Pure Land Buddhism, see the bibliographies listed by Joseph M. Kitagawa, in Adams (ed.), *A Reader's Guide to the Great Religions,* pp. 170, 178-9.

Nos. 247 ff. On Zen Buddhism, see D. T. Suzuki, *Manual of Zen Buddhism* (Kyoto, 1935); D. T. Suzuki, *Essays in Zen Buddhism,* 3 vols. (London, 1927,

1933, 1934); Heinrich Dumoulin, A *History of Zen Buddhism*, trans. Paul Peachey (New York, 1963).

No. 251. On Muhammad's ascension, cf. Miguel Asin Palacios, *La escatologia musulmana en la Divina Comedia* (2nd ed.; Madrid-Granada, 1943); George Widengren, *Muhammad, the Apostle of God, and His Ascension* (Uppsala, 1951).

Nos. 252 ff. On Islamic mysticism, see the bibliography of Charles J. Adams, 'Islam,' in his A *Reader's Guide to the Great Religions*, pp. 326 ff.

Chapter 11: *Speculations on Man and God*

Nos. 260, 262, 272-3. On Egyptian religious speculation, see J. H. Breasted, *Development of Religion and Thought in Ancient Egypt* (London, 1912; Harper Torchbook, 1959); John A. Wilson, *The Culture of Ancient Egypt* (Chicago, 1951; Phoenix Books, 1958). Henri Frankfort, John A. Wilson, Thorkild Jacobsen, *Before Philosophy* (Chicago, 1946; Pelican Books, 1949), discuss and compare Egyptian and Mesopotamian myths and theoretical speculations. See also Henri Frankfort, *Kingship and the Gods* (Chicago, 1948); Henri Frankfort, *Ancient Egyptian Religion* (New York: Harper Torchbook, 1961); pp. 59 ff., 88 ff.; S. G. F. Brandon, *Man and His Destiny in the Great Religions* (Manchester, 1962), chap. 11.

Nos. 264 ff. On Indian religious thought, see Franklin Edgerton, *The Beginnings of Indian Philosophy: Selections from the Rig Veda, Atharva Veda, Upanishads and Mahabhárata* (Cambridge, Mass., 1965); J. N. Farquhar, *An Outline of the Religious Literature of India* (Oxford, 1920); Louis Renou, *Religions of Ancient India* (London, 1953); S. Radhakrishnan and Charles A. Moore (eds.), *Source Book in Indian Philosophy* (Princeton, 1957); Wm. Theodore de Bary (ed.), *Sources of Indian Tradition* (New York, 1958); Surendranáth Dasgupta, A *History of Indian Philosophy*, 5 vols. (Cambridge, England, 1922-55); S. Radhakrishnan, *Indian Philosophy*, 2 vols. (London, 1927); H. Zimmer, *Philosophies of India*, ed. J. Campbell (New York, 1951). See also the bibliographies compiled by Norvin J. Hein, 'Hinduism,' in Adams (ed.), A *Reader's Guide to the Great Religions*, pp. 56 ff., 68 ff.

On the interpretation of the Bhagavad Gītā, see Franklin Edgerton, *The Bhagavad Gītā* (New York: Harper Torchbook, 1964), pp. 105-94.

No. 265. On myth, religion and philosophy in ancient Greece, see W. K. C. Guthrie, *The Greeks and Their Gods*, chaps. X-XII; W. K. C. Guthrie, *The Greek Philosophers, from Thales to Aristotle* (London, 1950; Harper Torchbook, 1960); R. B. Onians, *The Origins of European Thought about the Body, the Mind, the Soul, the World, Time and Fate* (2nd ed.; Cambridge, England, 1954); Bruno Snell, *The Discovery of the Mind: The Greek Origins of European Thought*, trans. T. G. Rosenmeyer (New York: Harper Torchbook, 1960); S. G. F. Brandon, *Man and His Destiny in the Great Religions*, op. cit., chap. V.

No. 267. On Roman religion in relation to philosophy, see the bibliography in Frederick C. Grant, *Ancient Roman Religion* (New York, 1957), pp. 59-60.

Nos. 269, 270, 305-6. On Muslim philosophy, see the bibliography of Charles J. Adams, 'Islam,' in his A *Reader's Guide to the Great Religions*, pp. 312-16. Also Henry Corbin, *Histoire de la philosophie islamique* (Paris, 1964), pp. 348-63, bibliographies.

Bibliography

Nos. 270-1. On archaic philosophical speculations, see Paul Radin, *Primitive Man as Philosopher* (New York, 1927; enlarged ed., New York: Dover Books, 1957); Marcel Griaule, *Dieu d'Eau* (Paris, 1948); P. Tempels, *Philosophie bantoue* (1949).

Nos. 272, 273, see under nos. 260, 262.

No. 275. On Jainism, cf. Walther Schubring, 'Der Jainismus,' in A. Bareau, W. Schubring and Chr. von Fürer-Haimendorf, *Die Religionen Indiens*, vol. III Stuttgart, 1964); Walther Schubring, *The Doctrine of the Jainas* (Delhi-Benares-Patni, 1962); Helmut von Glasenapp, *Der Jainismus, eine indische Erlösungs-religion* (Berlin, 1925, 1964); A. L. Basham, 'Jainism,' in de Bary (ed.), *Sources of Indian Tradition, op. cit.*, pp. 38-92.

Nos. 276 ff. On Ashoka, see V. A. Smith, *Asoka, the Buddhist Emperor of India* (Oxford, 1901); J. Przyluski, *La légende de l'empereur Asoka* (Paris, 1923).

Nos. 280-1. On religions of China, cf. the bibliographies compiled by W. A. C. H. Dobson, in Adams (ed.), *A Reader's Guide to the Great Religions*, pp. 31-44.

Nos. 282-9. On the Buddhist philosophies, see the bibliographies by Richard A. Gard, in Adams (ed.), *A Reader's Guide to the Great Religions*, pp. 124-8.

No. 303. On the Zoroastrian doctrines, cf. the bibliographies cited for Nos. 37-9.

Nos. 305, 306, see under nos. 269, 270.

ETHNIC AND GEOGRAPHIC
CROSS-REFERENCE INDEX